APPLAUSE FOR SYD FIELD AND
HIS CRITICALLY ACCLAIMED BOOKS
FOUR SCREENPLAYS

"A book that writers will stand in line for and studio executives will Xerox."

—James L. Brooks, writer-director-producer, *Terms of Endearment, Broadcast News, The Mary Tyler Moore Show, The Simpsons*

"Theory comes alive with this hands-on approach to what makes four great screenplays tick."

—Deborah Newmyer, senior vice president of development, Amblin Entertainment

"A first-rate analysis of why good screenplays work: a virtual must for aspiring screenwriters."

—Linda Obst, producer, *The Fisher King, Sleepless in Seattle*

"It's a fascinating view into the most overlooked process of film making."

—Michael Bresman, executive vice president of production, TriStar Pictures

"One of the very best books I have read on movies and screenplays. Syd writes both with passion and an astute understanding. . . . I only wish he'd written his chapter on *Thelma & Louise* before I started work on it because it would have made my contribution a lot better. But then, by reading Syd's book I get the chance to carry some of the clarity he brings to a project forward into my future work."

—Hans Zimmer, film composer, *Thelma & Louise*

Please turn the page for more extraordinary acclaim. . . .

SCREENPLAY

"Quite simply the only manual to be taken seriously by aspiring screenwriters."

—Tony Bill, co-producer, *The Sting*; director, *My Bodyguard*

"The complete primer, a step-by-step guide from the first glimmer of an idea to marketing the finished script."

—*New West*

"A much-needed book . . . straightforward and informed . . . facts and figures on markets, production details, layout of script, the nuts and bolts, are accurate and clear, and should be enormously helpful to novices."

—*Fade-In*

"Experienced advice on story development, creation and definition of characters, structure of action, and direction of participants. Easy-to-follow guidelines and a commonsense approach mark this highly useful manual."

—*Video*

"Full of common sense, an uncommon commodity."

—*Los Angeles Times Book Review*

SELLING A SCREENPLAY

"Syd Field is the preeminent analyzer in the study of American screenplays. Incredibly, he manages to remain idealistic while tendering practical 'how to' books."

—James L. Brooks, scriptwriter, *The Mary Tyler Moore Show*, *Terms of Endearment, Broadcast News*

"An informative, engaging look at the inside of the dream factory. This is a terrific aid for screenwriters who are trying to gain insight into the Hollywood system."

—David Kirkpatrick, producer, former head of production, Paramount Pictures

"A wonderful book that should be in every filmmaker's library."

—Howard Kazanjian, producer, *Raiders of the Lost Ark*, *Return of the Jedi, More American Graffiti*

"If I ever decide to do something crazy, like try to sell a screenplay, this is the book I'll stuff in my back pocket when I go to market."

—Steven Bochco, producer, *Hill Street Blues, L.A. Law, NYPD Blue*

BOOKS BY SYD FIELD

The Screenwriter's Workbook

Screenplay: The Foundations of Screenwriting

Selling a Screenplay: The Screenwriter's Guide to Hollywood

Four Screenplays

The Screenwriter's Problem Solver: How to Recognize, Identify, and Define Screenwriting Problems

Going to the Movies: A Personal Journey Through Four Decades of Modern Film

Going to
the Movies

*A Personal Journey
Through Four Decades
of Modern Film*

SYD FIELD

A Dell Trade Paperback

A DELL TRADE PAPERBACK

Published by
Dell Publishing
a division of
Random House, Inc.
1540 Broadway
New York, New York 10036

Dell books may be purchased for business or promotional use or for special
sales. For information please write to: Special Markets Department,
Random House, Inc. 1540 Broadway, New York, NY 10036.

DTP and the colophon are trademarks of Random House, Inc.

LIBRARY OF CONGRESS CATALOGING IN PUBLICATION DATA
Field, Syd.
  Going to the movies : a personal journey through four decades of
  modern film / Syd Field.
      p. cm.
  Includes index.
  ISBN: 0-440-50849-5
    1. Field, Syd.   2. Screenwriters—United States—Biography.
3. Motion picture industry—United States—History.
4. Motion pictures—United States—History.   5. Motion picture
authorship.   I. Title.

PS3556.I3967 Z468 2001
812'.54—dc21
[B]   2001028730

Printed in the United States of America
Published simultaneously in Canada

October 2001
10 9 8 7 6 5 4 3 2 1
FFG

To all the Siddha Masters
who walked the path
and keep the flame burning . . .

and to Aviva,
who helped show me the way . . .

go'-ing to the mo'-vies *ger. phr., n.*
[a subjective conditional experience]
(1.) an American pastime; (2.) the
collective experience of personally observing thrills, chills and spills ema-
nating from a large screen in a
darkened theater, <*i.e., Titanic*>; (3.)
the desire to be entertained driven by
hope and expectation, <*i.e., Casablanca*>;
an intense longing to be trans-
ported to another time, another
place, <*i.e., The Wild Bunch*>; (4.) an
audience connected by the *community
of emotion*, <*i.e., An Affair to Remember*>; (5.) expectation dashed by disappointment, <*i.e., The Lost World*>;
an experience forgotten within ten
minutes, <*i.e., Wild, Wild West*>

Contents

"This is my life. It always will be. There's nothing else. Just us and the cameras and those wonderful people out there in the dark. All right, Mr. DeMille, I'm ready for my close-up."

—BILLY WILDER AND CHARLES BRACKETT
Sunset Boulevard

Introduction

—————

*"My task . . . is to make you hear,
to make you feel—and above all to make you see.
That is all, and it is everything."*
—Joseph Conrad

It seems like I've spent most of my life sitting in a darkened theater, popcorn in hand, gazing in rapt wonder at the images projected on a river of light reflected on that monster screen.

I was one of those kids who grew up in Hollywood surrounded by the film industry; my uncle Sol was head of the Camera Department at 20th Century Fox, and our next-door neighbor was an actors' agent who, I was told, got my brother and me a tiny part in *Gone With the Wind*. I was probably about two at the time, my brother four years older, and we played the ragged and dirty children of a young Southern couple running away from the Yankees advancing on Atlanta. Unfortunately, the scene ended up on the cutting room floor. A few years later, while playing the trumpet in the Sheriff's Boys Band, like my brother before me, I was chosen to be one of the band members on the set of Frank Capra's *State of the Union*, starring Spencer Tracy and Katharine Hepburn. I don't remember much about the experience except that Van Johnson taught me how to play checkers.

Saturday afternoons were spent sneaking into the neighborhood Gordon Theater and watching those wonderful old serials of *Flash Gordon* and *Buck Rogers*. During my teens, going to the movies became a passion, a form of entertainment, a distraction, a topic of discussion, a place to make out and have fun. Occasionally, there would be unforgettable moments: watching the chemistry of Bogart and Bacall in *To Have and Have Not* or Walter Huston's mad dance as he discovered gold in the mountains in *The Treasure of the Sierra Madre* or watching Brando stagger up to the gangplank at the end of *On the Waterfront*. I went to Hollywood High School, where one of my best friends, Frank Mazzola, was chosen to be the "gang" consultant in Nicholas Ray's *Rebel Without a Cause*. Frank played the part of Crunch and the club I belonged to became the model of the gang in *Rebel*. That's when James Dean became one of the icons of my generation. We imitated his walk, his talk, the way he wore his hair and various other mannerisms. Yes, I can truly say that I was a child of Hollywood.

Later, going to the movies became a job, first as a documentary filmmaker, then as a film critic, which soon evolved into a career as a screenwriter. After many years of writing screenplays, I became a reader of screenplays, reading more than two thousand in a little over a year and finding only forty to submit to our financial partners. At that point, I became a teacher of screenwriting, then fused my experiences as a writer, reader and teacher into writing several best-selling books on the art and craft of screenwriting.

For the past thirty-five years, I've watched movies as they have become an integral part of our culture, part of our heritage, watched as they have become an international way of life. Once members of an audience are joined together in the darkness of a theater, they become one being, a single entity joined in a "community of emotion," an unspoken and deep-seated connection to the human spirit that exists beyond time, place and circumstance.

Going to the movies is both an individual and a collective experience, a collection of moments standing out against the landscape of time—whether it's a line of dialogue, like "Here's looking at you, kid," from *Casablanca* or the kid watching the video dance of a plastic bag amid the autumn leaves in *American Beauty* or the frogs falling in *Magnolia*.

Watching those flickering images flutter across the screen can bear witness to the entire range of human experience. It can be a moment of wonder and poetry, like the opening sequence of *Close Encounters of the Third Kind*, or one that captures the full scope of human history as the ape throws into the air a wooden club which merges into the spacecraft in Stanley Kubrick's *2001: A Space Odyssey*. Thousands of years and the evolution of humankind condensed into two pieces of film; moments of magic and mystery. Such is the power of film.

I've always felt that if we can understand what makes a good movie, those elements of form, action, character and situation, then we, as audience, will have a greater knowledge and appreciation of the movie experience.

For several years now, I've wanted to write a book that would explore the elements of the movies from the audience's point of view. What makes a good movie good and a bad movie bad. I must confess I'm appalled at how many bad movies make incredible amounts of money. Why do audiences go to these movies? I'm very happy when a good movie makes a lot of money, like *Titanic*, *American Beauty*, *The Matrix* or *Cast Away*, but when movies like *The Lost World* or *Men in Black* make so much money, it drives me up the wall.

The experience of seeing a good movie is more than just the quality of the acting, the music or the cinematography. Those elements, while important in bringing the movie to life, must be woven throughout the story line to be emotionally gratifying, like threads of gold accenting a rich tapestry.

I think James Cameron's *Titanic* is an excellent example of that. It's a great movie experience. Yet, when the film was playing around the world to packed theaters, many people, both critics and audience, publicly criticized the movie by criticizing the screenplay, making the assumption that people walked into a movie theater to see a great screenplay. As one famous producer told me, you don't drive down Hollywood Boulevard to see a great screenplay. You go to see a great movie.

I have this discussion with writer friends all the time: *Titanic* may not be one of the greatest screenplays ever written, but it's certainly a *great movie experience*. To be the most popular film of all time, winner of some eleven Academy Awards, more popular than *Star Wars, E.T.: The Extra-Terrestrial, Jurassic Park* or *Gone With the Wind*, requires an audience to see the film several times.

So, what attracts an audience to see a film like *Titanic*?

When I saw the film the first time, I noticed that almost 60 percent of the audience were teenagers. The sixteen-year-old daughter of a friend of mine told me she had seen it some six times. Curious, I asked what she liked about it. Was it Leo? Yes and no, she replied, then began to explain what she, and her friends, saw in the film and why she liked it so much.

Listening to her talk about *Titanic* was really an education, and during our conversation I began to understand the film from her point of view. First, she talked about Rose, the Kate Winslet character, who represented a woman searching for her place in life, a woman isolated, restricted and suffocated by the unwritten rules and regulations of an indifferent society. As her mother constantly points out, her primary ambition in life is to marry a wealthy man. No matter that he's a pompous ass; no matter what her personal dreams and goals are in life. She is *expected* to participate in the façade of a social convention that is supposed to look like happiness and fulfillment. Even though Rose rebels against that way of life, she is torn in two different directions. While she feels obligated to maintain the "proper" image of her upper-class heritage, she's a woman who wants to be set free from the restrictions of society. As the old Rose tells us, " I saw my whole life as if I'd already lived it . . . an endless parade of parties and cotillions, yachts and polo matches . . . always the same narrow people, the same mindless chatter. I felt like I was standing at a great precipice, with no one to pull me back, no one who cared . . . or even noticed."

Yes, she is the "poor little rich girl," and as Jack (Leonardo DiCaprio) tells her, "They've got you in a glass jar like some butterfly, and you're goin' to die if you don't break out. Maybe not right away . . . but sooner or later the fire in you is goin' to go out."

At that point in our conversation, the sixteen-year-old daughter of my friend told me she felt *Titanic* was a movie about "fate and destiny." I must have looked a little puzzled, so she patiently explained that Jack wins his place aboard ship in a card game, and his true purpose in the story is to unlock the spirit and individuality of Rose. That insight struck me deeply as I realized she had reached a level of understanding about the movie I had completely missed. Indeed, it could very well be a film about the ironies of fate and the force of destiny.

When I asked what her favorite scene in the movie was, she replied after careful consideration, "the flying scene," that moment when Rose and Jack stand on the bow rail facing the vast, unbroken sea and she raises her arms and starts "flying." I asked why, and she said, Rose puts her faith and trust in Jack and achieves a level of hope she had never experienced before. Jack makes her feel truly alive because he teaches her to believe in herself. Which is, of course, the very essence of freedom.

Visually, the moment is heightened by the sweeping movement of Cameron's direction, and the camera makes us partners in discovering the joy and freedom that Rose and Jack feel. In the screenplay it's written like this: "Rose gasps. There is nothing in her field of vision but water. It's like there is no ship under them at all, just the two of them soaring. The Atlantic unrolls toward her, a hammered copper shield under a dusk sky. There is only the wind, and the hiss of the water 50 feet below. . . . "

"I'm flying," Rose joyfully exclaims.

Jack and the ship seem to merge into one force of power and optimism, lifting her, buoying her forward on a magical journey, soaring onward into a night without fear.

When I first saw that scene I was just knocked out. The power of the images, the soaring emotion of the musical score magnified the unspoken commitment of Rose to Jack. When I read this particular scene in the screenplay, it brought to mind Edmund's speech from Eugene O'Neill's classic *Long Day's Journey Into Night*. Edmund tries to articulate his own feelings of merging into the absolute. He was on a ship heading for Buenos Aires, he says, and as *"I lay on the bowsprit, facing astern, with the water foaming into spume high above me. I became drunk with the beauty and singing rhythm of it, and for a moment I lost myself—actually lost my life. I was set free! I dissolved in the sea, became white sails and flying spray, became beauty and rhythm, became moonlight and the ship and the high dim-starred sky! I belonged, without past or future, within peace and unity and a wild joy, with something greater than my own life, or the life of Man, to Life itself! To God, if you want to put it that way."*

As I sat listening to my young friend trying to put her feelings into words, I glimpsed the same kind of passion etched in her luminous eyes. I knew within the very fabric of my being that her experience of seeing this movie could possibly have been a moment of a great awakening in her young life.

To me, this is the power of film. The themes, the images, the moments remembered in a movie experience like *Titanic*, are kind of a peak experience that can possibly influence a person's behavior for the rest of his life.

This particular moment led me once again to think about writing a book in which I could share with the reader and audience how to identify some of those particular moments that create great movie experiences.

Now, I know this is a noble idea, a wonderful idea, but I didn't have a clue about where to begin. Besides, would anyone really be interested? As I tell the writers I work with, a good idea is not a good idea unless it's executed properly. But the idea for the book kept nagging at me, and every time I went to the movies, I kept hoping I would find the key to some kind of an insight that would guide me along this path of discovery. What's so wonderful and mysterious about the creative process is that answers, or solutions to problems, often come when you least expect them. And that's what happened to me.

One night, as my wife and I were having dinner with a friend of mine, she asked what I was working on. I told her I had this idea about writing a book that would shed some light on the movie-going experience but didn't know how to execute it. She listened, smiled; and then, almost as an afterthought, she casually said, "Why don't you put yourself into it."

Her words struck me like lightning. Put myself into it? Why not? I could see tracing my own journey in film and writing about

the people and the films which have influenced me in the shaping
and executing of my ideas about the movies. I also saw I could isolate and define those elements found in all good movies and share
them with a larger audience. I started backtracking along my life in
film: where it began, how it began, where it took me and the things
that happened along the way.

Over the next few weeks, I began thinking about my life in film,
the people who guided and influenced me and the movies I'd seen
and studied. The more I considered the possibilities from this perspective, the more enthusiastic I became. The "capper" came one
night when I was watching Sam Peckinpah's great western *The
Wild Bunch* (Walon Green, Peckinpah) on television. As I watched
the movie I recalled the time I spent with Peckinpah while he was
writing *The Wild Bunch* and I was starting my own screenwriting
career. We had had long conversations at his home in Malibu about
the movies, especially westerns, as we sat nursing a beer and watching the sun set across the vast expanse of ocean.

Seeing *The Wild Bunch* again, many years later, even though it
had been edited for television, was a profound experience. The
images are so powerful, the characters so well drawn, that I still
remember some of the scenes he was writing, our discussions
about them and the joy and exhilaration I had watching them
unfold on the screen. Those memories kick-started me into recon-
structing the steps I've taken along the path that I'm still following
today.

It was a journey that began in the spring of 1960 during my second semester at the University of California at Berkeley. I was acting in a production of *Woyzeck*, and after a performance one night, I
was introduced to the great French film director Jean Renoir.

My relationship with Renoir changed my life. You know, there
may be two or three times during our lives when something hap-

pens that alters the direction of our lives; we meet someone, go somewhere or do something we've never done before, and those moments become peak experiences guiding us to where we're supposed to go. People say I was extremely fortunate to be working with Renoir, that it was a chance and fortuitous incident of being in the right place at the right time. That's true. But over the years, I've learned not to believe too much in luck or accidents anymore; I think everything happens for a reason. There's something to be learned from every experience we encounter during the brief time we spend on this planet. Call it fate, call it destiny, call it what you will, it really doesn't matter.

There's an ancient Sanskrit scripture that says, *"The world is as you see it"*; that means what's inside our heads—our thoughts, feelings and emotions—are reflected outside in our everyday life. In other words, the movie that's playing inside our heads is the movie we call our life. What we believe to be true, is true; accidents don't "just happen." I had been given the opportunity of working with one of the greatest filmmakers alive, and it was my relationship with Renoir that ultimately led me onto the path I'm still following.

For almost a year, I sat at Renoir's feet, watching and learning about movies through his eyes. He was always commenting on film, his opinions vocal and fervent about everything he saw or wrote as an artist, a person and a humanitarian. Being in his presence was an inspiration, a major life lesson, a joy, a privilege, as well as a great learning experience. Though movies have been a major part of my life, it was only during the time I spent with Renoir that I turned my focus to the world of film, the same way a plant turns toward the sun. Suddenly, I saw the movies in a whole new light, as a form to study and learn from, seeking in the story and images an expression and understanding of life. My love for the movies has fed and nourished me ever since.

"*Qu'est-ce que c'est le Cinema?*" is a question Renoir always used to ask before he showed us a movie; "What is film?" He used to say movies are more than mere flashing images on the screen; "they are an art form that become larger than life." During the time I spent at the graduate division of the UCLA film school, I approached my studies of the movies from the point of view of Renoir's question: "*What is film?*"

So, what makes a great movie experience?

That's what I wanted to explore in this book. For that reason, I've designed each chapter to be like a photograph, capturing a specific moment and insight in my life that occurred during a particular moment in time.

Hopefully, sharing the experience of my journey will illuminate and enhance your own perception of the movies, bringing forth a richer and more profound moviegoing experience.

La Grande Illusion

"The future is film."
—JEAN RENOIR

A ugust 1959.

The sun was high and it was very late in the morning when I finally got into my car and headed north on Highway 101 to Berkeley, California. It was a big step for me. For several years after my parents' death, I had been floundering, not knowing what direction I wanted to take in my life, not knowing what I wanted to be or do. My mother's last wish before she died was for me to become a "professional person," which meant, in that special, unspoken communication between mother and son, that she wanted me to become a doctor, lawyer or dentist.

Wanting to honor her wishes, and thus ignoring my own, I enrolled at USC in predentistry, but it took only a few weeks for me to discover it wasn't really for me. The courses I liked were English literature, but as my aunt, who was raising me after my mother's death, patiently explained, the only thing I could do with an English degree was teach. And what was the future in that?

A friend of mine from high school, Frank Mazzola, happened to be taking an acting class at a local theater, and convinced me it was something I should do. I sat in on just one session and, needless to say, loved it. Acting was an ideal opportunity for me to avoid dealing with all the future "life decisions" I was confronting. In exchange for the acting lessons, I was offered a "job" as stage manager for the little theater, and I jumped at it. I participated in many of the productions, as a walk-on or background extra, but I ran the stage with responsibility and efficiency. By the following summer, I had improved my acting skills to such a degree that I was invited to become a member of the Shakespearean Repertory Company at the Old Globe Theater in San Diego. I was seriously considering pursuing an acting career.

When my aunt, who promised my mother to take care of me, heard about this, she told me, "Acting may be a great hobby, but it doesn't pay the rent. What are you going to do for a living?" I had no idea, of course, and simply refused to deal with it. But I certainly knew what I didn't want: a "9-to-5" job in a bank or insurance company.

What did I want to do with my life? That was really the question. Should I become an actor? What about the promise I made to my mother on her deathbed? I had no answers, of course, and the pressure of trying to deal with these questions became too much, so I decided to just take off.

So, when the little theater finished its current slate of productions, I decided I would drive across the country and visit my brother, then attending Washington University Medical School in St. Louis. I loved that driving experience so much I decided not to return to school, and for the next two years I traveled back and forth across the country. It was really a time of freedom; I had inherited a small sum of money from my mother's estate and was very fortunate not to have to work. I just kept driving; I never knew where I was going till I got there. I had good times and bad times, and loved every minute of it. I was like a cloud on the wind, drifting without aim or purpose. But deep down, no matter how far or how long I drove, I was always aware that I would eventually have to come back to myself.

It didn't take me very long to see I was lost. I didn't know who I was, or where I was going. And then, one day, while driving through the Arizona desert, I realized I had traveled this same road before. Everything was the same, but different. It was the same stand of foothills in the same barren desert—but it was two years later. In reality, I felt like I had gone nowhere. I had spent two years ostensibly trying to get my head together, and still I had no aim, no purpose, no goal, no destination. I had no *direction* in my life. I suddenly saw my future—and it was nowhere.

Time seemed to be slipping away, and I knew in that moment that I had to *do* something, that it was time for me to stop wandering and go back to school. I thought that at least I'd give it a shot, maybe find something I liked, perhaps get a degree—not realizing then that the choices we make always take us to the place we're supposed to be going.

And so it was in that late summer of 1959 that I packed my belongings, said my good-byes, got into my car and began driving north to Berkeley. It was the first time in my life I truly felt I had some kind of direction, and I was both confident and unsure in the choice I was making.

Berkeley at the dawn of the sixties was an active crucible of revolt and unrest. Signs, banners, slogans and leaflets were everywhere: Castro's rebel force had just overthrown Batista, and signs ranged from "Cuba Libre" and "Time for the Revolution" to "Get Out of Vietnam," "Free Speech," "Abolish ROTC," "Equal Rights for Everyone" and "Socialism for All, & All for Socialism." Telegraph Avenue, the main street leading onto the campus, was always lined with a colorful display of banners and leaflets as I walked to class. Every day there were protest rallies, and when I stopped to listen I would see the FBI agents, trying to be inconspicuous in their shirts and ties, taking pictures of everyone. It was a joke.

Hunger strikes on campus protested the mandatory ROTC courses, and it didn't take long for me to be swept up in the activities and issues of the time. Like so many others of my generation, I was influenced and inspired by the "beats": Kerouac, Ginsburg, Gregory Corso, those poet/saints who were blazing a trail of rebellion and revolution. Inspired by their voices, and their lives, I, too, wanted to ride the waves of change. It wasn't too long before the campus exploded into a political frenzy initiated by Mario Savio and the Free Speech Movement.

One of the summer jobs I'd had a few years earlier was working in a heart research lab on the then-new heart bypass machine, and I really loved it. I had a notion that I might like to become a doctor, a cardiologist to be exact, but I discovered when I enrolled at Berkeley that I couldn't declare premed as a major. So I enrolled in English literature instead, got a part-time job working in a record store, and took my required premed courses like chemistry and physics, along with my English requirements. It worked out fine. I liked the school, the environment and the people.

One day, during the second half of my first year, as I was walking across campus I read a poster advertising an open reading for a university theater production of Georg Buchner's *Woyzeck*. I was restless studying, wanted to find a way to unwind, and since I had some spare time, I decided, why not? I would read for the play, without expecting anything because I was not part of the Theater Arts Department. So I joined the hopefuls, did my reading, and that was that. A few days later, I checked the casting board, and found to my surprise that I had been chosen to play the lead character, Woyzeck.

The rehearsals were intense, and when the play finally opened in Wheeler Auditorium, Berkeley's main theater, we played to full houses almost every night. One night, after the evening performance, I was introduced to the man who would soon become my mentor: Jean Renoir. As "artist in residence," Renoir would present the world premiere of his play *Carola*. Because of my work in *Woyzeck*, I was asked to read for Renoir's play, and while I knew it was a great opportunity, I didn't think too much about it. Not knowing anything about Renoir or his films, I read for the part, then learned I had been cast to play the third lead, Campan, the director/stage manager and lover of Carola.

What can I say about Jean Renoir? He was a man like any other, but what separated him, at least in my mind, was his great heart; he was open, friendly, a man of great intelligence and wit who seemed to influence the lives of everyone he touched. The son of the great Impressionistic painter Pierre-Auguste Renoir, he, too, had the great gift of sight. He literally opened my eyes to the world of film and theater, what it is and what it could be.

The rehearsals for *Carola* were held in the basement theater, and when I walked in for the first table reading, I noticed several well-known faculty members and press people hovering in the background, anxious to observe Renoir at work. Renoir, who reminded me of a warm, cuddly teddy bear, spoke with a pronounced French accent and walked with a slight limp—the result, I learned later, of a wound suffered in the First World War. I immediately tuned in to his presence, which emanated a sense of excitement that I found friendly and inviting.

Renoir sat the actors around the table and began to talk about his play. The action, he told us, takes place in Paris during the

German occupation in the Second World War. It was a time of fear and mistrust in Paris; the Nazis had installed the Vichy government to oversee the occupation, and the French secret police—the French Gestapo, as they were called—answered to no one.

The action of the play takes place backstage, in Carola's dressing room and just outside, in the adjacent hallway, before and during the performance, which takes place offstage. The play opens when Von Claudius, the German general in charge of Paris and former lover of Carola, comes back to see her. He is weary of the war, and is one of the instigators in the plot against Hitler. He wants to renew his love for Carola and run away with her to South America.

Carola was played by a young actress named Deneen Peckinpah, and since we had many scenes together, we spent a lot of time hanging out when rehearsals were over. We liked each other and developed a close relationship, both in and out of the theater.

My character, Campan, was the flamboyant, theatrical director/stage manager of the theater who is deeply in love with Carola; in the end, he sacrifices his life for her, for France and for the theater. Like most actors trained in the realistic approach of the "method," I liked to feel my way into the heart of the character, much like a butterfly circling a rock. During the early rehearsals, I read my lines simply, in a basic monotone, trying to find something—a word, a phrase, an emotion—I could latch on to.

Renoir was patient and persistent, saying, "Creating a part is like going into a store to buy a new jacket. First, you try it on and see how it looks and how it fits. Then, it needs alteration; you have to alter the sleeves, perhaps the length, maybe let out the back a little. Once it's altered, you try it on, and while it may fit, it feels a little tight under the arms, and the material is a little too stiff. It takes a few times wearing it before it really becomes comfortable, before it becomes an extension of yourself. It's the same in the creative process."

This image and his words have stayed with me. Facing the blank sheet of paper, I've learned to simply "throw down" thoughts, words and ideas, and gradually, a shape and form appears. Then I add, tighten, condense, hone and polish, and pretty soon I have something I can relate to. That's the creative process.

One of the first things I learned about Renoir was his aversion to the "cliché." The character of Campan was overly dramatic, and I had no experience to bring to that aspect of the character. So I played it as I thought it should be played, creating a character more from my imagination than from my experience. It didn't work. I wanted to play it more "real," but he wanted me to become more theatrical, "larger than life." It was a tough adjustment to make. Renoir was patient, nurturing. He would quote his father on bringing an idea into existence. "If you paint the leaf on a tree without using a model," the great Impressionistic painter once said, "your imagination will only supply you with a few leaves; but Nature offers you millions, all on the same tree. No two leaves are exactly the same. The artist who paints only what is in his mind must very soon repeat himself." If you look at Renoir's great paintings, you'll see what he meant. No two leaves, no two flowers, no two people, are ever painted the same way. It's the same with his son's films.

I learned to become observant, searching for people who would show me a kind of behavior I could draw upon, and it didn't take long for me to become adept at noticing mannerisms and behavior patterns. I would see a gesture, or the way someone walked, and try and incorporate it into my characterization of Campan. Over and over again Renoir would tell me to "avoid the cliché," and he constantly instilled in me, and every member of the cast, the value of my own experience. "Bring yourself to the character," he would say, because "an actor either plays 'true' or plays 'false.' If he plays 'true' he may allow himself all manner of exaggeration." Don't worry about being "too dramatic," he repeated over and over again; that's who the character is. He instilled in me a great understanding: as long as I avoided the cliché I could be true to the character and the situation. It was a lesson I still carry with me today.

Renoir often spoke about his love for the movies, about the theater, about art, acting and literature. *"Qu'est-ce que c'est le Cinema?"* he would ask over and over again; "What is film?" Is it art? Is it literature? He shared with us his view that movies "are a new form of printing—another form of the total transformation of the world through knowledge." And he would refer to Lumière, inventor of the early French motion picture camera, the *Cinématographe*, as "another Gutenberg."

During the year I was under his tutelage, he shared his experience of the movies and expounded upon the art of cinema. He insisted movies had the potential to be literature, but they should never be considered as "art." When I asked what he meant, he replied that "art" is the sole vision of one person, which in the scheme of the filmmaking process is a contradiction. He explained that one person can't do everything that's required to make a movie. One person can write the screenplay, direct the film, photograph it, edit it and score it, like Charlie Chaplin, but, Renoir continued, the filmmaker cannot act all the parts, or record all the sound, or handle all the lighting requirements and the myriad of other details that are required to make a movie. "Art," he said, "should offer the viewer the chance of merging with the creator."

As young students just learning from the master, we would literally sit at his knees and ask questions, share our ideas or discuss our opinions of life and art. He would answer everything. Every question, even the dumbest ones, were received with interest and respect. When a cast member asked, "How can we be true to our art?" he shared his personal philosophy that "art is in the doing of it." A simple answer, yet profound, relevant and true. It's only during the process of working, he explained—whether directing a film, composing a song, writing a script, painting a picture, whatever—that one "creates art"; art is the process of actually sitting down and doing it. Not talking about doing it, not thinking or fantasizing about doing it, but doing it. Only after the work has been completed, and exposed to public view, will it be considered a work of "art" or not. If you think you're "an artist" just waiting for the right project to materialize, you'll be waiting forever.

We had been rehearsing for several weeks when the Renoir film retrospective began. The question of "What is film?" is as relevant today as it was when I first heard it. "Qu'est-ce que c'est le Cinema?" How do we define it? Analyze it? What makes film a form larger than life? As I mentioned, I had not seen any of his films at that time, nor did I know anything about his film career.

One day, Renoir informed us there was going to be a special screening of his film La Grande Illusion for cast and crew, and needless to say, I was more than a little curious. After a short rehearsal, we went into the screening room, made ourselves comfortable and listened while Renoir told us a little about the history of La Grande Illusion. Produced in 1937, the film was viewed in Germany as an indictment of war. Joseph Goebbels, the Nazi propaganda minister, immediately banned it. He despised it so much that he labeled it "Cinematographic Enemy No. 1," and destroyed every European print he could find. Renoir thought he would never see the film again, but when the American troops marched into Munich in 1945, they uncovered a negative, preserved, ironically, by the Germans themselves. Several years later, under Renoir's supervision, the film was restored, duplicated, then released.

I could see the emotion engraved in his face as he prepared to show us the film that had survived the war. He finished speaking, paused for a moment, as if he wanted to add something, then changed his mind and took his seat. As the theater darkened, we could almost feel the tremendous physical and emotional energy he had expended to preserve his film.

At first, the images on screen seemed stilted and old-fashioned, the sound track scratchy, laced with static, the acting broad and theatrical. But all my judgments vanished quickly.

The situation depicting the barriers between the upper class, the aristocracy and the common man, the officers and the enlisted men, was sketched simply, without pretense or comment. As the film progressed, the ideas presented in it suddenly seemed so profound, so dynamic, so fresh and new to my consciousness, that I totally surrendered to the force of the images unfolding on the screen.

The story takes place in 1916, during the First World War. On a photographic reconnaissance mission, Marichal (Jean Gabin), an auto mechanic from Paris, and Captain de Boeldieu (Pierre Fresnay), an aristocrat and member of the military elite, are shot down by the German ace von Rauffenstein (Erich von Stroheim). They survive the crash, but are captured and sent to a German prisoner of war camp. When the war begins to turn against the Germans, the prisoners are transferred to another prison, a huge castle deep in the heart of Germany. In the kind of irony Renoir loved, the camp is supervised by von Rauffenstein, now wearing a bulky neck brace. The German is also an aristocrat, a member of the military elite, and the only gifts he's received for his glorious participation in the "art of war," he explains, is a fractured spine, three pieces of metal in his arms and a metal kneecap.

There are no distinctions between de Boeldieu and von Rauffenstein; both are aristocrats, both are of noble origin, and the fact that they are enemies is irrelevant. They are respectful and cordial to each other, and the French aristocrat is invited to the German aristocrat's personal quarters for brandy and conversation.

I began to see what Renoir meant when he talked about "avoiding the cliché." Showing von Rauffenstein, the "enemy," offering kindness and hospitality to his prisoner, and tenderly caring for his single geranium plant, reveals the German's own dedication to life and living. It presents a dimension of character that is enlightening in its simplicity. Caring for the geranium plant is the only thing that has meaning for him other than his conversations with de Boeldieu.

Another scene that reveals Renoir's genius in avoiding the cliché takes place on Christmas Eve. It's important to remember that during the First World War—the Great War, as it's called—the Geneva Convention was, for the most part, strictly honored. So it wasn't unusual for relatives, friends and family to send in crates of food and goodies to aid the prisoners in their health and comfort. What the prisoners received usually arrived intact, and they would usually share it with one another. And now, in this isolated fortress prison castle, Christmas is approaching. To celebrate, it is agreed that the French and English prisoners will put on a special Christmas performance for all the prisoners and guards of the prison camp.

A large crate arrives for one of the characters, Rosenthal, which is filled with women's clothes that will be used as costumes for the Christmas performance. As Rosenthal unpacks the crate, an English soldier removes a dress, tries it on, puts on a wig, applies some makeup and, with his pipe in his mouth, walks into the barracks looking for a mirror. Suddenly, the hubbub surrounding the arrival of the crates stops. All eyes turn and stare in silent wonder at the soldier in drag. No words need to be said. The contrast in image, emotion and desire dissolves into an exquisite moment of silence as the men realize how long it's been since they've seen a woman. It's a stunning moment.

This sets up a later scene, when the Russian prisoners of war receive a large crate, a present sent from the royal family. Anticipating vodka and caviar, they invite the other prisoners to join them in what they think will be a grand time. With great joy and enthusiasm, they remove the nails from the crate, open it, pull off the packing straw . . . and what do they find? Books. Books on algebra, philosophy; books on grammar; even cookbooks. The prisoners are outraged. In anger and frustration, they burn the books and curse the monarchy.

As the German guards rush to put out the fire, it is de Boeldieu who realizes that the fire creates an ideal diversion for escape. It is decided that Marichal and Rosenthal will escape, and it is de Boeldieu who will insist on creating a diversion, sacrificing himself for the sake of the others. He knows the class of the aristocracy is only a lingering echo of former times. As the Germans hunt down the French aristocrat de Boeldieu, von Rauffenstein begs the Frenchman to give up "this nonsense." During the distraction, Marichal and Rosenthal make their escape and begin their trek across the mountains to Switzerland and freedom. It's another one of Renoir's ironies that the German aristocrat should be the one to fire the shot that kills the French aristocrat. His action, of course, represents the death of an old way of life which has failed to survive the turbulence of the changing times. As one way of life ends, the two Frenchmen make their way to freedom to begin a new life. In that sense, the film is as relevant today as it was when it was made in 1937.

When the film ended and the lights came on, I was so moved I could hardly speak. I felt as if I was stoned, my mind overwhelmed with the dynamic expression of Renoir's ideas. No wonder critics have consistently named *La Grande Illusion* one of the greatest films of all time. Seeing this movie literally opened my eyes to what the movies could be: an intellectual and emotional experience, suffused with a truth and universal appeal that can transcend the boundaries of time.

"*Qu'est-ce que c'est le Cinema?*"

La Grande Illusion. That is film.

Looking back on that spring afternoon, I see it as a major turning point in my life. It was not so much the images of the movie, the grainy print and scratchy sound track or the seemingly old-fashioned acting style. It was the power of the ideas, the contrasting images between what was seen on the screen and the emotional undercurrents the characters were feeling and conveying. I left the screening and walked down Telegraph Avenue in a daze. It was late afternoon, and groups of students were gathering at street corners urging people to sign their petitions. The coffee shops were full, and the sound of jazz was playing in the background. But I hardly heard or saw anything; I was only aware of the power of the images and ideas that were echoing across the landscape of my mind.

I didn't know much about the First World War, but I did know that fighting this war was thought to be a brave and courageous act that would "end all wars." As we learned from Hitler and the wars following, that wasn't the case at all. Wars have always been part of our collective unconscious, since Grecian times. As I walked down that darkening street I became aware that the same thing was happening all over again: The revolution in Cuba had been successful and Castro had fought his way to power, replacing one dictatorship with another. And just the day before, I had signed a petition against sending U.S.-trained "advisers" on "training missions" in a Far Eastern country called Vietnam. To believe that the First

World War was fought as "the war to end all wars" is nothing but a grand illusion.

War was war: outdated, outmoded, to be sure, a political solution to an economic or social problem. What made such an impression on me was that Renoir's vision was articulated dramatically, through characters and action placed in a certain situation. It was truly a profound experience.

Over the next several months, the cast members were privileged to see many of Renoir's films: *Le Dejeuner sur l'Herbe (Picnic on the Grass)*, *Swamp Water*, *The Southerner*, *Nana*, *The Golden Coach*, *The River* and others. I began to gain an insight into both the man and the artist.

One afternoon, as we were preparing for our first dress rehearsal, Renoir started talking about a movie he had made called *Le Règle du Jeu (Rules of the Game)*. He told us the film had originally been produced in Paris in 1939 but that after the first public screening the audience was so outraged that the distributors felt compelled to cut the film drastically. The French and Vichy governments banned the film as being "demoralizing," and it was removed from every movie screen in Paris. During one of the Allied bombings, the original negative of *Rules of the Game* was destroyed. After the war, pieces of the negative were found, and once again the painstaking task of reassembling the film—from more than two hundred film cans, along with bits and pieces of the sound track—was undertaken. Renoir shared that just before he came to Berkeley, the restoration had been completed and new prints struck. He wanted us to be the first American audience to see the newly restored version.

Needless to say, the screening had a profound and emotional impact on all of us, including Renoir and his wife, Dido. It was a small yet select audience: the cast and crew of *Carola*, Renoir's son Alain, an English professor at the university, plus a few faculty members and friends. The first public screening would be offered a few weeks later.

The story takes place in 1938, and the winds of war are everywhere in Europe. The manners, morals and behavior that people live by are the "rules of the game," and in the turbulent times before World War II, the rules of society are in the midst of change.

The film opens as a daredevil flier lands in France in a single-engine plane, bettering Lindbergh's epic record. The pilot, Jurieu, is treated like a national hero. When he's interviewed about his courageous feat, he confesses that it was his love for a woman that inspired him to break Lindbergh's record. Then he complains to the assembled reporters that she was not even there to greet him. He really doesn't care that she's married and with her husband. For him to blurt out his love for his woman publicly is totally uncool. His best friend, Octave, played by Renoir, rebukes him for acknowledging his love. According to the "rules" of society, it's not the way you play the game.

At the large hunting-house party that is the centerpiece of *Rules of the Game*, Christine, the woman Jurieu's in love with, discovers her husband's mistress, and in a fit of anger and spite asks Jurieu to run away with her. The request is more an act of punishment of her husband than a sign of love for the aviator. In Christine's eyes, Jurieu is nothing more than a good friend.

Being hopelessly in love with her, he agrees, but insists upon telling her husband that they're running away together, so that it becomes an "honorable act." Christine can't believe that in Jurieu's mind it's okay to run away with someone's wife, but it's not okay unless you tell the husband first. Jurieu, trying to fit into a world in which he doesn't belong, doesn't understand "the rules of the game."

Renoir's point was that the "rules" and "laws" of society have changed and the old-fashioned concept of honor has disappeared.

Charm has become more important than feeling. The characters who live by the "old" rules of society cannot play the "game," and are unable to adapt to society's decay. The guests at the château house party seem to foreshadow the guests at the big hotel parties in later films—*La Dolce Vita, L'Avventura, La Notte, Last Year at Marienbad.*

What made such an impression on me was not so much the story or the characters or the acting, but how Renoir dramatized his ideas. Renoir had taken an intellectual idea and created a movie focusing on the concepts of love and relationships amid a changing social structure, a work of art incorporating farce, satire and tragedy. No wonder the film has been classified as one of cinema's most monumental achievements.

Renoir knew that with one world war history and another on the brink of happening, the antiquated feelings which had been the foundations of the "old" society no longer applied. The rules of the game were out of date, just like the aristocrats he depicted. I began to understand that this was a point in history in which sudden and dramatic changes were sweeping through all layers of society. People either had to adapt to this new way of life, the rise of the middle class, or die. That's the whole point of the movie. The great Russian playwright Chekhov wrote about these same themes in *The Cherry Orchard, Three Sisters* and other works.

A few days after seeing *Rules of the Game*, during a break in rehearsal, I asked Renoir how he found the ideas for his stories. He smiled and told me that when he wanted to create a story, he always "started with the environment; because it's only from the externals that I'm able to arrive at the creation of a character or a plot." By "externals," I understood he meant *situation*, the circumstances surrounding the story. Renoir shared that he had been absolutely astonished at the complacency with which the French had accepted the idea of the German occupation. That's why he felt the film was booed at the Paris premiere and banned by the French and Vichy governments. One critic wrote that "the film is a classic example of an audience's revulsion to a perceptive critique of their world." Renoir's intention, the critic continued, was to create "an exact description of the middle class of our time," and it seems pretty obvious he succeeded.

I saw *Rules of the Game* several times after that initial screening, and each time I saw it I understood more and more. I think that's why it is on every list of the greatest films ever made. The great French filmmaker Alain Resnais recently told me that seeing this film had been the most overwhelming experience he has ever had in the cinema.

When *Carola* ended its extended run, several things happened in my life. I had come to the university to find a direction in my life, and finally had to admit to myself that after my experience with Renoir, any aspirations I'd had for a career in medicine had only been a dream. It was time to give it up, time to just wise up.

With that realization, and not knowing exactly what to do, I decided to enter the graduate school in English literature, but it only took me a short time to realize I didn't fit in there either. I really didn't know what I wanted to do. I stayed in San Francisco a while, acted in the Actor's Workshop production of Samuel Beckett's masterpiece *Waiting for Godot*, playing the part of Lucky, and wondered what destiny had in store for me.

The next time I was in L.A., Renoir invited me to come up to his house and visit, which I did. When I arrived, the first thing I saw were some original paintings of his father's hanging on the walls—not only paintings, but wood carvings, fashioned by the great Impressionist's hand. Over the next few weeks, I spent many afternoons and evenings with Renoir and Dido. Finally, I summoned up enough courage to ask for help and guidance, and confessed that I seemed to have no direction in life and didn't know what I should do. Renoir looked at me for a long moment, walked over to his desk and started writing something on a piece of paper. Then he got up and handed it to me. When I read it, I saw it was addressed to the head of the Film Department at UCLA; it was a letter of recommendation.

"The future is film," he said simply.

The next thing I knew, I was attending classes in the graduate film program at UCLA.

By that simple act, Renoir pointed out the path through the forest and changed my life forever.

Movies 101

"Rosebud . . . Maybe that was something he lost. . . .
You see, Mr. Kane was a man
who lost almost everything he had."
—MR. BERNSTEIN (Everett Sloane)
speculating on the possible meaning of "Rosebud"
Citizen Kane (Herman Mankiewicz and Orson Welles)

Even though I grew up in and around the sound stages of Hollywood, I entered the Graduate Division at the UCLA Film School at the dawn of the sixties knowing absolutely nothing about filmmaking. The department itself was small, relegated to two reconverted bungalows, a few classrooms and a supply closet where we stood in line to check out the few 16mm cameras that never seemed to be available.

This is the future? I asked myself. I wondered what Renoir had had in mind when he wrote his letter of recommendation, whether he'd ever been on this campus, had ever seen or used the shoddy and makeshift equipment they issued us in the use of our "art." At that time, film programs at other universities hardly existed. Film studies, as it was then known, was not as "socially acceptable" as it is today.

The one thing I responded to immediately was the wonderful energy that permeated the classrooms and corridors by day and by night. Something was always going on—maybe a shoot in progress, or the screenings of dailies (the film shot the previous day), student or classic films—and everywhere there were lively discussions about film, life and art. Sometimes students would come into the editing rooms late and abscond with a Moviola so they could cut their films in the dead of night. The Film Department was always open, day and night, weekends and holidays.

There were no video cameras, no Super 8, no TV monitors, no electronic dubbing boards, no Avids at this time; everything was filmed with one of those old Bell & Howell 16mm cameras. Every class exercise we did, whether filming students walking on campus or reediting a scene from a produced movie, we paid for out of our own pockets. Sometimes, we were fortunate and got discarded "short-ends" from the movie studios, those unused portions of film stock left over from a movie production. Basically, we made do with what we had and what we could get. I began to understand the dedication, scrounging and finagling it takes to make movies.

I took all the required classes: film editing, film theory, film history, camera, sound and effects editing, as well as all the production classes. There were only about fifteen of us in our class, and we bonded fairly quickly. I learned about the great Russian filmmakers and theorists: Eisenstein, Pudovkin, studied the "step sequence" from *The Battleship Potemkin*, analyzed *The Great Train Robbery*, learned about D. W. Griffith and *Birth of a Nation* and was introduced to German Expressionism and *The Cabinet of Dr. Caligari*. I did my little two- or three-minute film exercises, screened them for my instructors, was critiqued by the other students.

It was really a great time of learning. I hung out with a guy by the name of Ray Manzarek, a rock musician, who was very interested in film, and we spent many days and nights exchanging ideas about art, film and music. He loved *La Grande Illusion*, and wanted to hear all he could about what it was like working with Jean Renoir. When I told him I'd met Aldous Huxley after one of the performances of *Carola* at Berkeley (he was a close friend of Renoir's), Ray told me his rock group called themselves The Doors, after Huxley's book *The Doors of Perception*. Jim Morrison, who sang and wrote most of the lyrics, Ray, Robby Krieger, the guitarist, and I had some good times together. I still see Ray occasionally, and of course, The Doors went on to revolutionize the music scene and become one of the legendary and classic groups of the sixties.

The early sixties was the time of the New Wave, a movement of young French film critics who started making films in revolt against the movies currently being screened. Their films literally exploded across the screens of the world, and changed the very perception of film. As one French critic put it, "The filmmaker/author now writes with his camera as a writer writes with his pen." The look, style and subject matter of film was beginning to change; instead of the Doris Day–Rock Hudson puff comedies of the fifties, or the grotesque *Lust for Life*, *The Ten Commandments*, *Around the World in 80 Days* or *Love Me Tender*, young, experimental filmmakers were rebelling and starting to express themselves with new voices and new visions. An explosion of ideas was swirling around the film school, and I was inspired by the New Wave movies coming out of France: Truffaut's *The 400 Blows* and *Shoot the Piano Player*, Godard's *Breathless*, Chabrol's *Les Cousins*, Rivette's *Paris Belongs to Us* and Resnais's *Hiroshima, Mon Amour*. I read and discussed critics like Andrew Sarris of the *Village Voice*, Stanley Kauffmann of *The New Republic*, Pauline Kael of *The New Yorker*, James Agee. I went to the midnight screenings at "art houses" around town to see what was happening, meeting Ray Manzarek and others there, and when the screenings were over we would sit for hours discussing what we had seen.

At the time, there were no intern programs available in which a few selected students would get hands-on experience in the craft of moviemaking. Our "intern program" was "learning by doing," and as part of the graduate school curriculum we were assigned to work on whatever thesis film might be in production. After we had finished our classes for the day, my classmates and I would go on the primitive sound stage and help set up lights or lay cables. Whatever we were asked to do, we did, whether it was taking film to the labs or picking up dailies from the previous day's shooting. Sometimes I ran the projector for screening dailies, or just sat in, basically observing all the parts that go into the making of a movie.

The first thesis film I was assigned to work on was written and directed by a young graduate student named Francis Ford Coppola. I knew nothing about him except what I had been told: he was a young filmmaker of extraordinary promise. I was chosen to lay cables and move lights, so I had a good view of the young virtuoso in action. What impressed me most, I think, was his focus— his concentration and his unerring effort to achieve what he wanted. I remember watching him set up a shot the DP (director of photography) said was "impossible." Francis went into a corner, picked up the script and started looking it over. Though he knew every word and shot by heart, I could see he was buying time. He looked around, then down at the pages he held in his hand, and then looked as if he were searching for something. All eyes were fixed on him.

Finally, he put the script down, walked back to the DP and said, "This is the way we're going to do it." He had the crew build a low, makeshift platform with two-by-fours mounted on bricks. Then he had the cameraman slide underneath this makeshift floor, and that's how he achieved the low-angle "floor shot" he wanted.

Coppola's thesis film at UCLA was the precursor to one of his first studio films, *You're a Big Boy Now*. The story basically deals with a teenager's passage into manhood, and when the film opened, it seemed most critics sensed he was a major talent. This particular theme, dealing with the rites of passage to manhood, seems to run through most of Coppola's work. You can see and feel it in his major movies, from *You're a Big Boy Now*, to *The Rain People*, to *The Godfather* and *Godfather, Part II*, to *The Conversation*, to *Apocalypse Now*, to *Rumble Fish*, *The Outsiders* and others.

It was in my second semester at UCLA that I took my first screenwriting class. I had never written anything before except term papers, but I had discovered and fallen in love with the plays of Eugene O'Neill and Henrik Ibsen when I was at Berkeley. I had written many term projects about the influence of Ibsen on O'Neill, and I found the issues and themes of their plays very powerful. And I had a feeling, somewhere at the back of my mind, that I might like to write a play. But a screenplay? I had never read one, much less thought about writing one. I had no idea what to do or how to do it.

My instructor for the screenwriting class was Dorothy Arzner, a well-known director who had made several notable films in the twenties with such luminaries as Clara Bow, Fredric March and Rosalind Russell. She was intelligent, patient and insightful, and instilled in me the willingness to make mistakes. She insisted that writing the screenplay was only a start point, and not the end point, and wanted me to try things that might not work. This concept is an integral part of my teaching method to this day. "Writing a screenplay is always a work in progress," she would say, "because it never ends."

Dorothy Arzner knew what she was talking about. She emphasized that film has its own language, and that it's essential to learn the proper grammar and vocabulary before you write anything for the screen. So she began by giving us an action to write, like a car running out of gas or a relationship disintegrating, then let us shape it into visual images. I think I started my screenwriting career like everybody else: by letting the characters explain through their words who they are, what they're doing and what they want. Talking heads to the extreme. Even as I was writing these little exercises, I saw that this kind of writing did not work. It was explanatory, and made me so uncomfortable I wanted to puke. It was terrible. As an actor, I knew that the function of dialogue was more than simply explaining what was happening. What about all those thoughts, feelings and emotions that could be explored below the surface of dialogue? How could I capture those?

Gradually, I started thinking more in pictures than in dialogue. When I approached the idea of writing my own screenplay for class, I had the notion that I wanted to create an event (influenced from watching Kurosawa's *Rashomon* and Orson Welles's *Citizen Kane*) that would trail through my character's life, influencing his actions at various stages. I'd always been interested in time as a relative phenomenon, where an hour seems like a minute, a minute like an hour.

With that in mind, I wrote what's now called a "nonlinear" screenplay for my term project, about a young boy's witnessing a murder committed by his uncle, then inadvertently saying something to the authorities which leads to his uncle's arrest. I told it through several different stages in my character's life, using flashbacks as well as crosscutting between various time periods: the witnessing of the murder, the accidental admission to the authorities, through his marriage, his success, divorce, loneliness and, finally, death. À la *Citizen Kane*. I called it *Time, Forever*. Dorothy Arzner liked it and told me I should seriously think about becoming a screenwriter.

Writing this script made me aware once again of *how* I looked at the movies; no longer did I simply go to a theater, passively sit back and watch the story unfold. As Renoir taught I began to look for things within the movie itself; if I saw something I liked, I wanted to know how the effect was achieved, how it was set up, how certain scenes revealed, or influenced, character. It was a major transformation in the way I studied and looked at film. I saw movies differently now, as if I had changed the prescription of my glasses.

Filled with so many new ideas about film, I often visited the Renoirs, and over a coffee or a glass of wine we would have long and wonderful discussions about the New Wave films being made in Europe. The small theaters which had been showing foreign films for years, the "art houses," were receiving a lot of attention because of these films.

One night after class, several of us went to see the late screening of Ingmar Bergman's *The Seventh Seal*. It had recently burst upon the scene and was being talked about by the entire Film Department. I had never seen a religious allegory that was so visually arresting and intellectually challenging. The story of a Knight returning after ten years in the Crusades, searching for God, spiritual redemption and a purpose in life, hit me on a very deep, personal level, and I found it riveting. When Death appears before the Knight and tells him it's time to leave this plane, the Knight is not ready and challenges Death to a game of chess. If he wins, he gains an extension so that he can search for something to believe in, "the meaning of life." If he loses, Death wins.

After the screening, we started talking about the film. During the discussion, I realized I had responded to this dramatic situation as if it were a Eugene O'Neill play. Intellectually, I understood the artist's point of view: life is chaos, a random series of incidents, filled with selfishness and violence. I had read about it, studied it, seen literary examples of it, but the truth is, I'd never emotionally "got it." I had never *experienced* it on a gut level; it had only been an intellectual exercise. But in *The Seventh Seal*, I *saw* how Bergman viewed the world; the film revealed his personal point of view. Life, according to Bergman, is pain, suffering, torment and unhappiness, woven together with unrealized dreams and unrealistic expectations. If this is the case, how does a man find the faith within himself to endure? And what, then, is the meaning of life?

As our discussion continued into the early morning hours, I saw that the images Bergman presents, the various scenes and sequences, support the point of view of the main character; we see the world the way he sees the world, through his eyes. For that reason, he's a passive character, an observer, watching the tableau of life unfold in front of him. He is the eternal outsider. He comments on the action, reacts to the events but does not participate in them.

I understood that *The Seventh Seal* expresses the character's point of view visually—through pictures, not words. We see what he sees, learn what he learns; the audience and character are connected in a bond of discovery.

Because of my English literature background, I had been *reading* the points of view of great authors: D. H. Lawrence, Henry James, James Joyce; the plays of Strindberg, Ibsen and O'Neill. It took me a while to understand that the forms of the novel, the play and the screenplay are as different as night and day. To understand the distinction between them, I felt, would be the first step in understanding the language of film.

Later, when I started teaching screenwriting, I went back to this experience and began to isolate and define the way a novelist writes his or her story; I did the same with the play, and the screenplay. It was a great exercise. I reread novels and plays, saw lots of movies and read whatever screenplays I could get my hands on. I began to see the distinctions between the three forms. I found that when I read a novel, for example, the dramatic action usually takes place *inside the character's head*, through what I term the *mindscape* of dramatic action. The character's thoughts, feelings, emotions, dreams, fantasies, memories, basically form the internal action of the novel, and take place inside the character's head. We see the story through the eyes of the characters. And many times, the point of view shifts from that of one character to that of another.

When I went back and read some of the Eugene O'Neill plays, I saw that the action of the play takes place onstage, under the proscenium arch, and that the audience makes up the "fourth wall." The dramatic (or comedic) action is revealed through the words of the characters, through their dialogue. I recalled that as an actor I had always been listening to other characters explaining their thoughts, feelings, emotions, memories and dreams. The action in a play, I saw, is expressed through the *language of dramatic action*, through *words* spoken by the actors.

When I contrasted and compared the novel and play with the screenplay, I began to notice something different. Movies are *stories told in pictures*, and while the action and dialogue are integral parts of the screenplay, the story line unfolds through the visual images. An event happens, and then we see the characters' reaction to that event; that's the story which unfolds from beginning to end.

I had just begun to understand and define these distinctions at school when I saw a movie that pushed my understanding into a new, and deeper, perspective: Akira Kurosawa's masterpiece *Rashomon*. The movie is set in eleventh-century Japan, and focuses on a single event as seen through the eyes of four major characters:

a wife, the spirit of her murdered husband, a bandit and a wood-cutter.

Rashomon was screened in a tiny, dusty, run-down screening room on campus as part of our film history course. I watched the story begin to unfold around the key incident of the movie, the rape of the wife and her husband's murder. Four people had seen the same event, and four people had seen something entirely different. The idea behind the movie was so simple, yet so mind-blowing; I had never seen anything like it before.

Over the next several days, I couldn't get the film out of my mind. I couldn't figure out how Kurosawa achieved such an emotional effect. Was it the idea that truth is "relative"? Or, was it the psychological insights he had gleaned from each of the characters in this particular circumstance? Was it the way he framed the story? I kept sifting the various pieces of the film through my mind, hoping to gain some insight and clarity into the response I was having.

Was it, I wondered, the way he opened the film, during an intense rainstorm, as three men seek refuge under the crumbling ruins of the Rashomon Gate? In his opening, one of the men, a priest, tells the others about a crime that has been committed, where a woman has been raped and her husband murdered. As the priest tells the story we flash back to the reenactment of the event as told through the eyes of the four main characters: the victim, the bandit accused of the crimes, the spirit of the victim's dead husband and the wood-cutter who claims he witnessed the murder. Of course, the "truth" changes, as revealed through the eyes of each character.

I think what intrigued me so much is that Kurosawa had found a visual metaphor which explores the philosophical concept of the nature of truth. The more I thought about the film, the more I saw that all four characters are involved, in some way or other, in the events of the rape and the murder. Each of the characters faces the camera, as if speaking to a judge, and recites his or her own version of the sequence of events. And each story is reenacted from the point of view of the character telling the story. Kurosawa implies it's the audience who must decide the relative truth of each character's testimony—if there's any truth at all.

The action in *Rashomon* revolves around the way each person sees the same event, and that's what visually creates the dramatic action. The event is the event; it remains the same, and thus becomes the start point of the movie. I've come to learn that many movies revolve around, or are initiated by, one particular incident. In dramatic terminology, the event which initiates the story line is called the "inciting incident."

What this incident is, how it's set up and the dramatic function it serves became clearer when we screened *Citizen Kane*.

I first saw the Welles classic on a Friday night in a large, bare screening room with the other students in my film history class. These Friday night screenings were the high point of our week. We saw most of the film classics, those movies that influenced the evolution of filmmaking from a historical perspective. Hugh Gray, a noted and delightful philosophy professor, as well as a film historian, taught the class. As we piled into our seats he told us that of all the films we'd seen during the semester, *Citizen Kane* would probably be the one that would stay with us the longest and influence us the most. He briefly described the history of the film, and told us a little about Orson Welles, from the rise of the Mercury Players to the radio presentation of the phenomenal *War of the Worlds*. When he finished, we sat back in our seats and watched an old scratchy print that revealed the life and times of Charles Foster Kane.

Hugh Gray was right. The film was a virtual encyclopedia of film knowledge. *Citizen Kane* is truly a story told with pictures, a search for the mystery of one man's life that revolves around the last words Kane utters on his deathbed. From the very beginning, I was aware of the deep-focus photography, the high and low angles and the wide-angle lens shots. I had never seen anything like it before; "I want to use the motion picture camera as an instrument of poetry," Welles had said, and I knew what he meant.

After the screening, Ray Manzarek and I, along with a few friends, went out for a beer and discussed the movie. There was so much I personally responded to in the film; thinking about the way the story is built and put together, I started to understand what Dorothy Arzner kept telling us in our screenwriting class, that it's not necessary *to explain* everything, that sometimes things are better left unsaid.

From the very first frame of the movie, I saw that Kane's character is *set up visually*; the first thing we see is the high, wired chain-link fence bolstered with the initial K, and, deep in the background, the isolated mansion high on the hill. As we move closer we see boxes and crates of ancient antiques, artworks and artifacts stacked everywhere. Huge pens house exotic animals, and then we're inside Kane's enormous castle, so full, yet so empty of life. Then, we cut to an extreme close-up of Kane's lips and mouth as he whispers his last word, "Rosebud." The glass paperweight falls from his fingers and breaks open, and we see snow, the first glimpse of his lost childhood.

Like a classic mystery, the story thus begins. Who is Charles Foster Kane? What is he? Who or what is Rosebud? As if in answer, Welles cuts to a darkened screening room filled with chain-smoking reporters, and we watch newsreel footage of Charles Foster Kane, a man larger than life, a man of total excess. The great director Robert Wise (*The Magnificent Ambersons; Curse of the Cat People; Executive Suite; Run Silent, Run Deep; Odds Against Tomorrow; West Side Story; The Sound of Music; The Sand Pebbles,* to name just a few) edited the film and told me in one of our conversations that Welles shot all the simulated newsreel footage and then, to make it appear more "real," had Wise crinkle it up and drag it across the cutting room floor. It lent an authentic, credible look to the film. Kane's entire life is visually set up in less than a minute—through pictures, not words.

Another thing that stood out for me was the way Orson Welles used his transitions, those moments where the film goes from scene A to scene B—from an intimate dialogue scene, for example, to a scene of intense action and suspense. The purpose of a transition is to connect two separate, independent scenes so that the story keeps moving forward. Transitions bridge time and place and move the action forward quickly, visually. Many years later, during my own screenwriting career, showing the passage of time was one of my most difficult tasks.

Of all the great cinematic techniques in the film, I think my favorite is the "marriage montage." Kane's marriage is revealed in one incredible transition. The sequence begins with the marriage and honeymoon of Kane and his first wife. We see them at breakfast having an intimate conversation. There is a *swish pan* (the camera swishes quickly out the frame) and we see them in different clothes talking and reading the paper at breakfast. *Swish pan* and we see them at a slightly larger table having a very heated discussion. *Swish pan* to them having a more vocal argument about him spending so much time at the newspaper. *Swish pan* to them at a much larger table, both silent, both reading the paper, he reading *The Inquirer*, she reading *The Post*, his primary competitor. She asks him something and he simply grunts in reply. *Swish pan* to them at a very long table, eating in total silence. The sequence tells us so much in so little, using pictures instead of words. It's an extraordinary example of bridging time, place and action. The sequence sets him up for his love affair which, when discovered, dashes his political ambitions.

Every time I went to the movies after seeing this film, I began looking for transitions. They are the nuts and bolts necessary to move a story forward. Even today when I go to the movies, I'm keenly aware of how the writer and filmmaker go from one scene to the next, and how the various transitions are effected.

Though Welles took credit for writing most of the screenplay for *Citizen Kane*, it was probably cowriter Herman Mankiewicz who scripted the bulk of its incisive, witty scenes and dialogue. Yet it was Welles's extraordinary insight and genius into the various corridors of Kane's life that I found so astute. I call it "an emotional detective story," because the search for who and what "Rosebud" is leads us to uncover the life of Charles Foster Kane. It's this question that begins the movie and acts as the inciting incident.

At the end, after Kane's death (which is where the story really begins), the warehouse is being cleared of what seem to be endless piles of junk, curios, furniture and unpacked crates. As the camera moves into a darkened corner, we see a huge collection of toys, paintings and statues. Slowly, the camera pans Kane's possessions until it reaches the blazing furnace. Workmen are tossing various items into the flames. One of the items is a sled, the very one Kane had as a boy in Colorado. When it's thrown into the fire, the camera closes in tight on the sled, and as it catches fire the name "Rosebud" is revealed. Only then do we recall that when Mr. Thatcher, the youthful executor of Kane's estate, first describes his meeting with Kane as a boy of ten or so, young Charles was sledding down the hill in the snow. It is an emotionally riveting moment, emblematic of the lost youth Kane had been searching for, but had never found. Then we cut outside the huge mansion as smoke from Kane's lost youth curls upward into the night sky. The film ends with the same shot of the iron fence that opened the film. "I was with him from the very beginning," Mr. Bernstein (Everett Sloane) says during the film, and "Mr. Kane was a man who lost everything he had."

It was after that first year in film school that I knew without a doubt that I wanted to be in the arena of the movies. Seeing *Citizen Kane, Rashomon* and the other classics was memorable, for it allowed me to see and understand the language of film with "new eyes." Finally, I had found something I truly loved and believed in.

What I had hoped for on that day I had gone to see Renoir for guidance had come true: I had found something I loved, something challenging and inspiring. I had found a direction in life. And direction, I would soon learn, is a line of development.

As excited as I was about my new "direction," school was still school, and I was feeling antsy and stifled by the academic rigors and requirements. I felt the faint stirrings of restlessness, and I could tell it was time for me to move on. Though I didn't know exactly *what* I wanted to do—whether it was in the arena of writing, producing or directing—I was content; when I totaled up the years I'd spent in school, I knew I had had enough and was ready to move on.

To what, I wasn't quite sure.

Catching the Wave

"I believe now that I'm no longer capable of writing. It's not that I don't know what to write, but how to write it. That's what they call a 'crisis.' But in my case it's something inside me, something which is affecting my whole life."

—Giovanni (Marcello Mastroianni)

TO Valentina (Monica Vitti)

Antonioni's *La Notte*

It was late, and I sat at my desk staring at the blank sheet of paper in front of me and wondered what I was trying to do. What I *wanted* to do was write a film review of Michelangelo Antonioni's film *La Notte*, but I was not having any success at all. I had been sitting at my desk for hours and I was angry, frustrated and perilously close to the deep edge of depression. It was all I could do to stare at the wall in front of me.

Writing. I never thought it would be so difficult. I thought about what had so moved and inspired me about the movie, and remembered those incidents and events which had led me to attempt putting my thoughts, words and ideas onto a blank sheet of paper. How and why did I end up here?

The whole process had started a few months earlier. Since I'd left UCLA I'd been trying to get a job and couldn't find one anywhere. I had gone from production company to production company, interview to interview, read the trade papers diligently, made up endless lists of names to call, had called, was told to send in a resumé or the calls were never returned. I had been fortunate to get a few interviews, which I thought had gone well, but nothing had happened. I had dressed appropriately, rehearsed my answers, polished my resumé, was polite and punctual, but couldn't get a job to save my life.

To bolster my spirits, I reread a biography of Henrik Ibsen and the wall of resistance he had endured while becoming "the father" of modern playwriting. Ibsen, author of *A Doll's House*, *The Wild Duck*, *An Enemy of the People*, *Hedda Gabler* and other plays, had struggled alone, in solitude and anonymity, for years, all the while seeking someone to believe in him and his work. But no matter how hard he struggled, or how difficult the times were, he did not give up, and continued to write his plays in the face of no agreement. Although his faith wavered, deep within himself he knew that when he was ready to be discovered, something would happen; someone would find him. That was the Law of Destiny. Reading about his struggles reinforced my own faith and renewed my determination. I just had to be patient and keep trying to get a job. Grace only comes through self-effort.

Finally, after several months of nothing happening, I surrendered to the fact that I was hitting a stone wall; I couldn't do it on my own. I needed help. So, in desperation, I went to talk to my uncle Sol.

Sol Halprin—"Solly," as he was called—had married my mother's sister and was currently the head of the Camera Department at 20th Century Fox. He had held that position for more than fifty years. Originally from New Jersey, he had come to Hollywood when he was sixteen, and learned the camera business from the inside out.

He started as a lab assistant at the old Fox Films lab, was promoted to assistant cameraman in 1921 and worked on every single one of the old Buck Jones and Tom Mix westerns. He was smart, and he was tough. I had seen pictures of him as a young man, wearing a white suit and straw hat, holding a baseball bat in his hand at one of the early strikes in Hollywood. He looked like an ex-prizefighter, with a broken nose and cauliflower ears, but in truth he was the epitome of the tough-crusted man with a heart of gold.

He became a director of photography in 1928, and from what I was told had been the first cameraman to hoist one of those old Mitchell 35mm cameras onto his shoulders and let himself be lashed to the tail of a biplane, from which he took some of those wonderful aerial shots that were in those old silent movies about World War I.

I had many reservations about asking Uncle Sol for help getting into the movie business. I had heard him say on more than one occasion that he would never help any member of his family get into the movie industry. He had seen too much, endured too much, and did not want his family to be subjected to the harsh realities of "the business." As head of the Camera Department, he was in a position where everyone asked favors of him: producers, directors, heads of studios, stars. Whenever anyone had a problem dealing with a camera, or a film stock or a cameraman, they called Solly. He was on call twenty-four hours a day, handling camera breakdowns in the middle of Africa and broken generators deep in the heart of the Sahara or high in the mountains of Wyoming.

By the Second World War he had climbed through the ranks to become an important member of John Ford's Naval Film Unit, and would often hang out and play cards with Ford and his buddies: John Wayne, Ward Bond and others. I still remember having cookies and milk at John Ford's house as a kid while Solly and Ford, blustery and intimidating with that black patch he wore, discussed business.

In 1953, Solly won an Academy Award for coinventing the CinemaScope wide-screen process, and served as the president of the American Society of Cinematographers for many terms. He was honored, revered and appreciated by every single studio head he worked for.

From my perspective, Uncle Sol was a man who had an opinion about everything, which is why it was so difficult to talk with him about anything relating to the movie business. I knew from past experience that whenever I would ask for advice, he would make a point of telling me about the downside of everything, and when I was in his presence I always felt insecure, awkward and out of place.

After talking with my aunt Gladys, Sol's wife, I decided that if I was really serious about getting a job in the movie business, I'd better bite the bullet and swallow my pride. Besides, what was the worst that could happen? He'd tell me that the movie business was not for me, that I was wasting my time and he wasn't going to help me. I took a deep breath and decided I didn't have anything to lose. So Gladys set up a time for me to have breakfast with them one Sunday morning.

I washed the car, dressed nicely and drove to their house. I sat down, trying to be cool, made some small talk and over the course of breakfast filled him in on my time at UCLA. He listened, asked me a few questions about the cameras we were using. During a lull in the conversation, I took a deep breath and nervously told him what I wanted to do and whom I had talked to, and asked if there was any way he might be able to help me get a job. It didn't matter what, I said, I just wanted to get a foot in the door. He grumbled and mumbled, told me how foolish I was, that I should be a "professional" person like my family wanted me to be. In truth, I could tell my aunt had already briefed him on my request. He appeared supportive, but made no promises, and we simply left it at that.

I knew that while Solly might be able to help get me a job, in order for me to keep it I would have to perform well above the line of duty. If he was able to help me get in the door, I was going to have to make sure I was not embarrassing him. Hollywood is a small town, and he occupied such a high position that by helping me he'd have to "call in" one of his favors.

So I continued looking for a job, but at the same time I was anxious to do something. Since I'd gotten my degree in English literature, I decided to try writing film criticism. When I was at Berkeley, I used to read a magazine called *Film Quarterly*, published by the University of California Press, whose perspective and point of view I admired. I contacted the editor, who told me to go ahead and write something; they were always open to reviews, he said.

Where do I start? I wondered. How do I set out to write a film review? The answer to both questions was obvious. First, I needed a film to write about. Second, I needed a way, or a point of view, to start the film review. I recalled a literary criticism class I had taken at Berkeley which had been taught by the noted American poet Josephine Miles. She said the basis of all literary criticism is composed of answering a simple question: *Do I like it?* If so, why? And if not, why not?

She emphasized that answering this question is really the start point of all literary criticism. If I liked something, what did I like about it? Was it the characters? The action? The dialogue, the situation, or premise? On the other hand, if I didn't like it, what didn't I like?

So I began seeing movies, all kinds of movies, always asking myself whether I liked them or didn't like them: I saw Truffaut, Hitchcock, Chabrol, Resnais; I saw *The Hustler*, *Hud* and many, many others. The more movies I saw, the more aware I became of the elements that made them work or not work, what I liked about them and what I didn't like. It was the start of a wonderful learning experience.

But in all those movies I saw during this particular time, there were only a few that really stood out. The most daring and original, I thought, was *Breathless*. I first saw it at UCLA during my second semester. Originally released in 1959, it was made by the great young French filmmaker Jean-Luc Godard, one of the former film critics of the famous magazine *Cahiers du Cinema*. Seeing it again at the Los Feliz Theater, I was captivated from the very first frame. It was new, it was fresh, it was alive and it was daring; it was a film that took the existing visual language, smashed and modified it, then offered it up in a new fashion. It is truly a landmark film.

Jean-Paul Belmondo plays an amoral petty criminal who models himself after Humphrey Bogart. He steals a car, senselessly kills a highway patrolman, chases after some money that's owed to him so that he and his young American girlfriend (Jean Seberg) can escape to Italy.

As outlaws, their efforts to escape are farcical and halfhearted. I totally related to their nonchalant attitude. Somehow it captured the moral ambivalence of my generation, which was rebelling against the surface niceties of the times. It seemed that Godard's characters really didn't give a damn about anything; they had no moral foundation, no political ideology. They went from one thing to the next without worrying about whether their actions were "good" or "bad," or "right" or "wrong." They were literally rebels without any cause whatsoever, and that appealed to me.

Great lines were everywhere: "Between grief and nothing," Seberg says, "I will take grief." To which Belmondo replies, "I'd choose nothing." In the famous bedroom scene, Seberg looks deeply into Belmondo's eyes and says, "When we look into each other's eyes, we get nowhere."

It was so cool. The film never stops moving. Even the title seems to be a visual metaphor: *À Bout de Souffle* literally means "out of breath," and Belmondo never stops moving until he's finally shot down, and only stops breathing when he's "out of breath." To emphasize this fast-paced tempo, Godard inserts jump cuts to speed up the action into a disparate, disjointed jazz riff. The first time I saw it I thought the print had been cut. It was only later that I understood that the jump cuts were intentional.

I went back to see *Breathless* over and over again, and thought this might be a film I could really write about. But before I could even outline my thoughts and ideas, I saw a movie that changed the entire landscape of my thinking.

It was a film called *La Notte*, made by the Italian filmmaker Michelangelo Antonioni. I had read about Antonioni, but had never seen a film of his before *La Notte*. I had a deep-seated emotional response to it; it just hit me in the gut. For days, certain images from the film stayed with me, always a sure sign, I knew, that there was something important for me to learn.

As I went back over the film in my mind, I began to understand that it worked on two different levels. One level was the visual surface level, portrayed through those ordinary events that make up our day-to-day existence. The other level, deeper and far richer, occurred below the surface details, and dealt with the emotional action and interaction between the two characters. It was this second level, the emotional state, that revealed the true nature of what the characters were thinking and feeling. In that regard, I saw that what was left unsaid was more important than what was said.

At the first viewing, I only sensed this emotional state; I had no words to express it, only these vague, haunting images. Seeing it a second time, I felt that maybe Antonioni had uncovered some kind of new visual language and was using images to create an emotional response—something felt, not spoken. Later, I would discover that this subterranean emotional level was called the *subtext*, something I had known about and practiced as an actor in some of the roles I had played.

In the film, Giovanni (Marcello Mastroianni) and Lidia (Jeanne Moreau) have lived in Milan during their ten years of marriage. Giovanni is a successful novelist whose new book has just been published, but emotionally, he is in a crisis. He feels his best years are behind him, and he's stuck in the meaninglessness of writing a new novel. Lidia feels empty, and tells Giovanni that she no longer feels the same way toward him.

It took me several viewings to understand one of Antonioni's hallmarks: his characters see themselves in each other. Their dying friend tells Giovanni and Lidia that being in the hospital has given him time to think and that what he has come to understand is that he is a person who "lacks the courage to get to the bottom of things." He could really be speaking for Giovanni, as the way they respond to each other is really a mirror, or reflection, of their own lives.

Antonioni demonstrates the power of silence in film, and shows how it can be much more effective than words. The chasm in their marriage is conveyed visually. Visiting their dying friend in the hospital, as they ride in the elevator they carefully avoid looking at each other—two people, together but separate, without emotional bonds of sympathy or support. Later, when Giovanni and Lidia leave the hospital and take a long drive to a party celebrating the publication of his new book, we sense the distance between them again, as they drive in absolute silence.

At the publication party, Lidia, feeling the outsider, leaves and wanders through the city. We see what she sees, and sense her alienation from her husband and herself. The empty landscape of the city echoes her state of mind. So simple, yet so rich; I responded to it on both an emotional and intellectual level.

Many critics and reviewers did not understand this long walk. To me, it represents another aspect of the journey into insight and clarity. Everything in *La Notte* is part of a journey: a journey to hope, despair, fulfillment or freedom; a journey seeking an emotional connection to other people; the journey from night to day. After all, the journey from night to day, from darkness to light, from ignorance to knowledge, is all part of the journey of life.

Later, at an evening party given in honor of Giovanni by a wealthy industrialist, Lidia is tempted by a rich playboy, while Giovanni is tempted by Valentina (Monica Vitti), the daughter of their host. When it begins to rain, many of the partygoers seek a diversion by leaping into the pool. Giovanni and Valentina share some pleasant moments together and, like many strangers, share their most intimate thoughts. He tells her, "I believe now that I'm no longer capable of writing. I know what to write but not how to write it." Like many of Antonioni's characters, Giovanni's personal life is reflected in his inability to work; he is what he does. It's not his ideas and convictions that have been lost, but the force, the energy and the inner fire to create a work of art. Ideas are part of his makeup; they may change, evolve, come and go, but they are never lost. It's in the physical act of producing his work that Giovanni has become powerless.

Meanwhile, Lidia telephones the hospital to find out how their friend is doing, only to learn he has just died. She goes to tell Giovanni, but sees him kissing Valentina and turns away.

As they leave the party in silence and walk out into the cold, gray light of dawn, she tells him of their friend's death. Then she addresses Giovanni directly: "If I want to die, it's because I no longer love you. That's the reason for my despair. I would like to be old already, to have devoted my whole life to you. I don't want to exist anymore because I can't love you." He replies, "I have given you nothing . . . I amount to nothing. I have wasted and I'm still wasting my life, like an idiot, taking without giving anything or giving too little in exchange. . . . It's strange that only today did I realize that what we give to others comes back to ourselves."

At the end of the film, as they sit at dawn on a deserted golf course, she reads him an old love letter, moving, poetic, from the heart. When he asks, "Who wrote it?" she looks at him for a long moment, then confides, "You did." (A little overstated, true, but it allows us to realize the depth of his despair.) He turns to her and tries to force his love upon her, in an attempt to recapture their lost passion. As day breaks, the script reads, "A sort of animal passion, a memory of that which was and which will never be again, grips them." Fade-out.

I had no words, or language, about what I felt at the time I first saw *La Notte*, but as I studied the film over and over again, I grasped that something new was at work here, something profound, a different way of telling stories in pictures. Antonioni seemed to tell his stories internally, revealing the language of the heart through visual images.

A lot of people did not like *La Notte* because "nothing really happens"; there is no plot, no action and it's way too long, they felt. Some critics asserted that the film is simply an "empty testament of modern life," not even a "slice of life," and they viewed Antonioni as a filmmaker who is too internal, focusing on *what does not happen* rather than on what *could* happen. Whatever that means. As in *Rashomon*, everyone saw something different.

My response to the film had been so powerful that I was dreaming about it, and kept jotting notes down in my journal. Looking back, I think what I responded to most were the characters and their search for meaning in life.

Seeing *La Notte*, I discovered a visual metaphor for the search for love. As I became more familiar with some of Antonioni's later films, I began to see that many of his movies deal with this theme. The question he raises is simple, yet profound—how does a person live in the modern world, in a world of change, cynicism and technology, with integrity, values, faith and love?

Whether in *L'Avventura, La Notte, Red Desert, The Eclipse, Zabriskie Point* or his last film, *Beyond the Clouds*, Antonioni always deals with this same theme. F. Scott Fitzgerald once wrote that we write only one or two stories during our lives; no matter how many books we write, or how many movies we make, we end up exploring the same themes over and over again.

While I admired *Breathless* for its fervent energy and ideas, compared with *La Notte* it was a movie that didn't touch me; it was Godard's ideas and technique that I responded to, not the emotional intensity of the story and characters. Ingmar Bergman once remarked that film is very much like poetry: it bypasses the mind and goes directly to the heart, then rises to the mind, at which point we can begin to analyze its meaning and relevance.

If I was going to write about a film that touched and inspired me, there really was no choice at all. *La Notte* showed me something I felt inside. It was a film, I felt, that blazed the trail of a new cinematic language, a language of the heart, a language that once learned would reveal a great deal about the moviegoing experience.

Many years later, after my introduction to *La Notte*, I had the opportunity to meet Antonioni. The German ministry of culture had invited me to Berlin to teach a workshop for a selected group of screenwriters. I had been there for over a month, and when it was over I decided to go to Italy to visit some friends. During my

stay, we traveled to visit Assisi, home of the poet-saint Francis of
Assisi, whose writings I had studied and admired when I was at
Berkeley.

As I was walking around the beautiful Church of St. Francis, I
saw a man walking across the square toward the church. He was
moving with difficulty, holding on to the arm of a woman, and she
was very careful not to rush him. It was a beautiful day, and the sunlight splashed on the pinkish-colored stones which are so unique to
Assisi. I watched for a moment, drinking in the scene, and then my
gaze turned back to the man and woman. His left hand was stuck
in his pocket, and he was dragging his left leg as he walked. The
woman led him to a chair underneath the ancient wood overhang,
shielding him from the sun, and he sat down.

He seemed nervous, his face tense, drawn tight in concentration;
each step seemed an effort. He looked vaguely familiar, but I didn't
place him. Yet something kept nagging at me, and suddenly I recognized him.

I got very excited; I did not know he had suffered a recent stroke,
so I was surprised at his physical condition. I watched as his wife,
Enrica, settled him in the chair. I watched respectfully, and after a
short time I walked over to introduce myself. Usually, I don't do
things like that, but I was so thrilled to see him.

It didn't even occur to me that he might not speak English,
and, of course, he didn't. He understood a lot, and his wife—his
production designer on *Blow-Up*—interpreted his responses for
him. Enrica told me he had just suffered a paralyzing stroke. She
explained that they were waiting for someone, and that I was
more than welcome to wait with them. He was very friendly, open
and patient, and Enrica encouraged me to share with Michelangelo my thoughts and ideas about his films. Even though he was

partially paralyzed, even though he couldn't speak English, even though he was in great physical and mental pain, we spent over an hour together. For me, it was one of those magic moments. The light in Assisi is incredible, and the light changed as we talked. I saw firsthand Antonioni's amazing power of perception: it seemed he could isolate every visual detail, from the number of tourists in the square to the shades of light and shadow moving across the area.

I kept referring to his movies, and I could tell he enjoyed the interaction. A few years later, Enrica told me how appreciative she was that I had come forward to speak with them. Because of Antonioni's stroke, she said, he seemed to be losing his will to live; life was becoming very difficult for him, and she was concerned. It almost sounds like a situation out of an Antonioni movie, but Enrica told me that during the brief time we had spent together, he'd felt much better.

A year or so later, I met the Antonionis again in upstate New York over the holidays, and we had Christmas dinner together. I had studied all of Antonioni's films, so I decided to ask him something I had been curious about ever since I'd seen L'Avventura. I asked him how he got the idea for the film, and in his characteristic fashion he smiled and shrugged his shoulders. Then, I asked him what happened to Anna, the character in L'Avventura who disappears at the end of the first act, the incident that really initiates the dramatic situation and begins the movie. He laughed, shrugged his shoulders and said: "I don't know; someone once told me she committed suicide, but I don't believe it," and we had a good laugh together.

Antonioni told me that he considered L'Avventura a "detective story back to front," so that what happened to Anna was really unimportant. It was what happened between her fiancé and her best friend, Claudia (Monica Vitti), which is so important; that's what the movie is all about. Searching for the missing girl brings them together, and it's that situation, their falling in love, which powers the entire movie. That's when the story really begins. Antonioni is truly a master of creating powerful and dramatic situations.

It was the essence of *La Notte* that I was trying to capture on paper for my first film review. But staring at that blank sheet of paper brought me back to the present. I wanted to write a review, a critical analysis, of Antonioni's film, and I was so stuck in my resistance that I couldn't write one word. Word after word, sentence after sentence, paragraph after paragraph, read terribly; it was trite, contrived and academic. I kept making mental judgments about how terrible my writing was, how I was unable to capture my true feelings on paper, and I could feel those dark clouds of depression beginning to surround me. It all seemed so ordinary. Was I kidding myself in thinking that I could write a film review?

I was in a terrible battle with the critical voice at the back of my mind; the *critic's voice* was insisting every sentence I wrote had to be perfect, intelligent, insightful and brilliant. I failed to understand that I was learning a new form, and that it was okay to write some shitty pages. I had to give myself permission to explore so that I could learn what I wanted to do. But this particular lesson only comes from experience. I was climbing up a mountain of resistance; I must have cleaned the refrigerator, sharpened pencils and washed the kitchen floor hundreds of times.

After struggling for days working on this review, I had had it; I pushed back the chair and in a fit of frustration threw my pen against the wall and went running. I must have run for over an hour, up and down streets, angry, frustrated, my self-esteem shattered and battered. When I returned, I was exhausted, totally drained. I took a shower and lay down on the bed, ready to cry. All of a sudden, a particular phrase wafted across my mind. At first I didn't pay much attention to it, but it grew, became stronger, and I realized it would be a good opening sentence to the review. I jumped up, rushed to my desk and started writing. For hours, I couldn't stop. When I had finished, I had written several pages—rough and awkward to be sure, but at least it was a first draft. It was a start point. As King Lear says: "Nothing comes from nothing." I learned you can't change something from nothing. You've got to have something before you can change it. And that gave me a place to begin.

I spent the next few weeks rewriting the piece, honing, polishing and getting it to a point where I felt it read well. I finished the review and, with a sense of accomplishment, and great expectation, sent it off to *Film Quarterly*.

A few weeks later, I got a very nice reply telling me thanks but no thanks; they liked the piece but had already gone to press on an entire issue devoted to the films of Antonioni and would I like to write something else for the magazine? If I saw a movie I liked, the letter went on, please feel free to call the editor.

At first, I was crushed. But after I read and reread the letter I understood that while it was a rejection letter, it was also an invitation.

What made that writing experience so important to me was the realization that there are two sides to writing. One side can be discouraging, full of pain, doubt and despair. The other side is the knowledge that with patience and discipline and the willingness to let material gestate, it will emerge when it's ready. That was a huge lesson for me.

About a week after I received the letter from *Film Quarterly*, my uncle Sol phoned. He told me I should call a small television production company called Wolper Productions and make an appointment to see the business affairs person.

When I went in for my appointment a few days later, the man I met with asked when I would be available to start; I told him that I was ready right now. He smiled at my enthusiasm and told me to come in Monday morning. I didn't know it at the time, of course, but this interview would become another one of the major turning points of my life.

More important, I was going to work, and I was elated.

4

Shadows
on the Wall

"Suppose you're in your office. . . . A pretty girl you've seen before comes into the room and you watch her. . . . She takes off her gloves, opens her purse and dumps it out on the table. . . . She has two dimes and a nickel—and a cardboard match box. She leaves the nickel on the desk, puts the two dimes back into her purse and takes her black gloves . . . just then your telephone rings. The girl picks it up, says hello—listens—and says deliberately into the phone, 'I've never owned a pair of black gloves in my life.' She hangs up . . . and you glance around and suddenly see another man in the office, watching every move the girl makes—"

"Go on," said Boxley smiling. "What happens?"

"I don't know," said Stahr. "I was just making pictures."

—F. Scott Fitzgerald
The Last Tycoon

The first thing I saw at Wolper Productions the morning I arrived was an ambulance parked in front of the building, red light swirling. I walked into the front lobby, where a number of people were standing around talking in muted, hushed voices. I watched as two ambulance attendants wheeled a man on a gurney through the lobby and outside into the waiting ambulance. The attendants settled him inside, got into the vehicle and sped off. After a few moments, the people in the lobby began to disperse, and after what I hoped was a respectful pause, I walked over to the front desk and introduced myself to the receptionist. I told her I was supposed to start work that morning. She smiled, made a phone call, then told me to take a seat; the person I was supposed to see was occupied with the recent medical emergency.

So I sat and watched. It was the fall of 1962, and at this time Wolper Productions occupied a beautiful old rotunda-styled building on Sunset Boulevard that is now the home to the famous Le Dome Restaurant. Under its high arching roof, the circular lobby was filled with black leather couches and coffee tables stacked with trade magazines. Soon, phones started ringing and people began walking through the lobby into the various offices on each side of the building.

A youngish-looking man holding a lit cigar in his hand and wearing bedroom slippers poked his head out of a large office and stepped into the lobby. He yelled something to somebody, then disappeared back into the office. This, I found out later, was David L. Wolper. After a short wait, I was called and ushered into an office by the man who was then head of business affairs. He apologized for the unusual welcome, jokingly saying that at Wolper no one was supposed to take any unnecessary time off—the man who had collapsed, he explained, had "only been working seventy-two hours straight." He laughed, told me I was going to have a lot of fun here and mentioned how much he admired my uncle Sol. Then he took me downstairs into the basement area, where I officially became part of the Shipping Department.

The downstairs area was a large open space, with small editing rooms lined around its perimeter. This seemed to be the central hub of activity; the phones rang constantly, and in the background I heard the distinctive sound of film being cut on Moviolas. Immediately, I liked the commotion, the busyness, the activity, the energy. I looked around, and realized that after seven years of college, as an almost published "film critic" in my mid-twenties, at a time when most people had already entrenched themselves in a career, I was starting out at the absolute bottom, one of the "gofers" working for $75 a week. And I loved it.

When I inquired after the person they had carried out on a stretcher, I was told he had collapsed from exhaustion. It was explained the company was producing a new television show, a half-hour documentary series called *Biography*, hosted by Mike Wallace. This particular episode, one of the first shows to be aired, was late for delivery, so the "production team"—the executive producer, writer/producer, associate producer and editors—had been locked in one of the tiny editing rooms for some seventy-two hours straight in order to make the delivery deadline. And they were still working.

Working around the clock to get the job done and meet television delivery deadlines was standard operating procedure at Wolper. We had no rules to follow, and since we were a group of young, bright and energetic filmmakers, we literally made things up as we went along. I think that's why our shows reached such high standards of quality; the next year, our *Biography* series won the prestigious Peabody Award, and some of those series episodes are still being shown today on A&E.

I started my career in the Shipping Department under the supervision of Arnold Shapiro, the future Emmy Award winner for such groundbreaking documentaries as *Scared Straight*, *Rescue 911* and *Scared Silent: Exposing and Ending Child Abuse*, to name just a few. The other person I worked with was Conrad Holtzgang, who would later become one of the finest line producers at Warner Bros. for their TV Movies of the Week.

During the three months I worked in the Shipping Department, I was trained to do everything; Bert Gold, then head of post-production, used to tell me never to "assume anything because you'll only make an ass out of you and me." Words to live by. I drove to the labs to pick up and deliver film, ran the projectors so the writer/producers and editors could see dailies, delivered packages or scripts or photos, picked up people at the airport. In short, whatever had to be done, I did.

On one "run," I delivered a package to Josef von Sternberg, the great German director of *The Blue Angel*, the man who had brought Marlene Dietrich to America and made her a legend. I drove to his house in Westwood and found him sitting in a tiny vault built inside his garage. He was gazing at an original Picasso hanging on the wall. I looked around and recognized a Renoir, a Monet, a Gauguin and other masterpieces. My mouth must have fallen open as I realized these were actually the originals, and therefore priceless. When I told him I had worked with Jean Renoir, he smiled, then very graciously gave me a tour of the paintings he had collected, complete with their history and significance. It was an abbreviated art history course of what was happening in Europe during the 1920s. In what other job could I have spent a couple of hours like that during the week?

When I was in film school I had read and heard about von Sternberg, but I had never seen any of his films, so a few days later I stayed late and screened *Morocco*, with Dietrich and Gary Cooper. Jack Haley Jr. and Marshall Flaum, then working on the TV special *Hollywood: The Great Stars*, came in during the screening, and we sat there literally floored by what von Sternberg had achieved in terms of lighting and composition.

I stayed in the Shipping Department about three months, learning the difference between negative and fine grain film and what the labs could and couldn't do with black-and-white nitrate newsreel footage. Most important, I learned you can cut two pieces of film together, connected by a cutaway or transition shot, and achieve a continuity of action and emotion effortlessly.

Though I wanted to be involved in the making of movies, I quickly learned that the dramatic principles of the documentary film are not so different from those of the fiction film. And that was the new concept David Wolper was bringing to network television.

Early in 1958, David Wolper came across an extraordinary collection of Soviet footage documenting the Russian space program. No one had ever seen this footage in the West, and Wolper thought it would make a great documentary. But when he tried to sell the idea to the networks, they refused, telling him that all network documentaries were made in their news departments. That didn't stop him. Seeking a sponsor, Wolper went to the Xerox Company, which agreed to sponsor the program if it was shown on one of the networks. Wolper went to work. With Mel Stuart, the documentary filmmaker from the noted series *20th Century*, Wolper rented a tiny two-room office and produced a documentary called *The Race for Space*. When it was complete, he went back to the television networks, but once again they refused to air the program because their policy prohibited the broadcast of any "outside," independent documentary. Refusing to accept no for an answer, Wolper lined up 150 independent television stations to air the documentary on the same day and at the same time, literally creating a "fourth network." Narrated by Mike Wallace, the show was broadcast in late 1958, and became the first television program ever nominated for an Academy Award.

David Wolper is an interesting man. He started out selling television shows right out of college, and it didn't take long for him to see the tremendous need for product on the airwaves. In 1960, Wolper bought the television rights to a movie (which had never been done before), *The Adventures of Martin Eden*, based on a Jack London novel, then started crisscrossing the country, selling it to over a hundred television stations. That sale began an absolutely new form of commercial programming: showing movies on television. Wolper is a man of extraordinary vision, astute in business, with an unerring eye for what will play and sell in the television market. He has what he likes to call "spontinuity."

Wolper next focused his attention on Hollywood and began production on a documentary special called *Hollywood: The Golden Years*. Then he turned around and sold this concept as a weekly series called *Hollywood and the Stars*. He hired some young, dynamic documentary makers—Jack Haley Jr., son of the famous actor who played the Tin Man in *The Wizard of Oz*; Mel Stuart, the dynamic news director out of the newsroom at CBS, New York; Alan Landsburg, Marshall Flaum and several others—and created the "entertainment documentary."

During my five years at Wolper, we made all kinds of television shows. When I started, *Biography* was the only show in production. As we became more successful, we branched out, doing various TV specials, including the *National Geographic* shows and the *Jacques Cousteau* specials. *The Making of the President, 1960* won an Emmy, as well as being proclaimed the "Program of the Year." At the request of President Lyndon B. Johnson, Wolper was asked to make a film tribute to the late President John F. Kennedy, called *A Thousand Days*, which was shown at the 1964 Democratic National Convention. Along with these specials, we did a number of series—*The Story of . . . ; Men in Crisis; Biography; Hollywood and the Stars*—along with several features, including *The Devil's Brigade; Bridge at Remagen; If It's Tuesday, This Must Be Belgium; Willy Wonka and the Chocolate Factory; Four Days in November;* and others.

A year later, David Wolper created the first "docudrama," a reenacted historical event presented on national network television; it was a show I ended up doing a lot of research on, called *They've Killed President Lincoln.* A few years later, Wolper sold his company, and subsequently went on to produce *Roots, Roots: The Next Generation* and *The Thorn Birds* (teleplay written by one of my students), and was invited to produce the opening and closing ceremonies of the 1984 Olympic Games in Los Angeles. Over the years, he's produced many other shows, spectacles and movies, the most recent being *L.A. Confidential,* winner of an Academy Award for Best Screenplay Adapted From Another Medium. During his career, Wolper has produced more than five hundred films, won more than a hundred and fifty awards—including two Oscars, fifty Emmys, seven Golden Globes and five Peabody Awards—and has been the subject of retrospectives at some of the world's greatest film festivals.

As I look back on this amazing era in Hollywood, I see now that it was a time of change and evolution. There were two places where the talent of this particular generation was being groomed. One was an acting class taught by Jeff Corey. Corey was a blacklisted actor during the notorious blacklist period, one of the darkest periods in Hollywood's history. During the early fifties, the fear of communism ran rampant through the U.S. Afraid the Hollywood talent pool would corrupt the moral fiber of our democracy, the House Un-American Activities Committee, under the leadership of Joseph McCarthy, started hearings to find out who was "sympathetic" to the evils of communism. During the infamous McCarthy Hearings, which began in the late fifties, people in Hollywood were asked to inform on friends and coworkers. Those refusing to "name names" were ostracized from Hollywood and forced to flee. Some writers, the so-called Hollywood 10, spent time in prison, then left the country to live in exile.

Jeff Corey was an actor who got caught in the hearings. He refused to name names to the committee and as a result was unable to work in his profession. So he did the only thing he could do: taught acting classes. And, oh, what talent he trained: Jack Nicholson started out there as did Robert Towne, one of the finest screenwriters in Hollywood, Warren Beatty, director Irvin Kirschner, actress Sally Kellerman and a slew of others.

From Jeff Corey's class, actors, writers and directors were given the opportunity of working for Roger Corman, the renowned producer/director of those low-budget, exploitation B movies like *Attack of the Crab Monsters*, *Carnival Rock*, *Teenage Caveman*, *Little Shop of Horrors* and *The Wild Angels*, to name only a few. Corman's production "factory" gave this new talent the "opportunity" of working in a professional situation for little or no money. But it was a unique opportunity that allowed them to explore their own creativity.

The second place that spawned this pool of creative talent was Wolper Productions. We were all trained and developed by Jack Haley Jr., Mel Stuart and Alan Landsburg, talented individuals who raised the bar of documentary filmmaking to a new level. During my years at Wolper, I had the opportunity and good fortune of working with talent like James L. Brooks, the extraordinary writer-director who, along with Allan Burns, created the incredible *Mary Tyler Moore Show* and other classic television programs. A few years later, Jim Brooks would win Academy Awards for writing and directing *Terms of Endearment*, *Broadcast News* and, most recently, *As Good as It Gets*. In addition, I worked on several shows with Walon Green, who would go on to cowrite *The Wild Bunch* with Sam

Peckinpah, and with David Seltzer, who wrote *The Omen, The Other Side of the Mountain* and many other feature films

One day, while I was still working in the Shipping Department, I was told to pick someone up at the airport—a young filmmaker from Chicago named William Friedkin. Friedkin had made a documentary about a convicted murderer called *The Life of Paul Crump*, and David Wolper wanted to hire him. I met him at the airport, and as we were driving to the office we struck up a nice conversation. After his initial meetings with Wolper, we were driving back to the airport when Friedkin asked my advice about whether he should work at Wolper. He really wanted to make feature films, he told me, and when I saw his film I understood why. I happened to be the projectionist when they screened his documentary, and as soon as I saw the first few minutes, I knew this man was a born filmmaker. I told him that if that's what he wanted to do, working at Wolper would be a great opportunity for him. Talent like that comes along only once in a while, and it was obvious that Billy Friedkin was a man born to film, like Steven Spielberg, John Milius, Francis Ford Coppola, Larry Kasdan, Frank Darabont and a few others. Friedkin would later become famous for directing *The French Connection*, creating one of the greatest chase sequences ever put on film; then he followed that with one of the best horror films ever made, *The Exorcist*.

After spending three months in the Shipping Department, I was promoted to do research on the *Biography* series. It was a good fit, because during the years I spent studying at the university I was taught how to use the library effectively. To this day, I use research to investigate those subterranean elements of story and character, and I stress the necessity of doing research to my screenwriting students over and over again.

One of my first assignments on *Biography* focused on the conflict in Cuba between the dictator, Batista, and the rebel leader, Fidel Castro, who had recently come to power in 1959. My assignment was to write a research paper and create a chronology of the events leading up to Castro's takeover. I went through whatever books and newspaper articles I could find, and began writing up a chronology of events as they happened. The result was a thirty-page essay.

That was fine for a research paper—but we were doing a television documentary, and we wanted footage to document the actual Bay of Pigs invasion. According to all the reliable newsreel houses I checked with, no footage existed, so I had to pursue another route. In my research, I read that many of the participants of the Bay of Pigs invasion were living in Miami, so I started calling the local newspapers in a search for survivors. I learned after many, many hours of investigation that there had indeed been a camera on board one of the boats. Now, if a camera was on board, there was footage taken. But since the participants had all been captured, who, I wondered, would have the footage? I made the assumption that the Cubans would have confiscated every foot of the film that was on board the landing crafts.

If the Cubans had the camera and the film, what would they do with it? I asked myself. The answer came immediately: use it for propaganda purposes. I figured a country that recognized the new Castro regime might help me in locating some of this footage. It was only a hunch, but worth checking out. I knew that Canada and Mexico were sympathetic to the new Castro regime, and I quickly tracked down the name of a *Time* magazine correspondent in Mexico City.

I called the offices of *Time* in Mexico City and told the reporter what we were doing and what I was looking for, and he agreed to go to the Cuban Embassy to locate the latest propaganda film from Cuba. When he viewed it, there it was: footage taken during the aborted Bay of Pigs invasion. He sent the reel to me, and the day it arrived everybody at Wolper wanted to see it. Our little screening room was packed, only this time I didn't have to run the projector. We viewed it, and there was no doubt it was the confiscated footage taken from the boat. Needless to say, we were jubilant. It was a real coup. We duplicated the footage and cut it into the show, and I sent the original reel back to Mexico, along with a very nice gift for the *Time* correspondent.

A few days after the show aired, I was called into Wolper's office. There were two men with him, both conservatively dressed in plain suits and ties. Wolper was very serious as he introduced me to the men, one from the U.S. State Department, the other from the FBI. They politely asked where I got the footage I had used in the show, and how I got it. I looked at them, then at Wolper. He nodded, and I started getting very nervous. A thousand thoughts started racing through my head. Had they come to get me? I had visions of being handcuffed and taken away to a dark basement somewhere and being questioned. I wondered whether I'd broken some kind of federal law, gone against national policy, or just screwed up?

I paused for a moment, debating with myself, wondering whether they were interested in the confiscated footage itself or in how I got it. When I asked, they replied that they just wanted to see the footage. Simple. Direct. When I told them how I got it, they remained totally deadpan.

After I screened the footage for them, they asked if they could have it, and of course Wolper agreed, so we gave them what we had (we had copies, of course). When the two agents left, Wolper took me into his office and told me how pleased he was that I had found the footage. From that time on, I had a more personal relationship with him. Whenever he needed something to be found or researched, he would put me on it.

In 1964, David Wolper sold NBC a half-hour series, *Hollywood and the Stars*, and after working on *Biography* for almost a year, during which I got to write and produce a few episodes, I was put on the new series, full-time. It was a new kind of show, unique in style and execution, and focused on all aspects of Hollywood. Conceived and supervised by Jack Haley Jr., it incorporated movie clips of the stars, with newsreel footage, home movies, stills and live interviews to create entertaining documentaries on the glitter and social influence of Hollywood's Dream Factory.

I was assigned to work with Julian Ludwig as an associate producer in training. Julian was Jack Haley's associate producer, and it seemed he knew everyone in Hollywood. Julian really trained me in the craft of film research, teaching me how to read newspapers and books to look for clues and the names of people I might be able to track down. He showed me how to make lists of those names and how to cross-reference to others, then had me start calling people. I learned very quickly that there were two things required to do good research: patience and persistence.

Under Julian's tutelage, I found the first film Marilyn Monroe ever did (under her married name of Norma Jean Dougherty), a little industrial film made for the Union Oil Company. After more than a hundred phone calls, I was lucky to find the very first modeling stills of Grace Kelly, taken when she was just seventeen, fresh out of a Philadelphia high school.

When *Hollywood and the Stars* first aired in the fall of '63, it was an immediate hit, and I was soon promoted to full-time associate producer. I did everything that had to be done: conducting text and film research; taking care of our host/narrator, Joseph Cotten;

working with the producers, directors and film editors; finding specific scenes, shots or pieces of footage we could use.

Even though I had been raised on the movies, I had a very sketchy background about the evolution of film history. While I had seen many wonderful movies when I was a child, it was only while working on this series that I was able to develop an overview of the evolution of various film genres: action adventure, thrillers, war films, westerns, film noir, love stories. I studied the great musicals like *Singin' in the Rain* and *An American in Paris*; westerns like *Shane, The Gunfighter, Duel in the Sun, Red River* and *The Treasure of the Sierra Madre*. Genre, according to the dictionary, refers to a particular type, or style: "a class or category of artistic endeavor, having a particular form, content or technique." A film's genre, I discovered, is its inherent nature.

My job description as associate producer was to "pull" scenes from great movies so that the writer/producers would have the visual material they needed for a specific episode. Usually, Jack Haley would give me a list of great movies and I would watch four or five of them a day in a darkened editing room, "tagging," or marking, the scenes I felt could be used in a particular episode. Today, if people ask what really started me on my career as a writer/teacher, I point to this particular period of my life as having the greatest influence on my understanding of film form and film content. Every movie I saw, regardless of genre, theme or execution, became a remarkable learning opportunity.

My first show as an associate producer was called *The Great Lovers*. My responsibility was to visually define who the great lovers were, then select clips from their various movies in order to substantiate their image. I began making lists of stars and films and searching for great love scenes.

What was it that made a great love scene? I wondered. Was it the kiss? Passion? Sex? Double entendres? Was it a scene like the fabulous beach sequence in *From Here to Eternity* where Burt Lancaster and Deborah Kerr kiss on the beach? Or that dynamic scene in *On the Waterfront* where Marlon Brando breaks the door down to reach Eva Marie Saint and they embrace in a frenzy of passion and misunderstanding? Or that incredible scene between Cary Grant and Ingrid Bergman in Hitchcock's *Notorious* where Ingrid confesses to Cary that she's being poisoned by her husband, Claude Rains, and they descend that long staircase clutching each other as the suspicious Nazis stand watching? Or, what about Bogart and Bergman in *Casablanca?* The subdued passion of Garbo and Robert Taylor in *Camille?* John Garfield and Lana Turner in *The Postman Always Rings Twice?* Or, that fantastic scene between Orson Welles and Rita Hayworth in *The Lady From Shanghai* where they speak of love inside the aquarium standing in front of the shark and barracuda tank?

Watching all these wonderful films, I became aware that great scenes make great movies. I saw that each episode I worked on was composed of different elements or parts which, when they're put together, make up the whole. I began thinking not only about the specific scenes but also about the elements that make up great stories. When I asked myself what all stories have in common, what their form is, my immediate answer was a beginning, middle and end. It's been that way ever since Aristotle wrote the *Poetics* and Plato described the allegory of the caves, in which people are huddled around a fire and the dancing shadows on the walls became the source and inspiration of the stories being told.

One night, I was working late, watching *Mildred Pierce* (Ranald MacDougall); the movie opens at night, with a shot of a house overlooking the ocean. The silence is suddenly shattered by the sound of gunshots. The front door swings open, and Joan Craw-ford staggers down the stairs, climbs into a car and drives away. What's happened? Who is she? All these things flashed through my mind as I leaned forward toward the screen, wanting to find out more.

That's when I really began to understand the necessity of having a strong opening. I started watching movies with new eyes, on the lookout for how the film opens, seeking some kind of dramatic incident, some kind of scene that grabbed the attention of the audience. I saw that the opening usually foreshadowed the theme of the movie. That element of a strong opening, I realized, seemed to be common to most films, regardless of genre.

With this in mind, I began to select scenes for the *Hollywood and the Stars* segments that would both grab the audience's attention and reveal the thematic subject line of the show. This "teaser" fed into a commercial, followed by Act I, then the act break and commercial, then Act II, another commercial, followed by an epilogue, and finally the closing on-camera narration by host Joseph Cotten. Even though it was a television documentary, I saw the form as being constant. I understood very quickly the reality of television: it's a medium that exists to sell products, and the shows are there to fill up the time between commercials. I saw how important it is to grab the attention of the audience quickly, within the first minute or two.

I also learned that these opening few minutes set the stage for what's going to follow. The more shows I worked on—like *The Great Westerns, The Gangsters, John Barrymore, Paul Newman, The Social Film* and others—the more I began to understand the relationship of the parts to the whole. I realized that if the first few minutes of the show are not set up correctly, the story will usually lack focus and fall apart, meaning the viewer will change channels. When I asked myself what kind of scene would grab the attention of the viewer, the answer that surfaced was so simple, so obvious, I was surprised. Conflict; that's what I should be looking for. I knew from my days as an actor that the basis of all drama is conflict; if there's no conflict within a scene, then it becomes dull or boring and doesn't work.

When I started screening movies for the episode on *The Screwball Comedies*, I searched for scenes that had conflict in them. The first film I viewed was the fabulous *Adam's Rib* (Garson Kanin, Ruth Gordon). What made Spencer Tracy and Katharine Hepburn so vital and alive in the battle of the sexes was their bantering and repartee. It dawned on me that to heighten the comedy, I had to set up the situation first and that then the conflict would follow naturally.

In the movie, Tracy and Hepburn are happily married and enjoying a healthy and loving relationship. Both are successful attorneys; he works for the DA, she in a private firm. She is a strong advocate of women's rights. The film opens with Judy Holliday tracking down and shooting her two-timing husband (Tom Ewell) in the middle of a crowded street. That little scene visually sets up the story. Tracy is assigned the case as prosecuting attorney, and Hepburn insists on taking up the cause of equal rights and defends Holliday, very much against her husband's objections. The legal question is simple: does Judy Holliday have the right to shoot her husband when she discovers he's having an affair with another woman? The result is hilarious, especially since Tracy and Hepburn can't keep their emotional, personal or professional lives separated when they're at home.

The next step was finding the best way to include the scenes in the episode. That's when I began to understand the significance of "film form." It wasn't enough to just put in scenes back to back to keep viewers' interest; they had to be built into some kind of story line, focusing on the theme, or idea, of the show. Watching screwball comedies like Howard Hawks's *His Girl Friday* or *The Philadelphia Story* or Preston Sturges movies like *Sullivan's Travels*, or the delightful *Thin Man* movies with William Powell and Myrna Loy, I saw that these movies *had a specific form*. There was a setup, conflict and resolution. The characters are set up in the beginning, the conflict is expanded in the middle, and that conflict is then resolved in the end. I saw too that these films' style, energy and wit revolved around a specific theme, or idea—in this case, the continual clash between men and women.

Now, I knew this was a generalization, but it gave me some kind of form to look for and identify. So I started pulling scenes from these comedies that illustrated the situation and the conflict arising from it, then basically strung them together into a line of action.

This new awareness raised an important question. If this form worked for a genre like screwball comedies, I wondered if it would work for all genres. Researching the next episode, *The Westerns*, I began looking at movies of that genre to see whether they fell within the same story form of setup, conflict and resolution.

Now understanding what I was looking for, I started looking for similarities between the form of the two genres. In most westerns, I found, the situation is set up immediately. In *Shane* a stranger rides onto a homestead and asks for water. Soon, he's embroiled in a conflict between a villainous cattle baron and a group of homesteaders. In Kurosawa's *Yojimbo*, the film opens when the Toshirô Mifune character reaches a crossroads and, not knowing which direction to take, tosses a piece of wood into the air, then follows the direction in which it points. The character arrives in a small village and immediately steps into the middle of a bloody conflict.

In each of these cases, the main character rides into town, enters a situation, is forced to take sides, reluctantly becomes enmeshed in the conflict and then is instrumental in resolving it. In a "contemporary" western like *Hud*, the story begins with a dead cow, and the story unfolds from this basic event. Seeing movies in this way became a wonderful lesson in understanding the nature of film story and film form.

It was understanding and defining the importance of film story which took me to the next step: understanding the nature and dynamic of the screen hero.

5

Movies,
Myths and Heroes

Rick: "Inside both of us, we both know you belong with Victor. . . . If that plane leaves the ground and you're not with him, you'll regret it—oh, maybe not today, maybe not tomorrow, but soon, and for the rest of your life."

Ilsa: "What about us?"

Rick: "We'll always have Paris. We didn't have it; we'd lost it before you came to Casablanca. We got it back last night. . . . Ilsa, I'm no good at being noble, but it doesn't take much to see that the problems of three little people don't amount to a hill of beans in this crazy world . . . someday you'll understand that. Here's looking at you, kid."

—RICK (Humphrey Bogart) TO ILSA (Ingrid Bergman)
Casablanca

Late one afternoon, after the first season of *Hollywood and the Stars* was winding down, I received a call to attend a special production meeting in David Wolper's office. When we had all assembled, David informed us that *Hollywood and the Stars* had been renewed for another season and that the new shows would focus more on the great stars: Cagney, Bogart, Bette Davis, Joan Crawford, John Wayne, Brando, Cary Grant, Jimmy Stewart—the list went on and on. We were told to look for concepts and ideas that would best capture the screen images of these great movie icons.

In our first season, *Hollywood and the Stars* had been dealing, more or less, with conceptual shows, like *The Great Musicals*, *The Gangster Movies*, *The Great Westerns*, *The Great Lovers* or *The Great Directors*. Now we were moving in a new direction, emphasizing the individual stars, their roles, their careers, their private lives and their impact upon the public consciousness.

We celebrated by having a giant water fight throughout the downstairs production office that left the entire area soaking wet; luckily, none of the shows currently in production were affected. It was a real mess, but we all had a great time.

As one of the associate producers on the series, I was responsible for text and film research, but with the new season I would be given more latitude in terms of influencing the thematic direction of the shows. My assignment for the new season was to select clips from the films of John Wayne, John Garfield and Humphrey Bogart. My only instructions were that the clips I chose should reflect the stars' attraction and their "public image."

At first, I was a little overwhelmed with the task, but as I started exploring the actors' careers, watching their films and researching their public image, I saw I had a creative choice. On the one hand, I could simply view their films, then select some great scenes that reflected their public persona. I felt I could choose any scenes from Bogart's or Wayne's films and I would satisfy the requirements of the show. On the other hand, I had always been inspired by the heroic stature of Wayne, Bogart and Garfield, so I felt that if I went a little deeper, exploring their attraction and larger-than-life images, I could possibly find a larger thematic context that had made these actors superstars.

I began by asking myself some questions. The term "star quality" had been discussed, defined and argued about for years, and I didn't want to get into that kind of show. But it started me thinking about the nature of a star's appeal. What makes a great star? Is it looks, personality, the roles he or she plays? I knew the answer as soon as I formed the questions: all of the above.

Since movies are a form of entertainment that is "larger than life" (on screen, the actor's image is at least twelve feet high), I wanted to explore the specific characteristics that made these actors the great stars they were. The more I thought about it, the more it seemed there were two basic elements that went into the making of a star like John Wayne or Humphrey Bogart. One was the actors' personality: their looks, camera charisma, mannerisms. The other was the roles they played.

Does the role affect the actor? Definitely. When I saw Humphrey Bogart in a western, for example, the image and part did not fit. Bogart "worked" when he played a tough guy with a heart of gold, as in *Casablanca* (Julius Epstein, Philip Epstein, Howard Koch), *Key Largo*, *To Have and Have Not* or as the tough private eye in *The Maltese Falcon*. The same with John Wayne, or John Garfield. I couldn't imagine Wayne in a suit and tie or tuxedo doing romantic comedy, for example, or Garfield in anything but a film noir, but early in their careers they played these kinds of parts. Sometimes an actor has a natural "affinity" for a part, and sometimes not.

What qualities go into making a great character on screen? The more I thought about it, the more it seemed "star status" was almost mythological in nature. Myth and the movies. I remembered a visit to New York several years before with an artist friend of mine, a man who was a close friend of the noted poet, author and essayist Robert Graves. Graves happened to be in town at the time, so the three of us met for dinner in Chinatown. I knew some of Graves's work from Berkeley, especially *The Greek Myths*, his novel *I, Claudius* and some of his poetry.

During dinner we were talking about film and I mentioned I had worked with Jean Renoir. Graves had long been an admirer of Renoir's, and thought *Rules of the Game* was an absolute masterpiece. During the course of our conversation, we started talking about the source of creativity, and I was very curious how Graves sparked his creative imagination. Graves became quiet, put down his chopsticks, looked at me for a long moment and mentioned that Stephen Spender, the English poet, used to sit at his desk with a rotten apple in front of him. Somehow, Graves said, the smell of that rotten apple invigorated his creative faculties.

At first, I thought he was putting me on, but he was completely serious. In his own case, he said, he looked outside himself for inspiration. What worked best for him, at least at that time, he said, was to fall madly in love with a woman and go through the intense permutations of the relationship. When the bonds of love began to splinter, he would sit down and in that great, tumultuous passion of pain and despair compose his poetry. "The White Goddess" and "The Black Goddess," two of his most powerful poems, had been written that way.

I had never really thought of creative inspiration that way, and I mentioned that Renoir had told me that great art comes from the distillation of personal experience. "It's the same thing," Graves said. Art springs from experience.

At that point in the conversation, we started talking about the influence of myth in our culture and its effect on literature. Graves pointed out how the context of a journey, as a form, worked on the shaping and molding of a hero. He mentioned *The Odyssey* and several other classics, then referred to a book called *The Hero With a*

Thousand Faces by Joseph Campbell. I had read the book a few years before, while I was at Berkeley, but had forgotten it.

Recalling my conversation with Graves, I wondered whether Campbell's book might help clarify my thinking about myths and the movies. I went to my aunt's house and dug through the several boxes of books I had stored there until I found my copy of *The Hero With a Thousand Faces*, then started reading.

Campbell had reached back through time, memory and culture to collect a series of myths from the ancient, primitive and contemporary traditions, culling them into a basic *form* which he termed "the hero's journey." Campbell found that in almost all myths and cultures, from ancient times to the modern, the hero travels along the same path and reaches the same destination: enlightenment and realization. As the hero follows this path, he encounters various obstacles that test the nature of his resolve and which serve to elevate him to a higher level of consciousness, a new level of being.

When I related Campbell's concepts to the movies, I understood that the hero of the story, the main character, is placed in a situation where he or she confronts a series of obstacles in order to achieve that higher state of consciousness. I saw it was not only a physical journey but a spiritual one, because it takes place inside as well as outside. On this journey the hero experiences a symbolic transformation of death and resurrection as he casts off the old parts of his life in order to be reborn and emerge into the "birth" of his new self. In mythological terms, Campbell says, the hero's journey is one of acceptance; he must accept his fate, his destiny, no matter whether it is life or death.

I wondered whether I might be able to use some of Campbell's ideas about the mythological hero as a sort of guide, or model, for the qualities which make a movie star "larger than life."

The John Wayne episode was the first of the three shows I had been assigned, and though I had never been a big fan of his, I admired his attributes and screen persona. Two of my favorite John Wayne movies, I realized, dealt with a journey: *The Searchers* (Frank Nugent) and *Red River* (Borden Chase, Charles Schnee). I'd always thought of Wayne as playing a kind of mythic, heroic figure who determinedly follows his path to achieve what is right, noble and just while remaining true to his beliefs.

I chose *The Searchers* as the first film I viewed within this mythic context because it dealt with a journey over the course of several years. I had seen the John Ford film several years before and liked it very much; I thought it akin to a Western *Odyssey*. Wayne plays a former officer in the Confederacy who searches for his niece, who had been kidnapped by a renegade band of Comanches. Wayne was the classic western figure—strong, rugged, silent, still engaged in the struggle between North and South. It is the search for his niece that gives his life meaning and keeps him going, just the way the beliefs and ideals of the Southern cause kept him fighting.

Watching *The Searchers*, I became aware that John Wayne's character doesn't change. There is no transformation in his character; he's exactly the same at the end of the movie as he was at the beginning. Wayne's image as a man of action, I saw, is heroic precisely because he does not change; he refuses to give up, bend or alter his ways until he accomplishes his mission: to find and rescue the kidnapped girl. At the end of the movie, when the family enters the house to celebrate the return of his niece, Wayne remains outside the doorway, a desolate, homeless drifter doomed to wander "between the winds."

I thought that blew my whole theory. In Campbell's analysis, the hero weathers every obstacle but returns home a wiser and better person, sharing his newfound awareness with his fellow man. That certainly didn't happen here. It took me a while to understand that Ford made *The Searchers* in 1956, when the Hollywood blacklist was still in effect. This horrific witch-hunt took its toll on the lives and careers of professional film people, who were forced to test their honor and integrity. Principles, self-respect, artistic freedom—those were the rallying cries of the screenwriters suffering the outrage and indignities of this period.

Wayne's film persona, I saw, was established by his code of honor. Life is simple; there is right and wrong, good and bad. And, if you're ever in doubt, let your heart guide you. It's easy to see that the screen image of John Wayne stands for everything good, everything right. The path he follows is akin to the path of *dharma*—the path of righteous action, according to ancient Buddhist and Hindu scriptures. I think this was one of the main qualities that made his star burn so bright in the Hollywood firmament. At the end of *The Searchers*, it is his very strength of character that leads to his isolation and loneliness.

The next film I watched was Howard Hawks's 1948 film *Red River*, one of my favorite westerns. It, too, revolves around a journey; it is set within the context of a cattle drive from the Red River Ranch in Texas across vast plains and hostile Indian territory to Kansas City, as the Chisholm Trail is forged. Viewing the film with Campbell's mythic journey in mind, I really began to see how the journey, as a context, establishes the mythic and heroic qualities of the character.

But something else is working in *Red River:* the relationship between the man and the boy, surrogate father and surrogate son. Wayne plays a loner by the name of Tom Dunson, a man who follows his own path. He and his friend Groot, played by Walter Brennan, are searching for land near the Red River when they find the lone survivor of an Indian attack, a young boy herding a single cow. His name is Matthew Garth, and he tells Dunson he managed to escape only because his cow had wandered away from the wagon train.

Amid the harsh obstacles of the untamed frontier, Dunson lays claim to the rich, fertile land and starts his herd; in a simple but elegant ceremony, he marks his bull and Matthew's cow with the Red River brand.

Years pass. Matthew, now a young man, played by Montgomery Clift, has returned from fighting in the Civil War, and during the years he was away, Dunson has amassed a huge herd. But times are tough after the war and there are no buyers for his cows. Desperate to sell his beef, he decides to hire a crew and herd the cattle to market. In one of the most stunning sequences ever put on film, the cattle drive of some six thousand animals gets under way and the long journey to Missouri, over a thousand miles, begins.

And this is where the story truly begins. Dunson, driven by his obsessive need to get his livestock to market or face the ruin of his lifelong dream, becomes a righteous tyrant, riding herd on both men and cattle relentlessly. It doesn't take long for him to alienate his men, including Matthew and Groot. We sense a split between father and adopted son. For here, riding herd on the trail, is the place where relationships are formed and loyalties established.

When I first saw the film, I was struck not only by the cinematic beauty of the images but also by the motivation of the Dunson character. The journey is certainly the type of frame Campbell uses to illustrate the quest of the hero. In *Red River*, Wayne plays a character obsessively driven to achieve his goal. It is the quest, the hunt for the Holy Grail, that drives him on and motivates him. The journey becomes the source of his character, as in *The Searchers*.

During my acting days I had learned about character motivation, and had always approached a particular role with the idea that the actor creates his or her own dramatic need within the framework of each scene. But I came to a new awareness of character as I studied this movie. I saw that the key to creating a strong character on the screen starts with establishing a strong dramatic need. To me, John Wayne's persona was often defined by this intense need, and the journey was often the context in which that need was explored and fulfilled.

That was a major insight for me. I wondered whether the character's dramatic need might be the engine that fuels the dramatic context of the story line. If it was, how could I describe the dramatic need of the character? And how could I relate this to capturing the "essence" of Wayne's image? I spent a lot of time thinking about that, and finally arrived at an understanding of dramatic need that seemed to encompass the essence of a strong character. Dramatic need, I determined, is what the main character wants to win, gain, get or achieve during the course of the screenplay. It's one of the keys that can unlock the dimension of the character.

In *Red River*, Dunson's dramatic need—to drive his cattle to Kansas and then sell them—establishes the force and depth of his character. Examining this further, I saw that dramatic need, by its very nature, becomes a source of conflict. As Dunson heads north to Missouri, he confronts obstacle after obstacle: storms, a stampede (a classic sequence), rivers, an attempted mutiny, Indians. During the drive, the men fall victim to his obsession, and most of them, including Matthew and Groot, begin to doubt Dunson's ability to lead the herd to market.

The real fracture between father and son occurs when the men hear the railroad has reached Abilene, Kansas. If that's true, Matthew knows, they can cut several hundred miles off the cattle drive. But no one has ever driven six thousand head of cattle across uncharted territory, and more important, Dunson says, nobody has actually seen the railroad there.

Because Dunson refuses to listen to the rumors, he becomes isolated in his obsession, and when his men begin deserting, he starts making errors in judgment. When Dunson wants to hang two of the deserters, Matthew steps in and forcibly takes the herd away from him. It is the ultimate confrontation between father and son. Matthew tells the men they're heading for Abilene, and when he leaves with the Red River herd, Dunson tells his adopted son to always look behind him, "Because I'll be there, and I'm going to kill you."

Everyone knows Dunson means what he says; he will never give up the herd, even if it means tracking Matthew to the ends of the earth. From that moment on, every shadow, every sound, heralds the possible appearance of Dunson.

And so Matthew sets out on the unknown Chisholm Trail. As they move closer to Kansas, they rescue a wagon train of women and gamblers being attacked by Indians. During the battle, a relationship begins between Matthew and a feisty, free-spirited young woman played by Joanne Dru. When Matthew and the herd finally reach Abilene, and the railroad, it's cause for celebration, except for one fact: Dunson has rounded up a group of men and is hot on their trail. It's only a matter of time before father and son come to their final confrontation.

The showdown happens at sunrise, on the streets of Abilene. John Wayne catches up with his adopted son, and in one of my favorite fight scenes, Dunson strides through the herd of cattle milling around the streets of Abilene and confronts Matthew. Dunson pulls his gun and fires at Matthew, narrowly missing, but his son never flinches. Dunson remembers a time when Matthew told him never to take his gun away from him, and when Dunson does just this, the two men explode into a ferocious fight. Matthew goes after his adoptive father with a frenzy. Before they can kill each other, Tess, the Joanne Dru character, stops the senseless mayhem by firing her gun angrily, telling them they're fools; anyone can see they'd never kill each other—they love each other too much to do that. The two men, lying amid the shambles of broken debris, look at each other, and Dunson sardonically says, "You better marry that girl, Matt." A little hokey, to be sure, but a wonderful scene.

Red River is one of the few westerns that Howard Hawks made, and as I thought about the characters and the forces that drove them toward their final showdown, I saw how Campbell's ideas could be applied to the modern "hero." *Red River* is a story in which the main character embarks on an unknown journey, leaving one way of life and replacing it with another. Both characters, Dunson and Matthew, undergo their own personal change, their own rites of initiation. By the time they reach their destination they have gone through a transformation of character based on their dramatic needs, a journey that is both inner and outer.

More than once I thought back to my dinner with Robert Graves and silently thanked him for pointing me in the direction of my own journey of understanding. The scenes I pulled for the John Wayne episode were all placed within the context of the hero's journey.

But while it worked with Wayne, I was not so sure it was going to work with John Garfield.

I've always liked Garfield's films. Something about his manner, the tough guy with a strong moral center, strongly appealed to me. The first Garfield film I ever saw was *The Postman Always Rings Twice*. Released right after the war in 1946, the film was adapted by Harry Ruskin and Niven Busch from a James M. Cain novel. I was struck with the energy and intensity of Garfield's performance. In the film, he plays a drifter who accepts a menial job in a gas station because of his attraction to the owner's wife, played by Lana Turner. Together, they decide to murder her husband, but after the crime has been committed, the forces of doubt and fear begin to seep into their relationship, and they get caught. It is a steamy, intense film noir, energized by the chemistry between Garfield and Turner.

As in many of Garfield's movies, he plays a character who is caught in circumstances beyond his control. The more I studied his films, the more I began to see it wasn't the outward journey that formed his dramatic need, but an internal journey fueled by his own passion. And often it's this very passion that leads him to become his own victim.

I became fully aware of this fact when I screened one of his early films, *Dust Be My Destiny* (Robert Rossen). In it, Garfield plays a character who tries to run away from his destiny, but the seeds of his fate have been planted early on. When we first meet him, he's just been released from prison, convicted of a crime he didn't commit, and enters the story knowing he can never escape from this mark on his character. It turns out to be a self-fulfilling prophecy. I could see that while his character was tough, energetic and forceful on the outside, on the inside he was a rebel who stands up and defies the "system," a rebel with a cause, who is ultimately crushed and subdued by the forces of society.

Other roles revealed this same quality of character: *Four Daughters*; *Body and Soul*, written by Abraham Polonsky and directed by the great Robert Rossen; *Humoresque* (Clifford Odets and Zachary Gold) and especially *Force of Evil* (Abraham Polonsky and Ira Wolfert).

Finally, I identified a common thread in Garfield's roles—his point of view, the way he looked at the world. In his strongest roles he played a character born on "the wrong side of the tracks," desperately reaching out for fame or fortune, but in the process discovering that in order to achieve his goal he has to sacrifice his moral center. In *Humoresque*, for example, he plays the youngest son of a poor family with a unique gift to play the violin. Tired of financially draining his family, and against his mother's wishes, he joins a professional orchestra, but learns he cannot overcome his basic nature as an outspoken soloist. When a wealthy woman, played by Joan Crawford, offers to become his "sponsor," he accepts, but the emotional price he has to pay as her lover to reach his artistic potential is too high. In the end, he has corrupted his moral and ethical standards, and he wants out. The ending, in which Crawford wades into the deep ocean at sunset, is right out of *A Star Is Born*—melodramatic to be sure, but effective nevertheless.

In *Force of Evil*, one of my all-time favorite Garfield films, he plays a sharp corporate attorney driven by greed who accepts corruption as a necessary part of life. Once again, the Garfield character is born on "the wrong side of the tracks," and we learn that his older brother, played by Thomas Gomez, has sacrificed his own dreams to put his younger brother through law school. When the story opens, Garfield is the attorney for a New York racketeer who runs the numbers racket. Garfield sets up a brilliant scam and tries to convince his brother to close his small private bank to protect him from bankruptcy. But his older brother refuses to double-cross his clientele, and when the preselected number hits the next day, he's wiped out.

Later, Garfield finds his older brother dead, lying on the rocks underneath a bridge. And there, the film ends; greed and corruption, he learns, lead only to death and betrayal. In many ways, this is a personal statement for Abe Polonsky, as he was one of the screenwriters whose life and career had been adversely affected by the Hollywood blacklist.

In relating Garfield's films to the mythic structure described by Joseph Campbell, I came to understand that the internal and external journey of a character are really the same. While the outer journey provides the shell, or the structure, for the inner journey to unfold, as in *Red River* or *The Searchers*, in Garfield films like *Body and Soul*, *Force of Evil* and *Humoresque* it was the context of the inner journey that made the transformation of his character so visceral. It was his point of view, the way his characters viewed the world, that led to the transformations that occurred.

I once again saw the importance of the internal journey when I began my preparation on the Humphrey Bogart episode for *Hollywood and the Stars*. Making a film list of Bogart's career, I flashed back to the first time I had seen him, in *The Treasure of the Sierra Madre* (John Huston). I was about fifteen, and a couple of friends and I went in to see it in a small theater on Santa Monica Boulevard. It was just the kind of story I loved, with action, humor, high drama and the most wonderful irony at the end. To this day, I think about the ending of that film and experience a little smile inside that totally validates what going to the movies is all about.

While I was pulling several scenes from *The Treasure of the Sierra Madre* for the Bogart episode, I saw *Casablanca* again and found the key to what I was looking for: what makes great character, and what the qualities are that make an actor larger than life and lift him into a mythological stature.

I had not seen *Casablanca* in its entirety for many years. While I was searching for scenes in *The Great Lovers* show, Jack Haley Jr., the producer, told me to pull the scene from *Casablanca* where Rick waits for Ilsa at the train station.

I remember watching the scene totally out of context. As Rick waits for Ilsa at the station, his face reflects everything he is feeling: happiness, anxiety, fear, concern. Just before the train leaves, Sam arrives, telling him Ilsa is nowhere to be found, but that she has left him a note. Rick opens it and starts reading as drops of rain splatter onto the paper, smearing the ink. I can still see Bogart standing in the rain, his face raw with the emotions of pain, love, hurt and betrayal; I think it's one of the great movie moments. As I prepared to select the scenes for the Bogart episode, I thought *Casablanca* would be the perfect vehicle to embody everything that made him not just a great lover but a character who was larger than life, a modern-day hero—in short, a movie *star*.

So, late one night after work, I sat down and ran *Casablanca* in the screening room. I didn't know what to expect, so I let the movie wash over me, soaking up the characters, the dialogue, the story and situation. It was wonderful. I left work that night totally blissed out; my mind was quiet, yet I was filled with an energetic excitement which I couldn't quite put my finger on. All night long, I was filled with images from *Casablanca*, searching for some aspect of the movie I could build into the TV show's episode.

It wasn't until lunch the next day that I found what I'd been looking for. As a few of us were sitting in the restaurant, we started talking about Bogart, and it suddenly dawned on me that in *Casablanca* Bogart sacrifices his love for Ilsa to serve a higher good, to serve a cause larger than himself.

I suddenly "got" the relationship between the movies, myths and heroes. In *The Hero With a Thousand Faces*, Joseph Campbell says the hero has "to die in order to be reborn." When *Casablanca* begins, Rick has been living in the past, harboring the pain and joy of a lost love affair. When Ilsa reenters his life, Rick laments, "Of all the lousy gin joints, in all the towns in all the world, she walks into mine," and we know it's time for him to embrace the past.

What makes Bogie so great in this film? I think it's the combination of the basic nature of the character he plays, his screen persona and the part itself which give Bogart mythological stature here. In their screenplay, Julius and Philip Epstein fashioned a character who is tough and fearless, with a strong moral center and the proverbial heart of gold. He's one of the "good guys," and his action at the end of the film, helping Victor Laszlo (Paul Henreid) and his wife Ilsa escape to Lisbon to continue their fight against the Germans, serves a much higher purpose than his and Ilsa's love affair. "I'm no good at being noble," he tells Ilsa, "but it doesn't take much to see that the problems of three little people don't amount to a hill of beans in this crazy world. . . ."

It's by his action, of course, that Rick is transformed; he has sacrificed his love and desire for Ilsa for the good of the Allies in defeating the Nazis. Victor Laszlo is a leader, a man of great spirit and integrity who serves the call of freedom. Through Rick I learned that action is character; what a person does is who he is. Film is behavior.

After lunch, I reread Campbell's book and found the passage about the nature of the hero—"A hero is someone who has given his or her life to something bigger than oneself." When I reflected on the template of the classical hero in myth and literature, I saw that Rick's action elevates him to the level of a contemporary hero. *"Life consists in action,"* Aristotle said, *"and its end is a mode of action, not a quality."* No matter what's in Rick's heart, it's his quality of character, his action, that drives the story line forward.

It is dharma, righteous action, as the ancient scriptures say, and it's this action that makes Bogart, Wayne and Garfield heroic figures. They—and the nobility of the human spirit they represent—stand as beacons that cross all barriers of time and culture.

6

In Search of
New Beginnings

"*Amos Charles Dundee is a tall, broad-shouldered, raw-boned man in his late 30s. Opinionated, strong-willed, quick-tempered, he is a realist who sees the world exactly as it is and can't get enough of it. An artist, perhaps a sculptor of battle, who knows that for him death is as close as the owl perched upon the thigh of night. It is a very personal world to Amos Charles Dundee and win, lose or draw, he will play it according to his needs and wants. Dundee is a soldier. He gives orders well and takes them badly. . . . A wise man who can be a fool . . . who will go his own way come hell or high water and so far has yet to look back or regret . . . who so far has yet to fail.*"

—SAM PECKINPAH AND OSCAR SAUL
Major Dundee

On a bright, sunny day in May, 1966, after more than four and a half years during which I participated in the making of more than 125 television network documentaries, I decided to leave the safe, comfortable haven of Wolper Productions. I had received an incredible education, worked with some of the finest talents in the film industry and climbed several rungs up the corporate ladder of success, but it was time to move on.

To what, I didn't know.

I had left Wolper because I was beginning to feel like I was in a rut. During the time I was there, I had written several film pieces for *Film Quarterly*, along with several book reviews for the *L.A. Times;* I could feel the forces of change and rebellion happening all around me, in music and film, and I wanted to be a part of that. The more I thought about it, the more I understood that I really wanted to write screenplays—not the normal "fluff" like the Rock Hudson and Doris Day *Pillow Talk* movies that were being made at the time, but screenplays that focused on ideas that I was passionate about; screenplays that dealt with real people in real situations. I wanted to write scripts that were strong and powerful, that captured the spirit of the artistic and political rebellion spreading across the land.

I also knew that I had to stay alive while I waited for that "spark of inspiration," so that I could pay the rent. I started taking freelance assignments writing proposals, stories or treatments (narrative story lines) for movies and TV shows. I wrote on-camera openings for a TV series called *The Westerner;* wrote a feature-length documentary, *Spree;* wrote stories for TV shows like *The Man From U.N.C.L.E., Amos Burke, Secret Agent* and *Batman;* spent a miserable three months in Ethiopia writing and directing a documentary and returned home with a dislocated left shoulder suffered in a fight with my cameraman. While recuperating, I was fortunate to find an agent to represent me, and in this way I joined the ranks of other unemployed writers.

Even though I was freelancing, my intention was still the same: I wanted to write original screenplays. But I had no idea of what to do or how to go about doing it. All the years I spent at Wolper had trained me to approach a show that already had a subject. I learned very quickly that it was a lot easier having a subject like John

Wayne or Humphrey Bogart to write about than creating a story line out of thin air.

I knew that before I could start writing a screenplay, I had to have a story, and that meant I had to have a subject to write about. What kind of screenplay was I going to write? Romance? Thriller? Action-adventure, detective story, western? Though I knew I was attracted to some kind of contemporary theme, in truth, I had no idea exactly what I was looking for.

But fate works in mysterious ways. A few months after I left Wolper, I received a call from the editor of *Film Quarterly* asking me to write a movie review of a film called *Lonely Are the Brave*, written by the great Dalton Trumbo and based on the novel *The Brave Cowboy*, by Edward Abbey. Produced by, and starring, Kirk Douglas, the film was a modern-day western, both in terms of execution and presentation. The story, about a "modern cowboy" who breaks into jail to see a friend, only to break out again and find himself being hunted down by the forces of society, is a strong and sympathetic statement on the high price of freedom.

Trumbo's screenplay depicts a man who stands outside the reach of society's conventions, a man who makes his own rules according to his own moral code. The theme of an individual refusing to bend to the conventions of society strongly appealed to me. Besides, I liked the movie and thought it would be fun to write about it. I went back to see the film again, liked it even more, then sat down and started outlining the review.

As I was writing my piece on *Lonely Are the Brave*, I got a call from the editor of the magazine asking me to see a film called *Ride the High Country*. He wondered whether I might be able to compare the two films in terms of style, theme and execution.

Ride the High Country, written and directed by Sam Peckinpah (with N. B. Stone), had been released in 1962 to very good reviews, then had simply disappeared from sight. Now two years later, I started searching for a venue where it was playing, and I finally found a small, run-down theater out in the suburbs. I was one of the very few people in the audience, but as soon as the film began, I was hooked. It had a strong subject and a great style, and was done with such color and humor that I was totally taken in by it. I loved it. As I was driving home I knew that if I could write a screenplay like that, I would be satisfied.

I compared the themes and style of the two movies for my review and began to seriously consider writing a western as my first screenplay. The more I thought about it, the more attracted I was to the idea. I liked the genre, and from my research at Wolper I knew there were certain time periods, like the turn of the century, or immediately following the Civil War, that provided good dramatic situations paralleling the spirit of rebellion that was now sweeping across the land.

All I had to do was find a story, or some kind of situation, I could mold and fashion into a screenplay. So I started hanging out at the library, reading about the West in newspapers, books and personal diaries. The aftermath of the Civil War, I saw, provided a strong dramatic backdrop. The idealistic conflict between North and South, between one way of life and another, often pitted brother against brother, friend against friend. It had potential for strong action, dynamic and colorful characters who would lay down their lives for their personal freedom.

The more I read and thought about it, the more it seemed that the aftermath of the Civil War really exemplified what the German philosopher Hegel intended in his famous theory of tragedy. Hegel maintained that the essence of tragedy was not derived from one character's being "right" and the other "wrong," or the conflict of good versus evil. True tragedy, he believed, occurs when *both* characters pursue actions that are right. As Hegel wrote, tragedy lies in the story of "good versus good."

I found that this same kind of moral dilemma existed during the period right after the Civil War. When the war ended in 1865, it left the people in its wake dissatisfied and disillusioned, restrained by new rules and a new way of life. In the South, the men who once wore the Confederate uniform with pride and dignity were now forced to sign loyalty oaths to the North, pledging their allegiance to the very principles and ideals they had fought so hard against.

It was a time of revolt. Those who refused to sign loyalty oaths, or to give up their guns as the law required, became "outlaws," retaining the pride and idealism that had prompted them to pick up their guns in the first place. So, even though the war was over and a treaty signed, it didn't change people's beliefs; their loyalty was intact, either to the South or the North.

This is the period of the mythic Old West as we know it from the movies, when the outlaw gangs of Jesse James and Billy the Kid and the Younger brothers rode the range. This era seemed a fertile story ground that reflected the social unrest and rebellion of modern times. After all, it was the mid-sixties, and when I walked down Sunset Boulevard at night, the pulsating energy of music hovered on the night wind. The songs of Bob Dylan and the Beatles were everywhere; "the times they were a-changin'." It was the "L.A. Scene," and a great place to be.

I remembered all those great classic westerns I saw when I was growing up. They always seemed to be about the loner running from his past, a man with strong morals, an unshakable sense of honor and humble dignity: *Shane, The Gunfighter, High Noon*. These stories portray the western hero fighting against the injustice of the system; he represented the true individual, true to himself and his ideals, an independent spirit, unyielding in the belief of freedom.

I think that's what attracted me so much to *Ride the High Country* and *Lonely Are the Brave*. I liked the theme of the individual against society in *Lonely Are the Brave*, but what appealed to me even more in Peckinpah's movie were his sense of humor, his grasp of situation, his language and the theme of "unchanged men in a changing time."

The more I studied *Ride the High Country*, the more I saw the simplicity of the story; it's the kind of morality tale that could easily have been derived from the Bible. The two main characters, played by Randolph Scott and Joel McCrea, were not the epic heroes in the classic sense that John Wayne was in *The Searchers*, but were two strong, independent men who were past their prime, relics of another time.

I became aware of the way Peckinpah told his story in pictures. It's noticeable from the very first scene. As the film opens we follow a lone rider, Joel McCrea, riding into town, where a carnival is in full swing. Suddenly, an old car turns the corner and the driver, dressed in a long coat and goggles, starts honking angrily for McCrea to move out of the way. Then a camel bursts into view, followed by a horse, and the two race neck and neck to a finish line, the camel winning by almost a full length. What a great opening, I thought. It was totally unexpected; a camel racing a horse grabbed my attention immediately. I thought this was a "new" view of the classical western, an image that reveals in one shot the entire situation of the movie: the future is already here, and new skills are required to adapt to the modern age.

The story line echoes this theme. Joel McCrea, a former lawman, has been hired to transport a shipment of gold from a mining town in the mountains to the bank in town. When he sees Randolph Scott, an old friend and an ex-lawman, working in the carnival's sideshow, he hires him, along with his young sidekick, to help transport the gold. But Scott understands that the times are changing and with no foreseeable future he sees this as an opportunity to steal the gold and retire with grace.

So the three men set out on their journey to pick up the gold. It's a long ride to the mining camp, and along the way they stop at a ranch where a young girl (Mariette Hartley), tyrannized by her father, pleads with them to take her to her fiancé at the mining camp. Reluctantly, they agree.

So far the film is relatively straightforward, but when they reach the mining camp, the visual tone of the film changes into pure Peckinpah. This camp sequence is really the centerpiece of the film. The fiancé has three brothers and the marriage is performed by a drunken judge in the camp's brothel. The interplay between the frightened girl, the whores and the violence of the four brothers moves the story forward. The brothers, believing in the adage "One for all and all for one," can't wait to get their hands on the girl. It's an extraordinary sequence.

McCrea and Scott stop the attempted rape of the girl by the brothers and take her back to her father's ranch. But the brothers are intent upon retrieving their "property" and vow revenge.

As they carry the gold down the mountain, waiting to be ambushed by the brothers, Scott tries to tempt McCrea into joining forces with him to steal the gold. The whole scene, I saw, is almost Faustian in intent, brilliant in its understatement. The exchange between the two old friends reveals an incredible insight into the characters. McCrea wavers, tempted, but holds out for what he believes to be right. He tells Scott that after floundering for years, lost in the morass of booze, "I learned the value of self-respect." "That doesn't bring much on the open market," Scott observes, but McCrea replies, "It means a great deal to me." Scott looks at him for a long moment, then says: "You know what's on the back of a poor man when he dies? The clothes of pride, and they're not worth a bit more to him when he's dead than when he's alive. Is that what you want?"

"All I want is to enter my house justified," McCrea replies. This may seem somewhat "clichéd," yet within the context of the scene, the words ring true; the language of the frontier and church have never come closer together. But that's the genius of Peckinpah.

Once again, I saw the value and dramatic effectiveness of conflict. As expected, the brothers follow relentlessly, bent on retrieving their "property." In the final shoot-out (a sequence which I think is the precursor for the shoot-out in *The Wild Bunch*), the two men and the kid take on the four brothers. McCrea is killed, but Scott has regained his sense of self-respect, and promises the dying McCrea that he'll deliver the gold to the bank. Scott's transformation is now complete, and the moral bond, of doing what's right, remains intact.

I think what I responded to so deeply in *Ride the High Country* was the way Peckinpah played against my expectations of what a scene should look like. A marriage taking place in a brothel, performed by a drunken judge? A horse race won by a camel? It gave me such satisfaction to watch, wondering what was going to happen next. I saw that this *contradiction* of the visual image, showing what's *not* expected, is woven into this theme of change.

One of Peckinpah's major themes is the situation of unchanged men in a changing time. I saw he found visual metaphors that really reflected the indicators of change. I think that's one of the ingredients Peckinpah brought to the contemporary western; he showed us bits and pieces of the character, woven into little moments of the visual action. I saw this in many of his later films:

The Wild Bunch, The Ballad of Cable Hogue, Straw Dogs, The Getaway, Junior Bonner, Pat Garrett and Billy the Kid and even *Major Dundee.*

Looking back, I see that when I was writing the article on *Lonely Are the Brave* and *Ride the High Country*, I was really learning the craft of writing a screenplay. What I had only intuited as a vague idea about screenwriting started getting clearer, like cleaning a thin layer of dust off a mirror and exposing the reflection of what lay beneath.

A few days after I turned in the piece, I got a phone call from Deneen Peckinpah. She was in L.A., she said, to pursue an acting career. I hadn't seen her for several years, not since we had acted together in Renoir's *Carola* at Berkeley. When we got together for lunch a few days later, I casually asked if she was any relation to Sam; she laughed and said yes, Sam was her uncle and she was staying at his house in Malibu. When I told her how much I liked *Ride the High Country*, and how I wanted to write screenplays like that, she smiled and said Sam would like to hear that.

A few nights later she invited me over for dinner. I had heard lots of stories about Sam, of course—about his drunken antics, the difficulties he had on the set with his crew, his sense of "perfectionism," the conflicts he had with the studios and producers—so I didn't really know what to expect when I met him in person. As we sat down for dinner, I found he reminded me a little of my uncle Sol—tough and honest, with a keen sensibility and understanding. He wasn't drinking the "hard stuff," he said, only two beers a day, and during our conversation I learned he had not made a film since *Major Dundee*, four years earlier. *Dundee* had been made right after *Ride the High Country*, and had been a traumatic experience for him. In his words, it had been a "personal disaster." It was while working on *Dundee* that he got the reputation of being "difficult"—meaning "unemployable," in the Hollywood vernacular. He couldn't get any work after that and was only now being given a chance to rewrite and direct a new screenplay called *The Wild Bunch*.

There were so many questions I wanted to ask him about writing a screenplay. I wanted to know how he created his characters; what he looked for when he was searching for a subject, or a story, to write about; if he artificially created the story's conflict, or if it was inherent in the story. The list went on and on, but I wanted to be cool, so I asked him only a few questions at a time. Sam was open and receptive and seemed to enjoy our conversation.

That summer, Deneen and I spent a lot of time together, most of it in Malibu, hanging out with Peckinpah while he was writing *The Wild Bunch*. It was an invaluable experience.

One day, drinking a beer and watching the sun go down, I told Sam about a story I had recently found in my search for the subject of a screenplay. It was a story about the "Hole in the Wall Gang," a group of bank and train robbers at the turn of the twentieth century. The times were changing, there was a recent device called the telephone, the railroad now spanned the continent and Henry Ford's invention, the automobile, was beginning to be seen even in the remotest regions of the West. The story I discovered was about two outlaws, Butch Cassidy and the Sundance Kid, who, when the changing times started going bad, decided to try their luck in South America.

Sam loved the idea. He thought it had everything a contemporary western should have and offered whatever help and assistance he could bring to the script. I was elated. I continued my research and after several weeks started laying out a story line. But a short time later I learned that William Goldman, the great screenwriter, was writing a script called *Butch Cassidy and the Sundance Kid*, and that was that.

I was very dejected. Sam simply shrugged and told me these kinds of things happened all the time. Be patient, he said, you might still find a way to use the material. Late that afternoon, as Sam, Deneen and I were talking about the way the studios operated, Sam shared his experience with *Major Dundee*. As he talked I could sense the sadness, the anger and the bitter disappointment begin to enfold him. I didn't know about what ultimately happened with it, but later, over dinner, Deneen told me how the studio had butchered the final film. Charlton Heston, she said, had returned his salary and Peckinpah had deferred most of his own salary just to film the opening sequence the way he had written it. The studio said no. The studio had also promised him final cut, then reneged on its contract and took the picture away from him. In effect, he was fired. Perhaps most embarrassing was the music sound track the studio used: the score was filled with sloppy violins and an absolutely inappropriate title song sung by Mitch Miller and his Sing-Along Gang. When I first heard the music, I couldn't believe how bad it was. In the overall scheme of things, I guess it was just the normal studio nightmare. When the film was released Sam demanded his name be taken off the film, but the studio refused.

Peckinpah didn't have the opportunity of directing another picture for several years, not until producer Phil Feldman wanted him for *The Wild Bunch*. His drinking and self-destructive behavior, his antagonism toward "the studio suits," made it difficult for him to get work. And his biggest fear, he once confided to me, was not being able to work. Directing movies was his life.

Late one afternoon, after Sam had finished his day's writing on *The Wild Bunch*, I asked how he structured his stories. He paused for a moment, then told me that he liked to "hang" his stories around a centerpiece. Typically, he said, he would build the action up to a certain event, about midway through the story, then let everything else be the result of that event. When I thought about the story of *Ride the High Country*, I saw that this centerpiece was the wedding scene in the brothel. Once he'd set up the story and characters, everything, all the action, led to the wedding sequence, and then the rest of the movie was the result of that sequence. To build a dramatic story line, I saw, I could "hang" the story around this centerpiece event. We discussed it for a while, then he left the room and returned a few minutes later holding a script. It was the screenplay for *Major Dundee*. "Take a look at it," he urged.

I took it home and read it that night. Reading this screenplay was an absolute revelation. As I sit writing this, I think that if there is any one script that taught me more than any other about the art and craft of creating a screenplay, it was *Major Dundee*.

I was impressed with the epic sweep of the story, the depth and dimension of the characters, the inherent conflict in the situation, the realistic dialogue, the ingrained sense of humor. I read *Major Dundee* over and over again, taking notes, studying it as if I were preparing for a final exam. It was an incredible education. I began *to see* things: how Peckinpah structured and set up the story in the opening sequence, how he established the characters visually and then built the story line to the centerpiece.

When I was at David Wolper's, I understood the importance of having a strong opening scene or sequence, something that immediately grabs the attention of the reader or audience. *Major Dundee* opens with a Halloween party at an isolated ranch on the western frontier just before the end of the Civil War; music's playing, people are dancing, laughing and having a good time while costumed children run around outside playing games. Then Sam cuts from the painted face of a child playing cowboys and Indians to the face of an Apache brave painted for war. Amid the music and dance, as children giggle and scream in joy and mock fright, the

Apaches launch their attack, killing everyone and everything except the male children and the horses.

It's a remarkable opening, something I term "pure Peckinpah." The contradiction between the images of the children in their Halloween costumes and the painted faces of the Apaches killing and scalping was horrifying. Kevin Williamson, the marvelously inventive screenwriter, imitates this opening in his *Scream* movies.

I marveled, too, at how Peckinpah introduces Major Dundee, the Charlton Heston character. The way he's described in the stage directions tells us everything we need to know: *"Opinionated, strong-willed, quick-tempered ... An artist, perhaps a sculptor of battle, who knows that for him death is as close as the owl perched upon the thigh of night ... He gives orders well and takes them badly. ... A wise man who can be a fool ... who will go his way come hell or high water ... who so far has yet to fail."*

I just love that description. In some way or other, I think all the screenplays I wrote during this period were influenced by Peckinpah's style and themes. By today's standards, of course, this description, already abbreviated, would be too long, too direct and too expository.

The story takes place right after the Civil War. Like the John Wayne character in *The Searchers*, Dundee is on a relentless quest to track down the renegade Apaches responsible for the massacre that opens the story and to rescue the hostage children. Dundee doesn't care how he does it, or the price he inflicts upon others, to achieve this goal.

How did Peckinpah achieve such a marvelous balance of tension, humor and color? That's what I wanted to explore. So the first thing I did was isolate the elements Peckinpah uses: the inherent conflict of a Union Army officer forcing his Confederate "enemies" to join him in marching against a common enemy, the renegade Apaches. Within this situation, he creates a variety of eccentric characters who give the story color and texture: a one-armed Indian scout; two Apache scouts who hardly speak, so that we never know whether they're friend or enemy; a gun-toting, rum-drinking preacher; a drunken horse thief; a young officer right out of West Point; and of course, a former friend of Dundee's, the staunch Confederate loyalist Benjamin Tyreen (played by Richard Harris), a prisoner of war still fighting for the Rebel cause.

Peckinpah describes Dundee as "a sculptor of battle," and as far as I was concerned, Peckinpah was a sculptor of film. I saw how he created the wonderful shadings and personal histories that add so much flavor to characters. I studied one sequence in particular, over and over again, because it seemed to embody Peckinpah's personal style. Not only is it the centerpiece of the film, but this one sequence was like an education in itself. On the trail of the Apaches, the makeshift unit is camped for the night. The sequence opens with the bugler writing in his journal, and we hear him, in a voice-over, talking about the quiet and peacefulness of the trek. In reality, he's surrounded by a flurry of activity and commotion; pots and pans are flying as the one-armed Indian scout and the Apache scout engage in a wrestling match. So far, the mission to annihilate the Apaches and rescue the children has been fruitless.

Suddenly, the call of a wild animal is heard, and in an instant, all sound stops: total silence. Then, emerging out of the darkness we see an old Apache. Straggling behind him are the hostage children Dundee has been seeking. The old man explains that the Apache chief, Charibba, has told him he's too old to ride with the renegades, and has sent him to "the white men." He gives the message to Dundee, who is dressed only in boots and underwear (another Peckinpah touch), and informs the Major that he will lead him to the Apaches' camp. Now, everybody knows the mission of the old man is to set the company up for an Apache ambush, but after a heated discussion, Dundee decides to follow him anyway.

When they reach the river separating the U.S. and Mexico, Dundee moves upriver to another location and crosses there. And it's here that they're ambushed. In a ferocious battle, the Apaches decimate Dundee's troops and when it's all over simply disappear into the night.

More than a third of Dundee's troops have been wiped out, most of the survivors are wounded and their horses are gone; only some mules remain. At the end of the sequence, Dundee leads a brief burial service, where the rum-drinking, gun-toting preacher says a few words over the dead. Then they mount up, ready to leave.

And here's where Peckinpah breaks the mood with a humorous episode that relieves the violence and tension we've just witnessed. As the straggly bunch mount, Dundee climbs on his mule and gives the command to move out. But the mule doesn't listen; he simply stands, then nonchalantly begins nibbling on the grass, while the column drifts to a halt, forming a circle around Dundee. Dundee prods and kicks the animal, to no avail.

Dundee orders two troopers to stand in front of and behind the mule. "Push and pull," he orders. They move into position, and start pushing and pulling. Suddenly, the animal gives a great kick, sending the man behind him sprawling, and the trooper in front, onto his back. Still, the mule refuses to move forward. Enraged, Dundee twists the animal's head and starts yelling at him eyeball to eyeball.

Finally the mule responds, leaping into the air "like a rocket, bucking, kicking, twisting, turning, churning, whirling, twirling through the troops—the brush—through anything and everything. The ornery mule bangs against trees, stands on its back feet, stands on its front feet, stands on its nose . . . Dundee holds, kicking the animal with all his strength . . . then suddenly, almost in slow motion, Dundee rises into the air, floats through the air, then hits the ground with a terrific impact." Around him, Dundee's troops laugh so hard they almost fall off their horses. The entire scene is done without a single sound, in total silence.

Slowly, Dundee gets up, dusts himself off, daring anyone to laugh, and remounts the mule. "Ho," he says and gallantly leads the troops forward.

I just love that sequence. After all the bloodshed and carnage Dundee and his men have gone through, I found myself laughing out loud, marveling at how Peckinpah manages to break the entire mood of the film in a single stroke. More important, this event unifies the men as a dedicated unit able to leave their personal differences and political conflicts behind. It is an extraordinary moment that brings life and dimension and humor to an otherwise grim event. I still marvel at the writing, the visual execution, the dramatic value and the sympathetic response. It's just great screenwriting.

The more I thought about this particular moment, the more I began to understand one of the "rules" of dramatic writing: a tense, suspenseful moment can be followed by a humorous episode in order to break the tension. Shakespeare does this in *Macbeth*, in the famous "knocking at the gate" scene. After the emotionally charged murder of the king, Shakespeare cuts to Macduff knocking at the front gate while the drunken gatekeeper waxes eloquently about how the "evils" of alcohol create the desire but take away the ability. It's called comic relief.

Today, I share this dramatic insight with my screenwriting students all around the world. I show them how a dramatic scene will often be followed by broad, humorous comedy. It's a way of opening up and expanding the story line, giving it more depth and dimension, more character.

About a week later, the next time I went by Sam's house, I told him how much I loved the script. We talked about writing screenplays for many hours after that and he spoke about what he wanted to do with *The Wild Bunch*.

Toward the end of the summer, inspired by Sam, I woke up feeling that maybe it was time for me to take the plunge and start writing my own screenplay. I had just made the decision when the phone rang. It was Deneen; Sam had just finished his draft of *The Wild Bunch* and had asked if I would read it.

The Wild Bunch

Pike: *"We don't get rid of nobody—we stick together—just like it used to be—when you side with a man you stay with him—if you can't do that you're worse than some animal— you're finished—we're finished—all of us!"*
—Pike Bishop (William Holden)
The Wild Bunch (Sam Peckinpah, Walon Green)

I drove out to the beach that warm summer afternoon in 1967 a little too fast, a little too recklessly, but I was anxious to read the first draft of *The Wild Bunch*. After hearing about it all this time, after reading and studying *Major Dundee* and *Ride the High Country*, after spending so much time with Sam discussing it, to actually have it in my hands to read would be a real thrill.

I passed through the Malibu Colony gate, turned onto the narrow asphalt street and felt a nervous knot forming in my stomach. What if I read it and didn't like it? What would I say? Would Sam be pissed, kick me out and tell me never to cross his threshold again? By the time I reached the house, parked my car and walked to the front door, I realized I was being ridiculous. I was simply being asked to read a script, and possibly give some feedback on it. After all, who was I to tell Sam Peckinpah what works and what doesn't?

A slight wind was blowing and the surf was up when I rang the doorbell, and I could hear the waves pounding the beach on the other side of the house. I was planning to pick up the script, go home and read it, but when Deneen opened the door, she was smiling. "Sam's at a meeting," she said, "but he should be back soon. He wants you to wait."

We went for a walk along the beach to pass the time. Deneen told me how much the script meant to Sam, about how he wanted it to be the best it could be. By the time we got back to the house, Sam had returned.

He was open and friendly, as he had always been, but underneath his demeanor I sensed he had an edge, and was a little nervous as he explained how he had been going over some preliminary ideas for the shoot with his production designer. We talked for a bit, then he gave me a copy of the script and was very straightforward: "Read it and tell me what you think."

I drove home like a little kid getting ready to read a book I'd been waiting months for. I put the script next to me on the passenger side and kept looking at it, finding it difficult to keep my hands on the wheel. When I got home, I read the first few pages, then reluctantly had to put it down so I could get ready for an appointment I had that evening.

The next morning I was up early. I made a big cup of coffee, sat down at my desk and started reading the first draft of *The Wild Bunch*. I read it in one sitting, totally engrossed by the action, the characters and the images that flowed across the pages. It was like seeing a movie on the screen of my mind—which, of course, is what reading screenplays is all about. When I finally put it down a few hours later, I knew that if the western, as a specific genre, was considered to be a footprint of the past, then *The Wild Bunch* was a step into the future.

The Wild Bunch consists of five outlaws—Pike (William Holden), Dutch (Ernest Borgnine), the two Gorch brothers (Warren Oates and Ben Johnson), and Angel (Jaime Sanchez). A planned bank robbery is going to be their "last job," but it turns out to be a total fiasco. In a magnificent action sequence that opens the film, the holdup is thwarted by a grubby band of bounty hunters led by Deke Thornton (Robert Ryan), an old friend of Pike's. The outlaws have been set up, ambushed by the railroad.

After their escape, they make a run for Mexico. On the way, they break open the money bags and discover they're filled with metal washers. Furious they had to shoot their "way out of that town for a dollar's worth of steel holes," Pike sets them straight about the truth of their situation: "We got to start thinking beyond our guns—them days are closin' fast."

After the characters and the visual context are set up, the real story of The Wild Bunch begins. Tired, hurt, angry, knowing they have a hefty price on their heads, their future clouded with uncertainty, the men enjoy a brief, lyrical interlude in Mexico. Seeking to recover their loss, they look for another score, then find and make a deal with Mapache, a corrupt Mexican general fighting the revolutionary forces of Pancho Villa. In exchange for stealing a gun shipment from the U.S. Army, they will receive $10,000. This, of course, leads to the ultimate showdown between the drunken Federales and the Wild Bunch, staged and shot in a poetic tapestry of violence and mayhem that leaves almost everybody dead.

So much for the broad story strokes.

When I went back through the script, the first thing I noticed was the way the story was set up. The script opens with a narrator (omitted in the final film) setting the tone: "To most of America in 1913, the Age of Innocence had arrived and the stories of the Indian Wars and the Gold Rush and the Great Gunfighters had become either barroom ballyhoo or front-porch reminiscences. . . . But on both sides of the Rio

Grande men still lived as they had in the '70s and '80s—unchanged men in a changing land."

A little direct, I thought, but I knew this idea of "unchanged men in a changing land" had always been Sam's theme. The script opens with a bunch of outlaws, led by Pike Bishop, wearing soldier uniforms riding into a small town. The stage description sets up Pike's character immediately.

Pike is a *"thoughtful, self-educated top gun with a penchant for violence who is afraid of nothing—except the changes in himself and those around him. Make no mistake, Pike Bishop is not a hero—his values are not ours—he is a gunfighter, a criminal, a bank robber, a killer of men. His sympathies are not for fences, for trolleys and telegraphs or better schools. He lives outside and against society because he believes in that way of life. . . ."*

But something else caught my eye. Pike is described as a man who "rides stiffly, always slightly in pain," who walks with a slight limp, the result of a failed bank robbery some years before. I wondered if this was part of his character, perhaps another way Sam wanted to establish a different aspect of Pike Bishop. Normally, I wouldn't have paid much attention to that little stage direction, but if Pike Bishop was a man who found it difficult adapting to the changes going on, I asked myself whether that physical deformity might represent an emotional state, the way Antonioni's use of landscape and setting did in *L'Avventura*. To me, it was a way of representing his dissatisfaction with himself. I thought about this description. Why did Sam draw attention to that fact? And as soon as I asked myself the question, I had the answer: Pike Bishop is an "emotional cripple." He is, like all the members of the Wild Bunch, an "unchanged man in a changing land."

I thought this might be a way of illustrating different levels, or layers, of character. If I wanted to create a character with an emotional fault, an "Achilles' heel," I could establish the character's emotional weakness, then create a physical ailment which reflects that flaw. Pike Bishop's limp, it seemed to me, was a visual representation of his inner state; he was an emotional cripple, living in the past as the present is changed all around him. That was a major insight for me.

I also saw that Sam sets up Pike with a sympathetic side from the very first shot; as the group prepares to enter the bank, he inadvertently bumps into a little old lady and knocks her parcels to the ground. Everybody freezes, but with the decorum of a gentleman, Pike picks up the lady's packages, extends his arm and helps the lady across the street. These were elements in the screenplay that gave me great insights, enhanced and expanded my knowledge of the art and craft of screenwriting.

The more I studied the script, the more I saw how Peckinpah set up the characters and situations in order to illustrate his theme. I could easily see the evolutionary influence of *Major Dundee*, as well as the Joel McCrea character in *Ride the High Country*, in Pike Bishop. Sam sets up the two main characters, Pike and Dutch, immediately. Within the first few scenes we see they've ridden together, stood by each other and fought each other; they have a history between them. Yet, they know the days of robbing banks and railroads are "closing fast," and they're locked into a dead-end future in which the only alternatives are death, prison or living out a meager kind of existence in a small Mexican village.

These thematic currents sweep through the action line— outlaws living by their word, "the evils" of alcohol, the idyllic, almost pastoral life of a small Mexican village—but these were merely the decoration surrounding the rigorous portrayal of outlaws on the run in Mexico.

In the opening sequence, for example, there are three separate elements: the holdup, the temperance parade and the scavenger bounty hunters waiting to ambush the Wild Bunch. As Pike and the others enter the bank, the paymaster is reprimanding a clerk. Normally, I would have thought this was simply a throwaway line, something to fill the scene that really doesn't mean anything to the action.

But when I looked closer, I noticed that one of the things Peckinpah does when he introduces a new element in the story—whether in the bank, at the temperance parade, on the roof, or as the children torture the scorpions—is to enter in the middle of the scene. When I asked myself why, I realized that starting the scene in this way tightened up the story line, making the action almost seamless as it flowed across the page. On the roof, for example, when the story begins, the bounty hunters have been waiting hours under a boiling sun for the Wild Bunch to arrive. They are hot and tired and ornery. It's at this point that we learn Deke Thornton has been forced to work for the railroad, that he must either help kill or capture the Wild Bunch, or the railroad will put him back in prison. And that's something he cannot endure. All these elements are set up and established as the action begins to unfold. It's only a matter of time before it all explodes into one kaleidoscopic action sequence.

When the Wild Bunch rides into town posing as soldiers, they pass a preacher standing underneath a tent preaching the evils of alcohol in an abbreviated Leviticus 10:9: "Do not drink wine or strong drink . . . lest ye die . . . it biteth itself like a serpent and stingeth like an adder." In almost every Peckinpah film, there is some kind of reference to the evils of alcohol. But of course, he never "throws in" a scene like this; he includes it as an integral part of the action, which in this case erupts once the temperance parade begins.

Integrating these different elements into an action sequence is what places Peckinpah head and shoulders above most other action directors. In the robbery sequence at the beginning of the film, as the men prepare to make their escape, Angel notices sunlight reflecting off the rifle barrels across the street. Pike and Dutch immediately know it's an ambush, and using the temperance parade as a cover they make their break, joining the marchers. That's when all hell breaks loose. The street becomes a confused melee as bandits run for their horses, bounty hunters open fire and men, women and children collide with each other, caught in the crossfire.

I think that's what struck me most about *The Wild Bunch*—the visual poetry of the explosive, unforgettable images: a bridge blowing up as horses and riders plummet in slow motion into the river below; an antique car driven by a drunken Mexican general; a buzzard perched on a dead man's stomach; the awesome beauty of the desert landscape. Despite the gruesome aesthetics of the extreme violence—which exceeded that of *Bonnie and Clyde* (David Newman, Robert Benton), released a few years earlier—Peckinpah made his characters seem heroic, larger than life, almost mythic in stature.

I had studied Sam's script of *Major Dundee* carefully, and I was paying the same attention to *The Wild Bunch*. I noticed he infused his characters with different shades of conflict: conflict among the characters themselves, conflict between the changing times and the bounty hunters. The conflict is shown between what the outlaws want—a last score so they can back off and "retire"—and the forces of society, of industrialization, which keep them from achieving their goal. Then there's the conflict between the individual characters and their behavior—conflict, basically, between the inside and the outside. In order to understand the nature of this conflict better, I went back to *Major Dundee* and began to outline some of the distinctions between the two films in the conflict among the characters.

I saw there's usually a conflict between the main character and the other characters—Pike and the Gorch brothers in *The Wild*

Bunch, for example, with their personality clashes, disagreements, distrust or plain old power struggle of who's right and who's wrong. The same in *Major Dundee*—the conflict between Benjamin Tyreen, who fought for the South, and Dundee, who fought for the North. Then there's the conflict between the character and what he wants to achieve during the course of the screenplay, his dramatic need. I saw that the conflict could also be an internal struggle: overcoming fear or an emotional obsession like revenge, or curbing desires, or lack of willpower.

Moreover, there's another force of conflict which stands alone and outside the characters. A background force—like a war, natural event or calamity; or changing times; or the conflict between the "rules" of society versus those of the individual—becomes the backdrop that plays against the canvas of action. Conflict, I saw, can be internal as well as external, or a combination of the two.

This was a major teaching. Without conflict, I was beginning to understand, there really is no action; and without action there's no character development or change; and without character, there's no story. And, of course, without a story, there's no screenplay.

I also saw how Sam had structured the story around a "center point," in this case the extraordinary train robbery during which the Wild Bunch steals the guns from the U.S. Army train. Peckinpah set up and designed the action of the first part of the screenplay in order to get to the train robbery. The robbery itself is an exceptional sequence executed almost entirely in silence; six pages of screenplay that take up almost ten minutes of screen time in the movie. I still marvel at the way Sam structured the tension and suspense of the robbery, the silence loud against the backdrop of the train as it stops for water. It's a breathtaking sequence that ultimately leads to the final showdown and the violent poetry of the last shoot-out.

I read the script several times, and each time I noticed something new. The characters in *The Wild Bunch* are men who live in the isolated dream that things will continue to stay the way they are; that the industrial age will not come, the migration west will somehow fade away and they will be able to "die with their boots on." But by the end of the story, the characters realize the dream is over. There is no choice left—either adapt or die. It's a new time, a new age, and they don't fit into the new "patterns of society," the new scheme of things. The handwriting is written plainly on the wall, and the only thing they have left is their code of life, the moral order of their own universe. Pike, Dutch and the Gorch brothers come to realize they're at the end of the line and that they should be honoring their values, honoring their allegiance to Angel, now being tortured as a prisoner of the Federales. Drinking, buying a whore for the night, being hunted and always on the run—Pike Bishop and Dutch finally understand that this is what the rest of their lives is going to look like. So they do what they must do: they face certain slaughter by walking into the middle of two hundred armed and drunken soldiers to rescue their compadre, Angel. "They'll be waitin' for us," Dutch says to Pike. "I wouldn't have it any other way," Pike replies. The ending of *Thelma & Louise* (Callie Khouri), released in 1990, is very similar.

As the outlaws make that long walk toward the cantina, they are joined together by a sense of purpose, a sense of mission and a sense of their own destiny. When they leave this earth it's going to be on their terms, not someone else's. "Good and evil are the same except in the fabric of experience," the great novelist Joseph Conrad once wrote. And in this epic, visual, poetic tapestry of action, the Wild Bunch go out in a proverbial blaze of glory. Better this way than living out the rest of their lives in a menial, borderline existence, like the Randolph Scott character working as a carnival sideshow barker in *Ride the High Country*.

At the end, with the smell of blood and death everywhere, we watch as the black-robed women walk among the dead bodies. The sun sets on the distant horizon, and a dejected Deke Thornton sits wearily against a rock without any sense of purpose or direction. The old man Sykes, played by Edmond O'Brien, looks at him for a long moment and then asks if he wants to ride with him. "It ain't like it used to be, but it's better than nothin'," he says.

The end of one thing is always the beginning of something else.

Even now, as I sit writing this, I can still recall that first reading of *The Wild Bunch*, and how emotionally drained I felt by the vibrancy of the experience. I felt I had taken a giant step forward in understanding the craft of screenwriting. *The Wild Bunch* is an extraordinary script, an extraordinary movie, and had become a major step in my education in the art of the screenplay.

A few days later I went back to Sam's, and we sat on the porch in the late afternoon, beers in hand, watching a luminous sunset. I told him what I thought about the script. I loved it, of course, and when we started talking about how I felt the story illustrated the theme and characters, he looked pleased. I shared with him how extraordinarily visual I thought the script was. And, I added, I thought the movie would blow everybody away.

After our discussion, I casually asked him about the origin of the idea (conceived by Walon Green and Roy Sickner), and that's when he told me he was trying to "tell a simple story about bad men in changing times." *The Wild Bunch*, I remember him saying, is simply "what happens when killers go to Mexico. The strange thing is," he said, "is that you feel a great sense of loss when these killers reach the end of the line." That sense of identification, the sympathy felt for these "killers," as well as the visual choreography of the final shoot-out, is truly memorable.

A few months later, in the late spring of 1968, Sam went into production. He shot the film, brought it in on time and under budget, then went on vacation in Hawaii. But conflict and controversy seemed to be Sam's middle name. No sooner had the film been delivered to the studio than Peckinpah found himself in the middle of another battle. The studio and the producer—the "suits"—considered the film too long. Sam's cut was a little more than two and a half hours in length, and they felt it had to be shortened.

So, while Sam was in Hawaii, after the original, uncut version had already been screened for the critics in New York, the studio decided to make cuts, bringing the film to what they felt was the "proper length." The cuts were purely economic; it's well known that a two-hour movie allows for more screenings per day, thus providing more profit to the studio and theater owners. Even Vincent Canby, the respected and knowledgeable critic of The New York Times, who saw the original cut, was dismayed when he went back to see the film again. All the flashback scenes had been omitted. While not really necessary to the progression of the story, these scenes illuminated the relationships between the characters, adding more depth and dimension to the story. At the present time, Sam's original cut is readily available on video, laser disc and DVD.

It was after my experience of reading The Wild Bunch and talking with Sam about the craft of screenwriting that I felt inspired to sit down and write my own screenplay. After all, I figured, I couldn't run away from it forever. Ultimately, I had to confront my fears and just sit down and write.

So that's what I decided to do.

The Blank Page

"It has never been my intention, in any film, to show the conflict between the human mind and technical progress. My interest is not in man facing machine, but in man facing man, with his acts, his story, his attempts at love. . . ."
—MICHELANGELO ANTONIONI
The Architecture of Vision

Even though I had committed to writing my first screenplay, I found I was still questioning what I was going to be writing about. I had two ideas I liked, both westerns. One was a story set right after the Civil War, with the notorious Younger brothers as the main characters. These four brothers fought for the South and refused to accept the laws of the victorious Union. When the war was over, they defied the law by becoming outlaws. They robbed and killed in the name of the South, then joined forces with Jesse James to commit the very first train robbery.

The other idea was to take the material I had researched about Butch Cassidy and the Sundance Kid and, as Sam had suggested, use that as the springboard for another screenplay. I could do that by writing a script about a fictional character who used to ride with Butch and Sundance. When Butch and Sundance leave for Bolivia my character stays behind, gets caught robbing a bank and goes to prison for three years. The story, I thought, could start in 1907, after the death of Butch and Sundance in South America.

I liked the color, the humor and the dramatic possibilities in the situation. I liked the theme of change, of trying to adapt to a new way of life. For months, it seemed, I had talked about it, discussed it, read about it, and finally, I reluctantly admitted to myself, avoided it. It was time to do what I wanted to do.

One afternoon, as part of my preparation, I decided to reread an article I had written for *Film Quarterly* when I was working at Wolper to see if I could glean any insights. I had called the piece a "print documentary" and focused on a film called *Outrage*, an updated, Americanized version of *Rashomon*.

The film was written by Michael Kanin and directed by Martin Ritt, whose work I had long admired, beginning with *Edge of the City* and later *The Long, Hot Summer*. Ritt had completed *Hud* a few years earlier, a film I thought significant in terms of being a bridge between the old style of filmmaking and the new. *Outrage* had a great cast: Paul Newman, Claire Bloom, Edward G. Robinson and Laurence Harvey. The director of photography was the legendary and brilliant James Wong Howe (a man I had literally grown up with through my uncle Sol) and the movie was edited by Frank Santillo (who edited *Ride the High Country*, among other films). The music was composed and scored by the brilliant Alex North.

I had begun the article by interviewing the writer, Michael Kanin. What was the source of the project? Kanin told me that when he had first seen *Rashomon* he thought it would be a perfect subject for a stage play. So he obtained the rights to the Kurosawa screenplay and, along with his wife Fay, also an award-winning writer, adapted it for the stage. Kanin and Ring Lardner Jr. had shared an Academy Award in 1942 for *Woman of the Year*, with

Spencer Tracy and Katharine Hepburn. Kanin also had written *The Cross of Lorraine*, *Rhapsody* and one of my favorites, *A Double Life*, among other screenplays.

When I asked him how he adapted the play into a screenplay, he replied, "Plays are written to be expressed in words and limited action. Motion pictures, quite simply, are pictures that move. They have to be done visually. The story has to move, not only with a forward thrust but from place to place, to sustain interest. Nothing is more important in a film than the underlying story line, its forward movement. It's like getting on a roller coaster. It goes somewhere—up, down, around, always moving, always going somewhere. That's what holds the audience's attention and makes for a dynamic and interesting film."

What Kanin told me on the day I interviewed him is one of the basic cinematic principles. I especially liked his analogy to a roller coaster ride, because that's what movies really are. A good film will keep me hanging on the edge of my seat, not really knowing what's coming next. Renoir used to tell me this all the time; I had just forgotten it.

"What is the truth of the motion picture?" Kanin went on. "As I see it, the truth is that there is no such thing as absolute truth. The truth is a many-faceted diamond. Hold it up to the light and it has various appearances. But it's still one diamond." And then he went on to say something really interesting about his approach to *Outrage*. "I believe that none of the four different stories of *Outrage* is a deliberate lie. All the stories are true, but each contains only a part of the truth—the truth as one person sees it. It's like the ancient fable of the three blind men and the elephant. Asked to describe an elephant, one blind man feels the trunk and says the elephant is like a large hose; the second blind man feels the side and says no, an elephant is like a wall; the third blind man feels the tail and says no, an elephant is like a rope. The fable points out that each man is right, but only within the context of his limited knowledge. Each can sense only a part of the whole."

I thought about that. Wasn't that what a good character personified in a movie—his or her own truth, from his or her own point of view? Isn't that what Peckinpah did in *The Wild Bunch*? In the *Yoga Vasistha*, an ancient Hindu scripture, the sages say, "*The world is as you see it.*" In other words, what's inside our heads, all those thoughts, feelings, memories and emotions, are reflected outside, in our everyday life. It's our mind, not the world, that is the source of our experience, the source of triumph or tragedy. The movie that takes place inside our mind is really the same movie that makes up our day-to-day reality. Inside and outside are the same. Which is what *Outrage* is all about. This was something I knew I wanted to create in my own characters.

My next interview was with the cinematographer James Wong Howe. A gifted and innovative cameraman, Jimmy had a most amazing career. While filming the boxing scenes in *Body and Soul*, he wanted to get closer to the action, so he put on roller skates, held the camera on his shoulder and skated around the ring. This novel technique totally altered the reality of moviemaking. Every film he did, whether it was *Sweet Smell of Success*; *The Rose Tattoo*; *The Last Angry Man*; *Bell, Book and Candle* or *Hud*, Jimmy viewed as an artistic challenge. Solly used to love having him do a picture for the studio; he was open to everything, totally loose and fluid, especially when it came to adapting to the needs of a given scene. "You can visualize certain things in advance," he said, "but the only way you can really see what you're going to have to cope with happens right there—on the set. . . . I can never arbitrarily say that I'm going to light a scene in such and such a way, because the lighting must fit the scene. I always have to conform to the action. It all revolves around the story. Like Shakespeare said, the action must fit the words and the words must fit the action. If it doesn't, then you have to change one or the other."

If there's any "truth" in the creative process, I think Jimmy's words sum it up best: don't be too attached to any preconceived ideas. The truth emerges from the creative well of the unconscious. It has its own life, and I began to understand that those little "tugs" of intuition were the ways in which the creative process asserted its true identity.

At the end of our interview, Jimmy said something that I now understood to be a basic truth about going to the movies. He said, "In the future there will be new cameras, new types of lenses, new types of film. Science will always be there to build us the new equipment, but then it's in our hands. We must master the technique in order to master the machine. And it's what we do with it that will determine the way of the future." Words to live by.

My interview with Frank Santillo, the film editor, pointed out another creative truth for me, one I've not forgotten. "If there's any basic rule in the creative process, it's this: the things you try *that don't work* will always show you *what does work*. Without trying things, without experimenting, there is no freshness, no spontaneity, no flavor."

Thinking back on my experience at Wolper, I recalled how the editor and I would cut a sequence: we would try it this way, then try it that way, and in the end it would be the sequence that would tell us the way it should be done. Frank Santillo's remark struck such a chord in me that I typed it up and put it on my desk lamp: *the things you try that don't work will always show you what does work.*

Reading these interviews again greatly helped me to define and articulate my own creative process; I felt that when I sat down to write I would have some kind of model to guide me. Before, I had always thought the creative act was something "mysterious," but now I understood there were tangible lessons I could learn.

When I put the article down and thought about which screenplay I wanted to write, I finally decided to write the story about the man who once rode with Butch Cassidy and the Sundance Kid. I chose it for a variety of reasons.

Around the turn of the century, Butch and Sundance had seen the writing on the wall. Times were tough and getting tougher—banks were harder to rob and most of the trains were under the protection of the Pinkerton Detective Agency. The telephone, telegraph, bonds, stocks, securities, the use of checks, the automobile, were making things far too difficult for the Hole in the Wall Gang to continue. Butch Cassidy knew that if they kept doing what they were doing, it was only a matter of time before they would be caught, jailed or killed. It was time for a change, time to start over. So Butch, Sundance and Etta Place, Sundance's girlfriend, a schoolteacher, boarded a ship and left for South America in the early 1900s.

I had done a lot of research on Butch and Sundance and the Hole in the Wall Gang, and it took me a while to see how I could use this period as the backdrop for a character who refused to bend to the changing times and to alter his way of life. I now saw what I had to do to make the script work.

Several years earlier, while at Berkeley, I had run across a quote by Heraclitus, the Greek philosopher, which stated, *"No man can step in the same river twice."* That really intrigued me. Did it mean you can't go back into the past, can't step back into an old way of life, something you've already outgrown and left behind?

This idea really intrigued me, and not surprisingly the screen-play I chose to write was about the problems of adapting to a new way of life. In my own life I had experienced how difficult it was to change. Whether it was moving to a new apartment, getting a new chair or changing the living room furniture, I found it hard to let go of the things in my life. This might have been the result of losing my parents when I was young, but I really didn't know. What would happen, I wondered, if I could just drop the past and step into the present, unencumbered by any old thoughts, feelings or emotions? If I could just drop it like a pair of old shoes and be totally free?

What stands in the way of achieving that dream? Is it the past? Does the past foretell the future? Or is it the fear of change that determines our future? Or a lack of self-worth? Maybe it's all of the above. I had been dealing with these questions for years, so the theme of a character's adapting to a changing time seemed like a perfect situation for me to explore.

I searched for a story line that would capture this theme's essence. In his late thirties, my character, Balinger, had ridden with Butch and Sundance for several years and thought their way of life would continue forever. When Butch and Sundance left for South America, Balinger was so angry he went out and robbed a bank. It was a disaster; he was caught and sentenced to prison. After three years, he broke out, determined to resume the only way of life he knew. The time was 1909, and in the early part of the story I had him learn that Butch and Sundance had been killed in a shoot-out in Bolivia.

To dramatize the idea that "no man can step into the same river twice," I wanted to show how the times had changed. While Balinger had been in prison, the banks had gotten stronger; they had armed guards and stronger vaults, and, according to my research, it was now common to trade in checks, stocks, bonds and securities, all of them worthless to someone like Balinger. In prison for the last three years, Balinger didn't know anything about these things. He found three young misfits and attempted to assemble them into a cohesive group. "One big score, then we'll back off" was his motto; once he'd accomplished his goal, he'd go to Mexico and live like a king.

Of course, things didn't work out that way. The gang's first job was a train robbery, but all they got were checks, a few stocks and bonds and some small change. Worse, the new technology of the telephone alerted everyone within a hundred miles about the robbery, and Balinger soon became live bait for any bounty hunter and lawman within reach. So he decided to head for the Pacific Northwest to rob a payroll from one of the large lumber companies. But sooner or later, the past always catches up to the present. After the last holdup, the story ended in a long chase sequence with a ragtag assortment of boats on the waters of Puget Sound. Balinger was hunted down and the story ended in wild crashes, explosions and finally Balinger's death.

I spent a few days avoiding sitting down at my desk to write this story, and then I woke up one day and knew I couldn't avoid it any longer. So I sat down to write. I spent three very tough days doing battle with myself—hitting my head against the typewriter, as I called it. All I had to show for it were a few lousy pages. I found it hard to come up with a style. I tried to be inventive in showing Balinger breaking out of prison, but it felt false and contrived. I was explaining more than I was showing, and I knew that's not what I wanted to do. The harder I tried, the worse it got. I was getting a little depressed.

A few days later, I was at my desk when I got a call from an executive at a production company who had been referred to me by someone from Wolper. He explained they had completed a documentary about Las Vegas, but felt the script needed a rewrite and were looking for someone to do it. Was I interested? It was an easy job, the money was good, and since I was looking for my next month's rent, I was relieved to put *Balinger* aside and went to take a look at the Las Vegas story.

When I screened what the producers had, and read the script of what another writer had written, I immediately saw there was no contextual overview for the movie. It was just a bunch of sequences strung together without any thematic construct. I met with the producers a few days later and told them my thoughts and what I might be able to do to fix the script. They liked my approach, offered me a deal, which I accepted, and shortly thereafter I began work on the project. What I wanted to do was to create Las Vegas as a complete fantasy, a mirage where all dreams can come true. I restructured the material according to this new concept, then went with a cameraman to Las Vegas, where we filmed some new sequences. Then I went home and started writing.

It took me several months to complete the new script, but once I'd finished it, the producers were very happy. The film was retitled *Spree*, and when it went into general release toward the end of the year, it was very successful.

A few weeks after I turned in the script, the producers called me into their offices and told me they had purchased the rights to a novel, a South African gold mining story, and asked if I wanted to adapt it into a screenplay. No problem, I said. The money I earned adapting the novel, and what I earned from *Spree*, would pay the rent while I wrote *Balinger*. Basically, I had the best of both worlds: I would be paid for learning how to write a screenplay. I could make my mistakes on someone else's money. How could I say no to that?

Once again, I sat down to face the blank sheet of paper. But this time I had to make more distinctions about the craft of screenwriting. What was the difference between adapting a novel and writing an original screenplay? After reading the novel and looking for visual clues, I understood that writing a screenplay adapted from a novel and writing an original screenplay were as different as an apple and an orange. Adapting a novel means there's already an established story line and established characters based on specific situations or events. I would have to go into that novel, explore it from a visual point of view, then find a way to maintain the integrity of the piece. Then I could see what I could use or not use. Basically, I had a subject to write about.

In an original screenplay, I had to create the subject, the premise, the theme, the action and all the characters. When I read the novel and started laying out its story line, I understood immediately that if I wrote the screenplay based on that material, it would be boring, long, explanatory and dull. No, I had to do something different. It was one thing to analyze and critique an original screenplay, quite another to write one.

The novel was straight action: a group of bandits robs a diamond shipment, only to discover that the diamonds are accompanied by four prostitutes in transit to the mining town, commissioned by the so-called mayor. The story details how the men of the diamond mines track down the bandits to recover their stolen property.

I started by doing research about South Africa and diamond mining, but the more research I did, the more I found myself getting away from writing. So, at a certain point, I took the information I had and began to lay out the novel in terms of its "center point." What was so interesting, I discovered, was that the story had all the makings of a classic western. Instead of diamonds, substitute gold. Instead of South Africa, substitute California, 1854, five years after the Gold Rush began. Introduce interesting characters, a colorful location, lots of action, and the elements would fit together very nicely. When I saw how I could change the novel into a western, I laid out the story and broached the idea to the producers. I pitched the changes to them, then learned something very interesting. They had bought the novel, they told me, not for the story or action or location, but because of one scene: an auction that takes place in a brothel, where the miners bid for the services of a girl who has just arrived. As long as I kept that and a few other scenes in, they said, I could make whatever changes I wanted.

Instead of four prostitutes, I simply changed the focus and had four mail-order brides being kidnapped by a renegade band of Indians. The rest was the same: the miners go after the renegades to recover their "merchandise." I began outlining the story, designing a strong action opening, a strong center point and a dynamic action scene at the end. Instead of setting the story in South Africa, I set it in a fictitious gold mining town called Desperation high in the Sierra Nevadas. The year was 1854, after the Gold Rush and just prior to the Civil War. As I was laying out the story line, I borrowed freely from certain elements in *Ride the High Country*.

In my research for *Balinger*, I had found some very interesting characters who had come to California searching for gold, a mix of bounty hunters, trappers, killers, prostitutes—and a Russian immigrant. I took the main character from the novel, made him an ex–Army man, then added some new elements to his characterization. He was going to be a Peckinpah character, I told myself. I created a Russian bear hunter, a cocky young gunfighter, all talk and little action, who was with his girlfriend, an ex-schoolteacher, faster with a gun than he was and not afraid to use it.

I asked myself what scenes stood out from the novel, then noted them on cards. Then I took the scenes I liked the most and matched them against the general story line. At that point, I reread the novel to see if I had missed anything, or if something else stood out. When I finished, I realized I had totally reshaped the novel, focusing on the visual while stripping away all the interior musings of the character.

I had no knowledge of screenplay structure at the time, so I laid out the story line according to the opening (the kidnapping), the center point (the miners' first confrontation with the renegades) and the ending (the rescue of the hostages), then laid in the scenes the producers wanted in what I felt was an appropriate arrangement of dramatic action.

Opening with the kidnapping of the mail-order brides was a strong action sequence which would lead me to establish the gold mining town, the main characters and the dramatic situation. My plan was to introduce the main characters dramatically, using a particular situation (like the opening of Kurosawa's *Seven Samurai*), that would bring the six main characters together by need, circumstance and desperation.

Getting them out of town was another matter. The story line was simple: the main character is hired to pursue the renegades and bring back the mail-order brides. He persuades the five other characters to go with him, so I created a situation where it would be better for each of the characters to join the group than stay in town. But by the time I introduced the characters, set up the situation and put them all together, I had written over 80 pages—more than half the screenplay. I only had about 120 pages to tell the whole story; if I kept going at my current pace I'd end up with a four-hour movie. What to do?

Looking over what I had written, I saw the problem immediately: I was trying so hard to be "fair" to each of the characters that I lost sight of the story line. For me, the real story was having characters overcome their personal obstacles and honor their commitments to themselves and the dramatic situation. I did not have one main character, I had six of them. If I wanted to shape the screenplay to length and make it work effectively, I'd have to do something; an ensemble piece, I saw, was definitely not going to work.

So I sat down and concentrated on the basic dramatic issue. Who was the story really about? All of them, obviously, but who did the action revolve around? Who would keep the group together and undergo the most change? The ex–Army man, who had been dishonorably discharged, was the main character in the novel and in the screenplay. His friend and sidekick would be a major character, as were the four others riding with them, but I decided they had to stay more in the background than the foreground.

That was my first real lesson in screenwriting: finding out who the story was about and keeping the focus on that character, both internally and externally. That's when I understood I had to know *who* the story is about before I could really show *what* it's about. So I went back to page one and started rewriting from this new perspective, cutting down and sharpening the action and secondary characters. The screenplay was now about a man who leads a group of five other men to track down and rescue four mail-order brides. I titled it *The Quest*, and it was heavily influenced by *Major Dundee* and *The Searchers*, but for me it worked as a period action-adventure.

Intuitively, I began to feel some kind of structure evolving in the story line, though I couldn't yet define it. My main focus was setting up the characters, and I only had about twenty-five or thirty pages to do it. At that point they had to be out of the mining town and on the trail, which is the true beginning of the story. One hundred and twenty pages, I saw, was not very long to tell the story. I had to condense, hone, sharpen and delete before I could really begin to do justice to the screenplay. The action in the mining town, I saw, was an individual unit of dramatic action; I had to dramatize the kidnapping, introduce the characters, then get them out of town so the story could begin.

That's when I understood that the unit of action which is Act I had to set up the story and introduce the main characters. Once I got them on the trail hunting the renegades, I could get more into the depth of their characters, à la Peckinpah.

It took me about six months to complete the screenplay, and when I turned it in the producers began shopping it around Hollywood. While there was a lot of interest, only one director made an offer: J. Lee Thompson, the director of *The Guns of Navarone*. But in the end, *The Quest* never made it to the big screen.

As soon as I finished the script, I wanted to get busy and start working on another screenplay. I thought about going back to *Balinger*, but I had just finished a western, and wanted to try my hand at something else. I thought it would be a good change of pace to write a contemporary story.

As mentioned, I had always been inspired by Antonioni's *La Notte*. I was looking around for characters, or situations, or incidents I could build into a screenplay, but nothing had really surfaced that I wanted to focus on. I thought it would be interesting to write something about the music business, even though I didn't know too much about it. At the time, I was totally into Dylan, the Beatles, the Stones.

One night, I was invited to a family gathering of a second cousin I hadn't seen in many years. When I arrived I met her sister-in-law, Marissa, who had married a man named Brian Stone. That night at dinner the three of us hit it off immediately, as if we had known each other our entire lives. Through their friendship and influence I was able to tap in to the creative currents of what was currently going on in the contemporary musical scene. I can truly say that Marissa and Brian sparked a major turning point in my life.

Marissa and I were almost related; her brother had married my cousin. Marissa was an amazing woman: a former model and *Playboy* Playmate of the Month, she was extremely intelligent, had a captivating sense of humor and unique way of seeing things.

Her husband, Brian Stone, had come to L.A. from New York and had ended up in the music business. In one of the many legendary stories about him, Brian and Charlie Greene, his partner, snuck onto a Universal Studios lot, moved into an uninhabited office and simply set up shop without anyone in the executive tower knowing anything about it. Two years passed before Greene-Stone Productions was discovered, and by that time they had a major client list and a deal at a record company.

Brian and Charlie were both fast talkers, street-smart wheeler-dealers who in the short span of a few years became extremely successful as business managers and promoters of popular musical acts. Their first client was Billy Daniels of "That Old Black Magic" fame, and as he started becoming popular, they discovered and signed a young husband-and-wife team who called themselves Sonny and Cher. A few months later, they happened to hear a young group playing on the Sunset Strip, and signed them that very night. The group was called Buffalo Springfield; the same thing happened with another group called Iron Butterfly. Brian and Charlie were among the main movers in forming the modern music business.

At the time, Brian was literally living in the office, handling these very hot groups, so Marissa and I used to hang out a lot together. It was through her that I really tuned in to the social, political and musical currents of the sixties. On Sunday mornings the three of us would have a late brunch at their house on Tower Road, the old John Barrymore house, and they would fill me in on "the scene."

I admired Brian greatly; he was intelligent, astute, a self-taught businessman. He was perhaps among the first millionaires under the age of twenty-five. Outside the office he was a loyal and compassionate friend. In business, though, he considered himself ruthless. I wondered whether he was the new model of success?

For many years, I had wanted to develop a screenplay around a character who has both everything and nothing. Hanging out with Brian and Marissa, I realized the high-stakes world of the music industry would make a perfect backdrop for the kind of modern success story I wanted to write, something like Ernest Lehman's *Sweet Smell of Success* or Paddy Chayefsky's *The Goddess*. I thought the best way to do this would be in a love story, where the drive for success overrides the desire for personal happiness. At the end, the character keeps his success but has lost what he was truly searching for—a meaningful and committed relationship.

The question was how I could create a conflict about a person afraid of personal commitment. I didn't know how I could do it, or whether it would be very dramatic. Would Hollywood even be interested in a contemporary character study like this? The more I thought about it, the more I liked the idea of trying to do an American version of what Antonioni did in films like *La Notte, L'Eclisse* and *Red Desert*—create an emotional drama that would be played out against the landscape of the American psyche.

I wanted my character to be a man who wanted to succeed at all costs, who believed that the ends justified the means and whose deepest fear was to fail. He drew no line as far as his moral or ethical behavior went; he did whatever he had to do to make the deal. But he didn't count on falling in love, especially with a woman who had a strong sense of identity and principles, and who was anchored in her own moral and ethical behavior. I envisioned her as a law student in her third year who was attracted to his confidence, his ability to make quick decisions and his success.

I knew if I put these two together there would be chemistry and conflict. That was the first level of the challenge. Who was this character? What did he do, how did he do it, what was his past and what were his goals? Those were the questions I had to answer. To help me, I turned to Antonioni's *L'Eclisse*.

Antonioni's study of a contemporary stockbroker is an extraordinary film, especially in its emotional subtext, in what is expressed but not stated by the main characters, played by Monica Vitti and Alain Delon. *L'Eclisse* is really a study in silence and image. The opening sequence is a masterpiece of understatement. In a large living room, the drapes drawn, Monica Vitti and her lover sit in total silence; only the slight whirring of a small fan is heard in the foreground. For almost five or six minutes, not a word is said. From this tableau, we know everything we need to know about the relationship; it's over, and there's nothing more left to say.

Monica Vitti leaves, then meets the attractive, dynamic young stockbroker, Alain Delon. During the film they form an intimate, loving relationship, and we think things are going to work out for them. At the end of the film, after spending an afternoon in Delon's office making love, they agree to meet each other that evening. The last sequence is literally a masterpiece of cinematic expectation. For more than seven minutes, we do not see the two main characters. We see the places where they used to meet, people walking with their backs to us who look like them; somehow we *expect* to see them again, but we don't. The last shot, a close-up of a large, bright streetlamp underscored with a harsh musical chord, is chilling. We know by the starkness of the image that their relationship did not survive; it was just a brief interlude of two people who meet, then disappear from each other's lives.

Studying Antonioni's film was a complete education. On the surface, nothing seemed to be happening, just the ordinary day-to-day events that make up our lives. But we know Monica Vitti is searching for a relationship in which she can love and be loved. She is hoping, as we are, that the Alain Delon character is *the one*.

That's the kind of character illumination I was striving for in my screenplay. Since this was the late sixties, I wanted music to be a major part of the script, so I hung out with Brian, attending some Buffalo Springfield recording sessions (they were recording the classic "For What It's Worth") to get a feel and taste of what such events were like. I wanted the main character to be in a glamorous profession in which he would be interacting with both music and film people. After thinking it through, I decided the main character should own his own public relations firm. Eliot, as I named him, was a man who liked to own things, and what he was striving for— his goal, or dramatic need—was to take an unknown rock and roll group and make them into a dynamic musical happening. I based this on Brian's efforts to promote Buffalo Springfield. I spent a lot of time with him in his office, observing how he operated, and sat in on several meetings to get a clear overview of what the working mode of my character would be.

I wanted to weave two lines of dramatic action through the story line. One would show him at work, successfully bringing his clients into the public eye. Secondly, I wanted to show him as a person who could not make a distinction between sex and love, who has no real moral center or sense of commitment. He was a man, I thought, who could not stand to be alone, a man who always had to be busy, so that when he meets a woman he truly likes, he can't really handle it. She is more than his equal—strong and independent, striking in looks and personality, with a strong sense of self-worth. She is an *equal*, not an object.

I called the screenplay *Lonely Is the Afternoon*, and as I was writing it I saw how the emotional dynamics of a character could be illustrated by behavior. My intention was to create a character where the dialogue, as a vehicle of action, became layered in subtext; I wanted to show that what *was not said* could reveal more about a character than what *was* said. Antonioni showed me there are two ways of revealing character: one by what he or she *says*, through the dialogue, and the other by what he or she *does*, through his or her actions and reactions. The character's dialogue may be cute, clever, witty or insightful, but I learned I could show more about a person through his or her actions than through what he or she says. That's not always the case, of course, but when the character arc takes place on an emotional level, when the change takes place inside, I found, it is a way of illuminating behavior. As I was beginning to understand, film is behavior.

It took me about six months to write *Lonely Is the Afternoon*, and when it was completed, a young producer optioned it as a vehicle for a young, up-and-coming director. Though never produced, it received a lot of interest and serious attention, and at one time had a well-known star attached to it.

I spent the next several years writing original screenplays. I considered myself fortunate, because each script I wrote was optioned either by a producer, actor or director, and I'd use that money to live on while I wrote a new screenplay. I wrote eight screenplays during that period, and two were produced: *Spree*, with Jayne Mansfield (I believe it was her last movie), and, several years later, *The Quest*.

I learned it was not the time to get the kind of a film I was writing made in Hollywood. The market was totally against what I was doing: the kind of films being made were big musicals like *My Fair Lady* and *The Sound of Music*, historical dramas like *A Man for All Seasons* or contemporary pieces like *In the Heat of the Night*. The small, character study scripts I was doing were considered too "arty," or too "English"—too much in the style of *Two for the Road*, *Look Back in Anger*, *Saturday Night and Sunday Morning* or *This Sporting Life*.

It took me a few years to get back to *Balinger*, and when I did, I approached it from a more confident position, creating deeper and richer characters and finding strong visual images to express the story line. When I finished it, there was a lot of interest, and it was quickly optioned by director Robert Aldrich, but he died before it got into production. After the option period, the rights reverted back to me.

I had been writing screenplays for a little more than seven years, and at the end of that time, I was beginning work on a new one when the reality of my situation hit me. The last three screenplays I had written had generated a lot of interest, but none had been sold or optioned. I didn't know where the next month's rent was coming from, and as I stared at this blank sheet of paper in front of me, I wondered what I was doing. My money was running out, I had no foreseeable assignments coming up and I was emotionally drained and devastated. As I sat going through my options, I suddenly realized that maybe it was time for me to take a break. There was no way I could continue what I was doing.

So, literally in mid-sentence of a new screenplay, I pushed my chair back from the desk, turned out the light and went looking for a job.

Sunset Boulevard

Betty: "I always heard you had some kind of talent."
Joe: "That was last year. This year I'm trying to make a living."

—SCRIPT READER BETTY SCHAEFER (Nancy Olson)
TO SCREENWRITER JOE GILLIS (William Holden)
Sunset Boulevard (Billy Wilder, Charles Brackett)

The address was 8155 Sunset Boulevard, and I was late pulling into the parking lot at Cinemobile Systems that spring morning in 1973. I was there to interview for a job, and that's all I knew. I had been looking for jobs the past few months—calling agents, setting up meetings, going on interviews—but was having no luck. Finally, once again surrendering to the fact that I needed help, I went to my uncle Sol and asked if he knew of any jobs I might apply for. He didn't promise anything, of course, but he told me he would look around and see what he could do, and we left it at that.

A few weeks later, he told me to call a man named Fouad Said at a company called Cinemobile. I called and was referred to a man named Eddie Rosen.

Ironically, Cinemobile was only about half a block away from where I worked at Wolper Productions. I was a single parent now, and with my ten-year-old son in school, this job, at least location-wise, would be ideal.

The Cinemobile building had a triangular shape and was three stories high, with a large lower level which housed the sales force and the maintenance bay for the Cinemobiles. I parked my car and entered the building from the rear, and immediately noticed the large Cinemobile units stationed in the parking lot. There were three of them, large Greyhound-type buses, modified to handle the various camera and lighting equipment needed to make a movie. Technicians and mechanics were stationed around and under the large vehicles, servicing them. I noticed the logo on the side of each unit—the globe of the world sliced by lightning-styled letters spelling Cinemobile. Little did I know how appropriate it was.

Though I had no idea what job I was applying for, I liked the feel and the energy of the place. It reminded me of my early days at Wolper, and I immediately responded to the environment. I checked in with the receptionist and walked up the narrow staircase to Eddie Rosen's office. Eddie was standing at the window looking out over the Los Angeles basin in the midst of a phone conversation, and he waved me in, indicating I should sit down. I noticed immediately that Eddie was high-energy; he was dressed stylishly, hair slicked back, wearing designer glasses and holding a cigarette in his hand. He finished his conversation with the words "Big changes, big changes" and hung up. He smiled and we shook hands. I found out he was a former literary agent who had been instrumental in coming up with the idea of "packaging" movies: putting the elements of a script together, then attaching the director and stars and taking that "package" to the studio for financing and distribution. Eddie knew everybody, and everybody knew Eddie.

Even though it was early Monday morning, the phone was ringing constantly, and the so-called interview consisted of his asking me a question, then answering the phone. When I asked what I would be doing, he said I would be his assistant, then asked if I knew anything about Cinemobile Systems.

I said no, and he explained that Cinemobile was a location facility, literally a studio on wheels. It provided "below the line" services, meaning all the technical and physical aspects of a movie's production. Fouad Said, the founder and CEO of the company, was Egyptian, a graduate of the USC Film School and the second unit cameraman on the television series *I Spy*, starring Bill Cosby and Robert Culp; he was responsible for filming the European location sites for the series. Fouad had created the company, I learned, as a way to simplify, streamline and economize the filming process. As he traveled around Europe filming different exteriors for various episodes of *I Spy*, he created a vanlike bus designed to house and carry the necessary camera equipment. He stripped the interior, then filled the inside with racks and a large storage area for the lights, cameras, generators and lenses, leaving enough space for the cast and crew. He refined and modified the Cinemobile to the point that it became economically feasible to do location shooting for both big- and low-budget movies. When I arrived on the scene, they had just completed building the Cine 8, a huge eight-wheel-drive bus that could climb up the side of a mountain, shoot whatever was needed and return, all in the same day. It revolutionized location shooting. It had been used to film the exterior locations on Sydney Pollack's *Jeremiah Johnson*, an outdoor action-adventure film shot mainly in the snow, high in the Sierra Nevada Mountains. Despite all the location problems, inclement weather and sensitive generators, the production values on that film had been superb.

Cinemobile transformed the way movies were made in the seventies. No longer was an army of supplies and support needed to fuel the production, and more important, it no longer took weeks to travel, shoot, wrap and return. If a producer wanted to film on location, he now would not have to deal with the logistical nightmare imposed by a studio at some distant outpost. With Cinemobile, it became economically feasible to let a filmmaker shoot on location and return in a matter of days. It could sometimes cut a budget by more than half.

Fouad's technology totally supported the vision of the new filmmakers: Francis Ford Coppola, Steven Spielberg, Martin Scorsese, Hal Ashby, Robert Altman, Warren Beatty, Peter Fonda, Dennis Hopper, Bob Rafelson and others. The company had become very successful in only a few years, and its reputation was growing so fast Fouad couldn't keep up with it. He was a real innovator, and was determined that his vision would manifest into a worldwide company serving the needs of filmmakers everywhere.

The year 1973 marked a new beginning for Cinemobile. Fouad had always wanted to produce his own movies. Now he could, so the first thing he did was hire a top-notch administrator, Bernie Weitzman, the former head of Desilu Studios, the old Lucille Ball and Desi Arnaz studio where the *I Love Lucy* shows were filmed. Then he hired Eddie Rosen to run the literary division, and created a new company called Film Guarantors, a completion bond company that guaranteed a film would be brought in on time, and on budget. If the production went over the allotted budget, the completion bond company would assume responsibility for the overage.

Eddie explained that Cinemobile was now in the process of creating another new company, which would be its film production arm. The new company would be called Cine Artists, and Fouad's partners were some of the biggest movers and shakers in the movie world: Salah Hassanein, one of the largest exhibitors in the country; the Naify brothers, owners of the United Artists theater cir-

cuit, with some 450 theaters across the country; and the soon-to-be
parent of Cinemobile, the Taft Broadcasting Company. Together,
they would provide several million dollars in production money so
Fouad could make movies. What they were looking for, Eddie told
me, was someone to read and evaluate the screenplays being submitted by agents, production companies, directors, studios, stars
and others. In short, in order to thrive and prosper, they needed
material and someone to read it. My job, he explained, would be to
read and find material. I was elated; as a writer taking a break from
writing, I would be able to read what other screenwriters were
writing. From my perspective, it was perfect.

After our meeting, Eddie and I went up to the third level of the
building to see Fouad. The large office at the top of the stairs had
windows on three sides overlooking the Sunset Strip and down-
town Los Angeles. On clear days, we could see the Pacific Ocean.

Fouad was a small, dynamic man, just over five feet tall, very
nice, polite and filled with nervous energy. The phones were ringing nonstop, and I was mesmerized watching his eyes trace their
flickering lights. Fouad was a man constantly on the go; if he was in
the office for more than six weeks, he would get antsy and get out,
traveling to our offices in London, Paris or Geneva, where crews
seemed to be shooting all the time. Or he would visit his best
friend, the King of Kuwait. He was a real globe-trotter. The more I
learned about him, the more impressed I became.

He had started Cinemobile with his own money because no one
in Hollywood would give him a break after he graduated film
school. Whether it was because he was Egyptian, or too young, or
whether production executives simply could not relate to his
streamlined vision of filmmaking, I don't know. After I'd worked
for him for almost a year, we were riding to one of the studios for a
meeting one day when he shared that my uncle Sol had given him

his first break, as a second unit cameraman on the old *Daniel Boone* series. Fouad never forgot a favor.

After we'd shared some small talk in his office for a few minutes, I watched Fouad's eyes race up and down the blinking lights on the telephone. Finally, he couldn't wait anymore and started punching buttons, and I knew the interview was over. What I didn't know was whether I had a job or not. But as we walked down the stairs, Eddie asked me when I could start and took me in to meet Bernie Weitzman so we could talk about salary.

The only instruction Fouad had given me, which Eddie constantly echoed, was to "find material." That was my job—find material. For the two and a half years I was head of the Story Department at Cinemobile, that was my mantra, my motto, my core of being. Eddie told me I was responsible for reading scripts submitted by various companies to determine whether we should put money in them, and whether for production services, completion bonds or partial or interim financing. In short, we made movies, and our success was measured by how many films we could get involved with. During my first year, Cinemobile was involved in the production of some 117 major movies, including *The Godfather*, *Jeremiah Johnson*, *American Graffiti* and *Alice Doesn't Live Here Anymore*, along with numerous TV shows.

As Eddie's assistant, I would read and evaluate the material, then send the coverage to Eddie so he could respond to the people who had submitted it. If I found something I thought was unique and good, I had to drop everything and tell him immediately. And, he emphasized, I was not to tell Fouad about anything I found until I first spoke to him. I learned quickly it was a twenty-four-hour-a-day job. We exchanged home phone numbers, and over the next two and a half years, we checked in with each other on a regular basis at least three or four times every weekend.

I was put into a makeshift office in the basement without windows, next door to the "pit," where the overhauling and maintenance of the Cinemobiles took place. After I got settled that first day, my ears ringing with the sounds of hammers and the whine of electric drills, Fouad came by and dropped about fifteen scripts on my desk. "Find material," he said, and vanished.

I looked at that pile of scripts sitting on the desk, and asked myself how I was going to do this. Obviously, I had to read the material, but how many scripts could I read in a day? And what kind of coverage did I need to provide? Was I going to synopsize each script in great detail, or was I going to summarize the story in a paragraph or two, then add my personal comments? I had no idea, so I just jumped in and started reading.

I reached for the top script on the pile and looked at the title: *W.W. and the Dixie Dancekings*, written by Tom Rickman. I'll always remember this script, because it was so good; the writing was visual and clean, the characters colorful, the dialogue sharp and witty, the locale interesting. There was just one problem: I knew I could not read the first script on my very first day and go racing up to the offices yelling, "Eureka, I found it, I found it!" I mean, I had nothing to compare it with, so I thought I'd better cool it until I had read several others and would be able to make some kind of comparison.

Ironically, that same day, Fouad walked in with another load of scripts, plunked them down on the desk and asked, "Find anything good?" I paused, then said I'd read a very good script, and the first words out of his mouth were "What's it about?" That question became a major learning experience for me. How do you explain a two-hour movie in a sentence or two? So, I started telling Fouad the story, about a con man in the deep South being pursued by a small-town sheriff. After a minute, I saw his eyes glaze over; he simply checked out, fidgeting with the phone line. I knew I had blown it. Fouad had an incredibly short attention span and I realized that in the future, if I ever found a script I liked, I would only have about thirty seconds to tell the story.

I was always seventy scripts behind. The pile of scripts on my desk was so high, I decided I would summarize the entire screenplay only if I felt the script was good enough. My job was to read, not to provide full coverage; I had to give Fouad and Eddie enough information to talk intelligently to the person who submitted the script. So that's what I did. After reading several screenplays I created a comfortable style for myself. For each script I read, I wrote about a page summarizing the plot and about half a page, or less, on my personal evaluation. Then I would make a comment about whether we should pursue the project or pass on it.

It was a major lesson in broadening my reading skills. When I found a script I liked, I passed it on to Eddie, and if he liked it too, we would plan to pitch it to Fouad. I would sit down and prepare my pitch, trying to describe the action of the screenplay in a few sentences. I used to call these presentations *pitchman pitches*, because when I pitched a project to Fouad, he was usually sitting behind his desk, ear glued to the phone with several calls waiting, and I knew I had a very limited time. No matter what story I was pitching, whether it was *American Graffiti* (George Lucas), *The Wind and the Lion* (John Milius) or *Rocky*, Cinemobile provided the location facilities, I knew I only had about thirty seconds. After that, he simply checked out; his eyes would glaze over and he would start looking at the telephone lights, just waiting to punch the next button.

I had been working for a few months when I began to realize that as much as Fouad wanted me to find material, he was reluctant to say yes to anything. It was his money, and he wasn't going to spend it simply because I liked the material. "See Eddie," he would say. And sometimes, he would pull a fast one on me.

One day, Fouad came in and threw a screenplay at me and told me to read it immediately. It was a script by Paul and Leonard Schrader called *The Yakuza*, a stylized drama that took place in Japan about an American girl kidnapped by Japanese gangsters. I was a big fan of Paul Schrader's, having read *Taxi Driver*, an extraordinary script. I liked it so much, I brought in Paul Schrader and Marty Scorsese for several meetings, then begged Eddie to plead with Fouad to see if there was some way we could get involved with the project. But the answer was always no. And that was that. No matter what I said, or did, *Taxi Driver* was a definite pass in our company. It took more than a year for producers Tony Bill and Michael and Julia Phillips to get it off the ground. Now, of course, it's considered a classic.

I read *The Yakuza* and found it very stylized and dry. When I finished, I went up to Fouad's office. Eddie was there. As soon as I walked in, Fouad asked what I thought. I told him it was an extremely stylized script that was so dense, so complex and convoluted, plotwise, that I didn't understand it at all. In terms of style, it was more Japanese than American, and since the main character was an American detective sent to Japan to rescue a kidnapped girl, I felt it had to be opened up more, in terms of both action and exposition; but doing that, I believed, would weaken the story. As written, I told him, it was a fascinating study of Japanese gangsters, but if we were in the business of making films that appealed to an American audience, we should pass.

Eddie immediately jumped in. This script, he said, was just sold to Warners for hundreds of thousands of dollars, and what did I have to say to that! At that point, I knew I'd been set up. I reminded Eddie and Fouad that I'd been after them to do *Taxi Driver* for months and they'd turned a deaf ear. Nobody, they'd complained, would see a picture about a "mentally defective" Vietnam vet. I stood firm, told them *Taxi Driver* had been extraordinary and *The Yakuza* was merely interesting, all style and no substance, well written, well conceived, but in my opinion not commercial at all.

Evidently, Warners felt the same. Several months later, Robert Towne was brought in to do a rewrite. When *The Yakuza* finally came out, it opened big, sank quickly and disappeared without a trace. It was what I call "an interesting failure."

A few weeks later, Eddie took me aside and told me that Fouad's edict of "finding material" gave me the opportunity of tapping in to the writing talents of the time. He said I needed to start cultivating relationships with writers I liked, writers I thought had a lot of potential.

When I read a script I liked, I made a point of calling the screenwriter, introducing myself and sharing with him or her what I liked about the screenplay. Then we would get together and discuss any other projects they might have, or any ideas they wanted to write. But I soon found out that while Cine Artists had a lot of money to make movies, we had no money to develop screenplays—that is, give money to a screenwriter to develop the idea into a script. Many good screenplay ideas came across my desk that I just had to let go. It didn't take long for me to learn that nobody in Hollywood has much of an imagination; it seems that most people can only see what's written on the page and can't see how it can be changed into a more powerful project. A good idea is not a good idea unless it's executed properly. I also found out that if one deal falls through, there's another one right around the corner. I didn't get too attached to any single project, except a book I loved: a Dick Francis novel.

I happened to be in Fouad's office one day when he received a call from Stanley Kubrick about some new lenses for a project he was doing. Kubrick, I learned, had started out as a photographer and liked to create and grind his own lenses, but he sought out Fouad to help him create several different camera lenses for *2001: A Space Odyssey* and *A Clockwork Orange*. Over the years, they had become good friends. I was a huge fan of Kubrick's, especially *The Killing* (Kubrick, Jim Thompson), *Paths of Glory* (Kubrick, Calder Willingham, Jim Thompson) and, of course, *2001*.

When Fouad asked what he was working on, Kubrick laughed and didn't say anything. Fouad pressed as only Fouad could, and Stanley reluctantly told him it was based on a novella written by Thackeray, a famous nineteenth-century English novelist. That's all he would say. So Fouad told him about Cine Artists and asked if he knew of any good material. Kubrick mentioned a Dick Francis novel. I didn't know anything about Dick Francis at the time, so I went out and read the novel immediately, but it took me some time to understand what Kubrick had seen in it. And when I did, I was just blown away. In this novel, the line between reality and the movies had been totally erased. To this day, Dick Francis remains one of my favorite authors.

When Fouad hung up, he told me about Kubrick's current project and asked if I knew anything about an author named Thackeray. I replied yes, he was the famous author of *Vanity Fair*. Fouad said he wanted to play a joke on Kubrick, so I should find out as much as I could about Thackeray. Over the next few days, I searched through the body of Thackeray's work and by a process of elimination presented Fouad with three alternatives which, I felt, could be the Kubrick movie. I gave him all the information, and when Fouad called Kubrick back, he told him what I had found.

Stanley freaked. In the end, though, they both had a good laugh. The movie was *Barry Lyndon* (written by Kubrick), one of Kubrick's most beautiful and, I think, most underrated films.

Fouad was typical of most producers in that he didn't like to read; he wouldn't read anything unless it was absolutely necessary to do so. That usually meant after the deal was made, when he was checking the script against the proposed budget. He always maintained that most movie budgets were "thirty percent fat" and could be trimmed. He had an amazing ability to look at a film's budget, whether it was three or ten pages long, and know immediately whether it was accurate, padded or thin.

To help myself catalogue the massive amount of scripts I was reading, I created a system in which I would read a script (I was reading three a day), write a short synopsis, send copies of the coverage to Eddie and keep a copy for myself in a notebook. If Eddie liked something, or knew Fouad had to speak to the person who submitted it, he would present the script with the coverage.

A short time later, I was given the script of *The Godfather* (Francis Ford Coppola, Mario Puzo) to read. The film was already in the midst of production when Paramount asked whether the company would be interested in putting up the completion bond and become involved in the production. I read the script, not having read the novel. The way the sequences were structured, the character insights and story progression, impressed me very much. It was a great script. But I knew even then that it wasn't what I thought about the script that mattered to Fouad, it was the deal. If the deal was good and I liked the script, he would commit immediately. If the deal was good and the script was bad, he would hesitate and negotiate for a stronger financial position.

What was important in my script coverage was to clearly state the obvious: namely, who wrote the script and what was it about. I called it *the brief* and it was usually a one- or two-sentence description of genre and story. If Fouad or Eddie did not have this to refer to, they were totally lost. So I quickly learned how important it was to synthesize the story line into a sentence or two; it was my *pitchman pitch.*

I think *American Graffiti* (George Lucas, Gloria Katz, Willard Huyck) was the first script where I actually managed to do this. Fouad came in one day, dropped it on my desk and said, "Read it— I've got to get back to them in an hour." So I dropped everything and read it. I opened the title page and saw that the script was written by George Lucas. I recalled that I had met George Lucas several months earlier, in the screening room at Warners when he was an intern, making a short film about Francis Ford Coppola directing *The Rain People.* He showed me his student film *THX 1138* (later remade with Robert Duvall), and I was struck by the fluidity and strength of the images. Even at that stage of his career, as a student in his early twenties, it was pretty obvious he was a filmmaker of great talent.

When I finished the script, I went up to see Fouad and told him we should do anything we could to help get this movie made. "What's it about?" he asked. I told him it was a story about a group of young people in a small town the night before they leave for college. "Did you like it?" I told him I did, very much, and thought we should get involved with it because it "could be made for a price." I knew "the pitch" I gave him had absolutely nothing to do with the story line; I would be generous saying it was even a one-line description of what the story was about. But I had learned certain things about Fouad in the short time I had been there. I liked the script of *American Graffiti* and thought it would attract a large audience. That was my opinion, and I stuck with it; otherwise, I wouldn't have been doing my job. He didn't say anything, just grunted and picked up the phone. Over the next week, I kept after him to get involved with the movie, and we finally did, thanks to Francis Ford Coppola. By our providing a Cinemobile during production, as well as the completion bond, the film was able to go into production.

Fouad once told me that making a deal in Hollywood is like digging a ditch: if you dig one shovelful of dirt each day, after many days of digging you'll have a ditch. The same principle applies to making a deal: one follow-up phone call every few days and pretty soon you're sitting down to negotiate. I'd never thought of it that way before, but it's a solid principle that applies to writing as well; writing is a day-by-day job, five or six days a week, three or more pages a day, and some days are better than others. That's the whole principle: a little bit each day and after a certain period of time there's a completed project, whether it's a song, symphony, screenplay, novel or painting.

To help Fouad keep focused on the "good" screenplays, I created a "hot sheet," a list of the top ten scripts I had read during the week. We had a number code, ranging from 1 to 10, 10 being the best, and if we were in a meeting with a producer, director or executive, at some point during the conversation, Fouad would look at me and say, "Is it a good script? A ten?" And I would reply, "Yes, Fouad, it's a good script, a seven, or an eight," and then he would know how far to go in terms of making a deal. He brought me into meetings because he never read either the material or the coverage, and he would always use me as the excuse if we decided to pass on a project. I learned it's important to have a fall guy. If I got calls from pushy producers or agents, even studio executives, telling me about a script that should be made, I would say, "I love the project, but I'm not going to lose my job over it."

It took a while before we established a smooth working relationship and an effective way of communicating. One day, during a meeting, I was telling him about a script I liked called *Alice Doesn't Live Here Anymore*. It had been submitted by Warners for Marty Scorsese to direct. I liked the Bob Getchell script, and told Fouad it was something we should become involved with.

"What's it about?" he asked. I told him. Then he asked me something odd, something I had never heard him ask before: "Any whammos?" I had no idea what a whammo was, and when I asked him, he simply shrugged his shoulders and changed the subject.

When I asked Eddie what a whammo was, he laughed and said he didn't have a clue. After that, whenever I read a script I liked and recommended it to Fouad, he would ask, "How many whammos? We need whammos," and he would emphasize the point like a baseball player pounding his glove. I was feeling bold one day, and when he asked me the question, I decided to test the waters. I said yes, this script has whammos. He looked closely at me, then told me he wanted to see a whammo chart. I looked at him, he looked at me, and I thought, Well, this is it, I'm screwed, because I still had no idea what he was talking about.

Then, a few days later, while Fouad and I were driving to a meeting, we started talking about the whammo. What is it? I asked. How does he see it, what function does it serve, how would he define it? He told me that when he was filming the *I Spy* series he found that in every good script there were "ten pages and a whammo, ten pages and a whammo. . . ."

It wasn't much, but it was a beginning. As I started thinking about it, I thought a whammo must be some kind of action scene, because the implication of "ten pages and a whammo" seemed to be that after a few scenes of dialogue there had to be some kind of scene to keep the story moving forward.

In order to define it to myself, I started with the name—whammo. It sounded active, like a verb, like action. It seemed logical, knowing Fouad, that a whammo must be some kind of action scene, or some kind of incident or event that creates tension and suspense. That was my start point. In my mind, a whammo became an action scene, or anything that propelled the action: a car chase, an explosion, a race or a chase—even, if done right, a love scene. How about the tension of the sound of a doorknob turning in the dead of night? Was that stretching it, or could that also be a whammo? Definitely, I decided.

At the same time, I figured, there could be a reaction, something that spun off from this basic action. Suppose, I reasoned, there's a bank robbery; it's tense, terse, taut. That's a whammo. Now, in addition, suppose the robbers race out of the bank and find their getaway car gone. Could that be a whammo? Or suppose they race out of the bank and suddenly find their car won't start. Is that a whammo? Or as the car speeds away, the street is suddenly blocked by a huge street-sweeper, even a parade. They're all whammos. And I thought back to the opening of *Major Dundee* and *The Wild Bunch*; Peckinpah used whammos all the time. I liked the definition, because it worked. A whammo could be either a car chase or a kiss, an action or anything that propels the action.

Once I had defined the whammo, I set about creating a whammo chart. Since Fouad liked to measure one thing against another, I decided to use the 1-to-10 scale that we used to rate scripts. I wanted to correlate it, or cross-reference it, to the specific page number in the script, so I created a graph. On the left side of the page I drew a vertical line with numbers ranging from 10 to 1, and on the bottom of the page I drew a horizontal line and put the page numbers 1 through 120. That way I could locate each whammo by page number, then rate it on a scale of 1 to 10.

Ten pages and a whammo, ten pages and a whammo—that was Fouad's motto. With this chart, I could go through any script and find those areas where something or nothing was happening and use it as an overview of the entire screenplay. Whenever I found a script I wanted to pitch to Fouad for production or possible financing, I always presented it with a whammo chart.

After I wrote out the pitch for myself in a sentence or two, I drew up a large whammo chart, then pitched the project. Fouad loved it, so I started using the whammo chart for all kinds of films, knowing, of course, they worked best for action-adventure movies.

I remember how absurd I felt at first about what I was doing. As a writer, I knew there was no way I could actually measure a screenplay in terms of the whammo; breaking a script down this way seemed totally unnatural, crazy. But I also came to see that there was a certain insane logic to it.

After I had done a whammo chart for several scripts, I realized that it was a unique way of analyzing a screenplay, not in terms of story, content or character, but in terms of dramatic structure. Fouad would look at the whammo chart and start evaluating the script based on the graph I had created. He would say, "Look at Act Two. For twenty pages, from pages thirty-five to fifty-five, there's not one whammo. It's all talk. We need a whammo here." And he would make a mark on the chart where he wanted some kind of whammo to occur. And I would protest, "Fouad, you can't arbitrarily put in a car chase, explosion or sex scene just because it's slow; you've got to maintain the integrity of the story." He would simply nod and wave me off, not even listening. Then it became my job to figure out what might work in terms of keeping the tempo and pacing together in a strong dramatic continuity. Of course, I had to convince the writer of this. No matter what my misgivings might be, I would try to help guide him or her to some kind of appropriate whammo, either a car chase or a kiss, that could possibly work. I found it to be a good exercise for fine-tuning my instincts about what kind of scene might be needed to heighten a particular moment of dramatic action.

As I became more and more comfortable with the concept of the whammo, I began to see that Fouad intuitively knew what he was talking about; you can't just have a movie of talking heads. There's got to be some kind of visual style that's expressed on the written page, and while "ten pages and a whammo, ten pages and a whammo" is not *the* answer, it certainly showed me the relationship between film style and film content.

It wasn't long before word about the whammo spread around town and I started receiving phone calls from various studios and production companies—and even the American Film Institute—asking if I would explain just how the whammo chart worked. The companies would invite their development executives and Story Department readers to a session in their conference room at which I would explain the concept and function of the whammo. Believe it or not, the concept still works. Joel Silver, the dynamic producer of such films as the *Lethal Weapon* series, the *Die Hard* films and *The Matrix*, uses the whammo chart as an integral part of the production process, and he's been very successful at it.

Creating the whammo chart was a major lesson for me in understanding what makes a good movie. But the real lesson was understanding that more whammos do not necessarily make better movies. In any film, no matter what the genre, there has to be a strong blend of character and action.

What I didn't know at the time was how the experience of creating the whammo chart would lead me to explore the landscape of what was for me an undiscovered country: what makes a good screenplay.

10

Turning Pages

———

"Gatsby believed in the green light, the orgiastic future that year by year recedes before us. It eluded us then, but that's no matter—tomorrow we will run faster, stretch out our arms farther. . . . And one fine morning— So we beat on, boats against the current, borne back ceaselessly into the past."

—F. Scott Fitzgerald
The Great Gatsby

During the two and a half years I was head of the Story Department at Cinemobile, I read more than two thousand screenplays and more than a hundred and fifty novels while searching for material to submit to our financial partners. Of those two-thousand-plus scripts, I found only forty to submit. Why so few? Most of the scripts were simply not good enough in terms of story or idea. Sometimes the ideas were good, but their execution was terrible—too talky, too wordy, too explanatory, with one-dimensional characters and contrived, predictable story lines. I learned that a good idea is not a good idea unless it's executed properly.

As a reader, I was there to do a job, to "find material," and I wanted to approach the task from the writer's point of view. I felt that if I wanted to improve my own skills as a screenwriter, I needed to find out what made a good screenplay—what makes it tick, what holds it together, how the story unfolds from beginning to end. After many years of writing and learning about the craft, I was now learning it through the reading of screenplays. And while I thought it would be an easy job, I learned I had to wade through a lot of terrible stuff, all those poorly written scripts, to get to "the good stuff."

One reason it was difficult to find good scripts to submit to Fouad was that Cine Artists was a new company and agents and producers were somewhat reluctant to submit their top material. They didn't know whether we were serious players or not. So we would get material which had been submitted and rejected all over town, and I learned very quickly that these recycled scripts were a real hard sell. That, clearly, was not the way to go. Especially if I wanted to keep my job.

In truth, the majority of screenplays submitted to Cine Artists were badly written. Not only were they poorly conceived and executed, most of them were imitations of movies that had already been made. Since I was the one who was evaluating the material, I had to make some clear and sharp distinctions about the screenplays I read. The scripts I submitted to Fouad and Eddie had to be good scripts, significant in some way or another, and they had to be of a good enough quality that I could stand behind my selection. Otherwise, I'd be out of there very quickly.

So I created an intention for myself: I would be as honest as I could in my evaluations, I would not submit anything I did not believe in and I would take full responsibility for what I submitted. I felt that if I could follow those guidelines, I would be okay. I had always known you can't make a good movie without a good screenplay. There can be an excellent movie made from a good screenplay, or an "okay" movie made from a good screenplay, or even a bad movie made from a good screenplay, but there ain't no way you can make a good movie out of a badly written and poorly executed screenplay.

I was determined to expand my ability as a writer by uncovering the elements that made up a good screenplay. From my own writing experience I knew that good screenplays contain a good story, strong action, interesting characters and sharp dialogue. I wanted to find a way I could use my writing skills to formulate my own values, judgments and opinions in evaluating the scripts I read.

What I didn't know is that reading a screenplay is a unique experience. It's not like reading a novel, play, technical journal or long piece in the Sunday paper. At first, I read the words on the page slowly, drinking in all the visual descriptions, character nuances and dramatic situations. I found it easy to get caught up in the writer's words and style. I learned that the scripts that read well, that were written in beautiful sentences employing stylish and literate prose and beautiful dialogue, were usually not the best screenplays. While they may have read like liquid honey across the page, the overall feeling was often like reading a short story, or a strong journalistic piece in a national magazine like *Time* or *Esquire*. And that's not what a movie is.

What I was looking for was a style that exploded off the page, the kind of raw energy exhibited in scripts like *Mean Streets* (Mardik Martin, Martin Scorsese), *Taxi Driver* and *American Graffiti*. As the stack of scripts on my desk grew higher and higher, I felt very much like Jay Gatsby at the end of *The Great Gatsby*, F. Scott Fitzgerald's classic novel. At the end of the book, Nick, the narrator, recalls how Gatsby used to stand looking out over the water at the image of the green light, beckoning him to those past memories of unrequited love. Gatsby was a man who believed in the past, a man who believed he could step back into that past and re-create it.

It was this dream that spurred him as a young man to cross to the other side of the tracks searching for love and wealth, searching for the expectations and desires of the past that he hoped would become the future.

The green light.

I thought a lot about Gatsby and the green light as I struggled through the piles and piles of screenplays searching for "the good read," that special and unique screenplay which would be "the one" to make it through the gauntlet of studios, executives, stars, financial wizards and egos and finally end up on the screen.

Every morning when I arrived at work, there would be a stack of screenplays waiting for me. No matter what I did, no matter how fast I read or how many scripts I skimmed, skipped or tossed, one solid fact always remained: I could never get through the pile.

Because of the enormous volume, I was reading three screenplays a day. I found I could read two scripts a day without a problem, but when I got to the third one, the words, characters and actions all seemed to congeal into some kind of amorphous goo of plot lines concerning the FBI and CIA, punctuated with bank heists, murders and car chases, with a lot of wet kisses and naked flesh thrown in for color. At two or three in the afternoon, after a heavy lunch and maybe too much wine, it was difficult to keep my attention focused on the action and the nuances of character. So, after a few months on the job, I usually closed my office door, propped my feet up on the desk, turned off the phones, leaned back in the chair with a script on my chest and took a catnap.

I must have read more than a hundred screenplays before I realized that I didn't know what I was doing. What was I looking for? What made a screenplay good or bad? I could tell whether I liked it or not, yes, but what were the elements that made it a good screenplay? It had to be more than a string of whammos laced together in a series of beautiful pictures. Was it the plot, the characters or the visual arena where the action took place that made it a good screenplay? Was it the visual style of writing or the cleverness of the dialogue? If I didn't know the answers to that, then how could I answer the question I was repeatedly being asked by agents, writers, producers and directors: what was I looking for? That's when I saw clearly that the real question for me was how do I read a screenplay. I knew how to write a screenplay, and I certainly knew what I liked or disliked when I went to the movies, but how did I apply that to the reading of a screenplay?

Over the next few months, I began making lists of scripts I liked, scripts I didn't like and scripts that were just okay. I kept a large notebook, keeping track of the screenplays and the writers I read and adding my comments and notations so I could create my own system.

I used as my start point something I learned while I was at Berkeley. I had taken a course in literary criticism taught by the famous American poet Josephine Miles. She was absolutely a wonderful teacher. Although she was confined to a wheelchair because of a debilitating illness, and her body was shrunken and misshapen, her mind was as clear and sharp as fine crystal. The way to approach literary criticism, she maintained, whether it be art, music, literature or film, was by asking a simple question: *Did I like it? If so, why? And if I didn't like it, why not?*

It was a lesson I took to heart. If I read a script I liked, the first question I asked myself was what I liked about it. Was it the action, the characters, the visual style or the dramatic premise? If I didn't like it, I asked myself what I didn't like about it.

It didn't take long for me to see that a lot of the screenplays being submitted were modeled after films that had already been made and that had been successful. After *American Graffiti* was released, I received a large number of submissions which utilized a similar story line but were slightly altered in terms of character, locale or action. In Hollywood, the success of a film meant there might be a large market for a similar kind of movie. Fear and greed—the two driving forces in Hollywood.

The problem with this kind of thinking, I discovered, is that films often take more than two years to complete. By the time a spin-off or sequel of a film is completed, there's already another trend in the marketplace. Once a script is purchased that's considered "new," or different, those in the industry will try to duplicate it, like *Volcano* and *Dante's Peak*. Then it becomes a race to see who hits the theaters first. This happens all the time in television: if one network has a period piece, then the other networks want a period piece, and more often than not, they'll show it on the same day at the same time in some kind of bizarre *mano a mano* competition. The result is that everybody loses.

As I sat there with my constant companion of seventy unread scripts, I made my first resolution. My rule was simple—*"hit 'em where they ain't."* Meaning if horror films were currently the rage, I was looking for a love story. Or if a hard-edged police drama was currently successful, like *The French Connection* or *The Godfather*, I was looking for a screwball comedy. I never wanted to follow a trend, or do a sequel, because I thought it was a lose-lose situation. It's better to begin a trend than follow one. Creating a trend, though more difficult, will be more rewarding, and I used as my examples *The Godfather*, *The Sting*, *Midnight Cowboy* (Waldo Salt) and *Easy Rider*, films which had all gone against the trend.

"Start out with an individual," F. Scott Fitzgerald wrote, "and you find you have created a type—start out with a type and you find that you have created nothing." The message seemed to be clear: follow a trend and it's doomed to failure. Like Gatsby, I believed in the green light.

When producers, writers, agents or directors asked me what I was looking for, I replied I was looking for something that I hadn't seen before. I wasn't being sarcastic or facetious at all. Something had happened while I was reading a lot of screenplays and seeing a lot of movies: after a while I found myself looking for some kind of differentiating aspect, some unique quality which separated that work from all the others. Something that was fresh and original, either in thought, execution, characters or locations.

When I started reading a screenplay, I looked for certain specific things. How did it look on the page? Was there plenty of "white space" or were the paragraphs too dense, too thick, the dialogue too long? Or was the reverse true? Was the description of the scene too thin, and the dialogue too sparse? Did I know what was going on? I looked for a visual style, an interesting premise and three-dimensional characters. Originality of thought, visual execution and interesting characters became the key factors in whether I recommended a screenplay or passed on it. That was the green light beckoning me as I devoured these seemingly endless stacks of screenplays looking for what I called the "good read."

The screenplays I liked kept me turning pages; screenplays which did not have a strong action line or strong characters bored me within a few pages. I wanted to see if I could find out what the qualities were that kept me turning pages. That's when something clicked. I began to ask myself how long it took before I made a decision about whether I liked the movie or not. If I could answer that question, maybe I could apply the same principle while reading a screenplay.

I'd been going to as many movies as I could, but now I went more as an observer than as a member of the audience. I saw about four or five movies a week. I went at night and on weekends. For a time I felt like I was back in that little editing room at Wolper screening all those movies for *Hollywood and the Stars*. Except now I wasn't looking to pull scenes, I was looking to see what the elements were that made something work.

Sitting in the darkened theater listening to the response of the audience, I began to get a real feel for the movie, whether it was too talky, too slow, or if the events and the action happened so fast I didn't understand the story line. It might be a fun ride, but as far as I was concerned, if it didn't work within the context of the story, then it wasn't working at all. Sometimes, I'd go to the movies and be caught up by the acting, the photography or the music and then when I walked out of the theater I'd have forgotten what I'd just seen. I called them "parking lot movies," because I didn't remember what I had just seen when I got to my car.

I gained a lot of information from this experience. I saw I had to be involved immediately. To understand what was going on, I had to know what was happening within the very first few minutes of the movie. If the story was not set up at the very beginning, and if I didn't know who or what the story was about, I was constantly playing catch-up. When that happened, I noticed, my attention started wandering, my focus shifted and I started getting restless. I found myself thinking about getting something to drink, or going to the bathroom. I started making judgments, having a little dialogue in my mind about the actors or the story. I found the two best critical tools I have are my bladder and my butt. When I started becoming restless, shifting my position in the seat, it was a sure sign the filmmakers had lost me, and that's when I'd start making judgments and decisions about the movie I was watching.

I began examining the elements that made this first unit of action so important. As I had learned from Peckinpah, the opening scene or sequence should grab the attention of the audience. At Wolper, television shows always opened with "a tease," a "grabber," that little scene at the beginning of the show before the title sequence and the first commercial break that tells the viewer what's going on in the story. If that scene doesn't grab me within the first few minutes, I'm out of there, reaching for the remote and surfing until I find something else.

So I started asking myself some questions. What elements need to be set up within the first ten minutes? The question answered itself; I wanted to know *what the story is about, who the story is about and what's going on.* If I see a movie with Clint Eastwood, Jack Nicholson, Robert Redford or Tom Cruise, I know they're the star and, in all probability, the main character, so the story is going to be about them. That means I want to see them within the first few minutes of the movie. I can't wait twenty or thirty minutes until I see who the story's about, or what it's about. I want to know who the main character is immediately.

Around this time, I was watching TV and *The Best Years of Our Lives* (Robert E. Sherwood), William Wyler's 1946 film that won several Academy Awards, was being shown. I hadn't seen it in a long time, and I was interested to see whether it held up. As I began watching it the first thing I saw was how well the movie was set up. The opening scenes revealed everything I needed to know. From the very first shot I knew that World War II was over and the servicemen were trying to find ways of returning home. One character, played by Dana Andrews, latches on to an air transport flight along with two other passengers, Fredric March and Harold Russell, and all three are plagued with memories of the war and doubts about the future. Right off the bat, we know it's a film about war veterans returning home and their difficulties in reentering a former way of life that the war has changed forever.

As I watched the film, I was moved again by that great sequence showing Fredric March's homecoming; done entirely in silence, it shows two people, married for some twenty years, trying to rekindle a relationship that the war has splintered. And then there's the sequence in which Dana Andrews visits a plane junkyard and climbs into an abandoned B-24. As he sits there the sounds of battle are played over his face, and we watch as he relives the pain of an unforgettable memory. It's truly masterful. Watching the film again showed me the value and necessity of setting up the story line instantly. Everything we need to know about the story, who and what it's about, is set up right from the very beginning.

From that point on, I began watching movies with a critical eye. I observed how the writer set up the story and characters and what happened in the first few minutes on screen. From my university days, I knew there are two ways to begin a story: one, with a dynamic action sequence like Peckinpah does in *The Wild Bunch*; or two, with a strong character scene like Robert Towne does in *Chinatown*. Both work effectively within the context of the story. An action sequence grabs me immediately and pulls me into the world of the movie. A strong character scene creates an emotional dynamic and carries me into the heart of the story through the point of view of the main character.

When the audience and character are joined together in discovering what's going on, it becomes a shared act of discovery. In *Chinatown*, Jake Gittes (Jack Nicholson) and the audience are joined into a single entity; we discover what's happening at the same time he's discovering what's happening.

One afternoon, I shared this observation with a writer who'd been around for years, and he told me *Chinatown* was an example of a "closed" story. The opposite of this, he said, is an "open" story. Hitchcock, he pointed out, was a master of the open story; in most of his films, the audience knows what's happening, but the main character does not, and the dramatic tension is heightened because we know what's going to happen when the character enters a particular situation. All we can do is hold our breath and wriggle in our seats and wait to see what happens.

Understanding what I was looking for in the first ten minutes of a movie led me to the next step: translating the movie experience into a reading experience. Now I began to analyze every screenplay I read in terms of how the story was set up within the first few pages. What information did I, as a reader, need to know for me to keep turning pages? The answers were obvious: *who* the main character was and *what* the story was about.

Reading the screenplay with this new approach was a revelation. I didn't have to linger over each word, each image, each line of dialogue. I read fast, yet efficiently. I found if I read the first ten pages closely, I could pick up the key elements that held the story together. The more I read, the more I understood. It got to a point where I would closely read the first ten pages, carefully read the next twenty pages, and at that point make a decision about whether I liked the story or not. If it took the writer more than thirty pages to grab my interest and attention, then I figured the rest of the screenplay didn't work. I didn't have the time or inclination to do the writer's job for him if the script wasn't set up right.

That's when I began to learn that one page of screenplay equals one minute of screen time. It didn't matter whether the page was all dialogue, all action or any combination of the two—one page of screenplay equals approximately one minute of screen time. If the writer did not set up the story within the first thirty pages, I pretty well knew the script was not going to work. That's the position I took. I couldn't imagine watching a movie for two-plus hours wondering what was going on and what the story was about.

When I mentioned this to friends and associates, they didn't like it at all. They complained that I couldn't make a valid decision about a script based simply on the first thirty pages; sometimes, they would tell me it takes that long just to get the story going. I disagreed, and found myself becoming very argumentative and opinionated about it. I knew the time and effort a writer needed to take to write a screenplay. Screenwriting is a craft, something that can be learned, but it takes diligence, patience, persistence and practice to understand the true necessities of the craft.

When I found a script I wanted to "sell" to Eddie and Fouad, I began breaking down the story in terms of action and character. I found that these qualities, if explained clearly enough, made it easier to talk about the material to agents, directors or producers. It also prepared me for the meeting with our financial partners.

At our first production meeting of Cine Artists, the partners had come to town to discuss ten scripts we had selected to recommend for production. Salah Hassanein was there, along with his chief assistant; the Naify brothers were there, with their lieutenants; the CEO of Taft Broadcasting was there with his executive assistant. There were about twelve of us in that small office, and if you measured their combined worth, it would be well over a billion dollars; the power and the energy in the room were palpable.

For several days prior to the meeting, Eddie and I had spent a lot of time preparing our material. I went over and over our synopsis sheets, polishing, tightening, shortening, making sure the one-line descriptions of the stories and the short paragraph summaries were easily readable. At the end, I added a brief "Why I recommend this project." When the meeting began, Fouad had Eddie present the projects and I did the gofer work, handing out the synopses of each of the films we were presenting.

Most of the projects we had chosen were action-adventure scripts with strong starring male roles. The next few hours were an education in terms of what exhibitors look for in their movie theaters. I had to explain every project in great detail, whether there was enough action, sex, laughs and tension. In some of the projects, I had to describe a particular moment that I personally responded to; I became the actor, the writer pitching a story, a comedian waiting for a laugh line, and at the end of all this I thought I began to understand why some scripts get bought and others don't.

I knew I had to grab their attention immediately, pitching the characters, the action and the situation. I saw very clearly that they couldn't "see" the potential in the project, just the way some people can't "see" a finished building through the design of the blueprints. I think it's a "Hollywood thing," because most of the executives don't actually read the scripts.

Out of all these scripts, most of which were produced later by other companies, we made only one; it was a film called *Aloha, Bobby and Rose*, written and directed by Floyd Mutrux, who later wrote *American Hot Wax*, *Hollywood Knights* and *Freebie and the Bean*, among other films. As soon as I read the first few pages of *Aloha, Bobby and Rose*, I knew it was fresh and original and could possibly reach a large audience. It reminded me a little of *Dust Be My Destiny*, the old John Garfield movie. *Aloha, Bobby and Rose* was about a teenager who accidentally kills another boy, doesn't know what to do and runs away with his girlfriend. In the end, the forces of law and order—"society"— claim him and he's killed in a police shoot-out. Many years later, this same idea would be brought up to date in *Thelma & Louise*, Callie Khouri's wonderful Academy Award–winning script. When the film had finished shooting and we were in postproduction, we laid a very hip sound track over the film, literally wall-to-wall music. *Aloha, Bobby and Rose* opened phenomenally well, and became one of the few pictures Columbia Studios publicly admitted made a lot of money at the box office. Ironically, I thought the audience for this picture would be those from eighteen to twenty-four, but I was totally wrong; it was the thirteen- to fifteen-year-olds who went back to see it over and over again.

Jean Renoir once told me that if he ever wrote something he felt was perfect, he would never write again. When a writer puts words on paper, Renoir said, it's never really finished. "Perfection exists only in the mind, not in reality" was the way he phrased it. Over the years, I've come to see the truth in that. Nothing is ever really going to be perfect; things are perfect only in their imperfection. When I looked back then at my own screenwriting experience, I saw that if I tried to make something "perfect," stylizing the words and phrases and images on the page, it was a dead read; there was no "juice," or energy, on the page. Reading so many screenplays, I became aware that a "good read" flows across the page. The story is set up from page one, word one: the characters are strong and defined, the images clean and sharp, the idea and dramatic situation embodied with clarity and skill.

Like Gatsby searching for the "green light," I kept wading through the mass of screenplays and novels, searching for material that would translate into a good movie. But now, I felt I knew what I was looking for. It may have been as ambiguous or fleeting as a cloud in the wind, but at least I had a direction, a line of development, a way of evaluating my reading experience.

In the end, even though I knew the forty screenplays I recommended to our financial partners were better than the other nineteen hundred and sixty, at least in terms of what worked and what didn't, I couldn't verbalize why. I sensed I was in new territory, and simply surrendered to the process. I felt as if I were climbing a mountain, and all I could see was the page in front of me and the pages behind. I had no clear overview of what a screenplay really was at that point, but I was beginning to distinguish the elements that would forge the trail and lead me to the "good read."

I knew that when the time was right, it would be revealed.

11

Sherwood Oaks

Eddie: *"I told you: I got drunk."*
Bert: *"Sure, you got drunk. That's the best excuse in the
world for losing. No trouble losing when you got a good
excuse. And winning! That can be heavy on your back
too. Like a monkey. You drop that load too when you got
an excuse. All you gotta do is learn to feel sorry for yourself. One of the best indoor sports: feeling sorry for yourself . . . a sport enjoyed by all, especially the born losers."*
—BERT (George C. Scott) to EDDIE (Paul Newman)
The Hustler (Robert Rossen)

I had just returned from a meeting with Eddie and Fouad when
the phone rang late one afternoon. I picked it up and the caller
introduced himself as Gary Shusett. He told me he was running a
school called Sherwood Oaks Experimental College, had gotten
my name from Paul Schrader and wanted to know if I would be
interested in teaching a screenwriting class. Since I had never
taught a class, I asked what it would entail. There would be about
twenty or thirty people, he told me, and all I had to do was talk
about screenwriting and answer some questions. And, he emphasized, I did not have to prepare anything. I told him it sounded
intriguing but I'd let him know, and we hung up. I went back to
work and promptly forgot about it.

About a week later, I got another call from Gary. Would I be able to come one evening next week to talk about screenwriting? he asked. I didn't have anything to lose except an evening, so I said yes. He gave me the date and the address and suggested I come a few minutes early.

That was the beginning of my relationship with Gary Shusett and Sherwood Oaks Experimental College. Sherwood Oaks was a new concept in Hollywood at the time. "Experimental College" was really a misnomer; in reality, it was a professional school taught by professionals: actors taught acting, producers taught producing, writers taught writing, directors taught directing. The purpose of the school, which didn't give credits and had no university affiliation, was to provide an opportunity for the professionals of Hollywood to share their experience and expertise with the community. At this time, in the early seventies, this was a radical concept, for it was the unspoken assumption that most people in the film industry would not share themselves in this kind of a public forum. As it turned out, everybody in the business came.

Where else could you take a weekend course taught by Paul Newman called "Acting for the Camera"? Or hear director Sydney Pollack talking about film directing? Or attend Lucille Ball's weekend seminar on TV comedy? Or listen to Paul Schrader, Waldo Salt, Robert Towne and Michael Crichton talking about the art and craft of screenwriting? Not a bad lineup.

As word of the school spread, many of Hollywood's top talents requested to come to this funky, dirty, run-down, second-floor storefront school, located in one of the most notorious sections of Hollywood. Every night, guests and students would be forced to "run the gauntlet" of the homeless, transvestites, hookers and winos just to get to the school.

The night I had been invited to speak, I went directly from work to Sherwood Oaks. It was located on Hollywood Boulevard, one block west of Hollywood and Vine, above a Florsheim shoe store. The area was so sleazy and shabby I thought I must be in the wrong place. I parked, walked through and around the sightseers, hookers and transvestites, then went up the stairs to the second-floor lobby of what had formerly been a large stock exchange. The lobby was dirty and unkempt and the place was swarming with people. Papers were strewn on the floor and the walls were flaked with chipped paint. I wouldn't have been surprised to see rats scurrying through the halls. A line from a Bob Dylan song wafted across my mind: "Oh, mama . . . to be stuck inside of Mobile with those Memphis blues again."

A man came up, introduced himself to me as Gary, then told me I was late and hustled me through the crowded lobby. He was of average height and wore glasses, but it was his clothes that got my attention. Everything was a mismatch: the jacket didn't match the pants, the pants didn't match either shirt or jacket, and I wouldn't have been surprised if his socks didn't match either. Every piece of clothing he was wearing was rumpled, as if he'd been sleeping in this outfit for weeks.

I followed him down the hallway and he led me into what had formerly been a conference room, where some twenty or thirty people were waiting. Before I could even say a few words to him, or ask what he wanted me to talk about, he stepped up and introduced me to the people, then turned around and walked out. I looked around the room and wondered what to say. Finally, I gave them a little personal background and talked about my work at Cinemobile and what it was like reading two or three screenplays a day. They asked me questions about the "business," and I answered as best I could. So began my teaching experience at the Sherwood Oaks Experimental College.

I really enjoyed it. The people were interested in screenwriting and liked hearing stories about the difficulties of breaking into Hollywood. They wanted to know what kind of scripts Hollywood was looking for, how to get an agent, how much money could be made selling a screenplay, how difficult it was to sell a treatment (a short, narrative synopsis of the story) and so on.

When the evening was over, people hung around asking me questions till after eleven. As I was leaving, Gary asked if I would be interested in teaching a longer screenwriting class, maybe an eight-week course. Unwilling to commit to anything, I told him I'd think about it and let him know. As I walked out the door, several people told me they'd learned more in this one class than they had in a full semester at UCLA. It was nice to hear, though I had no idea what I had said or done.

Over the next few days, I kept mulling over the experience. It was obvious that people were starving for information about the craft of screenwriting. But as much as I'd enjoyed the experience, I wondered how I could commit to teaching an eight-week class. I had never taught anything before, and the memories I had of my own teachers were not very flattering. The only effective models I had as teachers were Renoir and one of my English professors; only they had sparked the desire to learn in me. And I remembered a remark Renoir once said: a teacher is someone who teaches the student to see the relationship between things. Could I do that? Did I want to do that? And then the bigger question—what would I teach and how would I go about doing it?

I think part of my hesitation was knowing that I was just beginning to explore the craft of reading a screenplay. Yes, I had spent seven years writing nine screenplays, but as I was discovering, that didn't help me much in reading and evaluating a screenplay. So how could I be expected to teach a screenwriting class?

Then a few weeks went by and I didn't hear anything from Gary, so I assumed it wasn't going to happen and I forgot all about it and got back into the rhythm of my life and work.

But I'd underestimated Gary: he had the ferocity of a bulldog. He started calling, and when I became wishy-washy, not saying yes, not saying no, he kept calling back. He wouldn't let go. After several calls, I finally agreed to teach an eight-week class during the next session, even though I didn't know what I was going to do or how I was going to do it.

The more I thought about it, the more I saw that I could draw upon my experience as a writer and a reader. If this was going to be a course on screenwriting, how would I approach it? That was my start point. I saw I could approach the screenplay in terms of its evolution, from the inception of the idea to the finished script. I saw that if I did that, I would have several topics to discuss. I contemplated my own writing experience and the many discussions I'd had with Renoir and Peckinpah about converting the idea into the screenplay. I thought about my acting experience and retraced my steps in creating characters, and contemplated the various problems of writing in the proper screenplay form. It seemed everyone wanted answers for these questions.

I had eight sessions to prepare, so I broke the class down into specific categories: finding the idea, developing the characters, writing in screenplay form, building the scene and sequence and so on. When I finally walked into that first class and stood in front of some fifty or sixty people, I felt pretty confident I knew what I was doing.

But there was one thing I hadn't thought about: my attitude. Without being aware of it, I stepped into that class thinking I was going to be the "teacher." That was my position. Otherwise, I wouldn't be standing in the front of the room presenting this material, would I? It didn't take long for me to see that this attitude wasn't working, that all my thinking and preparation might go for naught. I found myself being righteous, opinionated and judgmental, and by the end of the third session people started leaving. The harder I tried, the worse it became. By the end of the eight weeks almost 80 percent of the class had left, numerous complaints had been lodged and a few refunds were being requested. I was devastated.

Gary thanked me for my efforts and told me he'd give me a call if he was going to offer another class. Which we both knew wasn't going to happen, because I had done such a terrible job.

I went back to reading my two or three screenplays a day, trying to define the elements of a good screenplay. But the teaching experience really rankled. What did I do wrong? I wondered. Should I have been more prepared? Less opinionated? More patient? Listened better? The more I thought about it, the more I saw that as I stood in front of that class I was mirroring the same attitude as many of my old teachers. Somehow, I realized, I must have expressed this attitude, either consciously or unconsciously, in my opinions and mannerisms, and that must have been why so many people left the course. When I thought about it from this perspective, the more convinced I became that this was what had happened.

This insight was a revelation. If I ever got the chance to teach again, I told myself, I was going to enter the classroom as the "student" and see what I could learn from my "teachers." When I decided that, I called Gary and told him that I'd be interested in teaching another eight-week class. He said he'd think about it, but he asked whether in the meantime I'd like to be the moderator for a screenwriting seminar that was going to be held the following month. I said yes immediately, and the next week he offered me the opportunity of teaching another eight-week course at Sherwood Oaks during the next session. I accepted on the spot.

The weekend seminar I moderated was one of many I did over the next few years. The Saturday morning panel I had been asked to moderate was with screenwriters Colin Higgins (*Harold and Maude*), Paul Schrader and Mardik Martin (*Mean Streets*). It was a fascinating experience, and it began a new kind of relationship with Hollywood screenwriters.

A few weeks later I was scheduled to start the new screenwriting course, and I began to spend a lot of time preparing for it. I made extensive notes about the screenplays I read at work, and noted the elements the writer must focus on when he or she sits down to write a screenplay.

As I prepared for the class I began to see that the process was helping me understand more about reading a screenplay. The more scripts I read, the more I saw there were two phases in organizing a screenplay: the preparation, and the actual writing itself. I went back into my own writing experience and broke down each of the elements I had used in the preparation of my screenplays, and began to list them as individual categories: defining the idea, building the story, creating characters. I broke each class down into one particular subject for the evening. My intention was to spend about ten or fifteen minutes discussing the subject, then apply it to current movies. I wanted the class to be an open forum where I could weave the subject into the general discussion. I had never been in a class like that, and wanted to see if it could work.

That first night of class, I walked into the large room, introduced myself to the people who were there and told them I wanted to find out what their backgrounds were. Some were writers, some were studio executives, some were in advertising and public relations and a few were professional people. With my mind set on being the "student," I started asking questions about what they wanted to know and what they wanted to learn during the eight weeks we would be together. I immediately felt an entirely new energy in the room.

In my first teaching experience, the people attending the course had been passive, listless, their body language rigid, tight, constricted. That had all changed. There was an openness now in the room, and once the wall of hesitation and shyness had fallen away, people felt comfortable asking questions, offering opinions, even starting a discussion about a current film. I just let them be. As I was standing in front of these people, feeling this sense of energy and excitement swirling around me, I thought that this must be what teaching is all about—instilling students with a desire to learn. It felt great.

By being the student, by listening and responding to the course participants' concerns about the craft of screenwriting, I mentally began designing a course based on what they wanted to know. No more would it be "us and them"; there would only be "us." I called the classroom the "big cooking pot," because everybody added stuff to it, then took out whatever they wanted to. It was really learning from each other. In addition to having the class experience, I asked them to go see various films of their own choosing. After that, we would have a discussion at the beginning of each class and talk about a particular aspect of a film a student might have seen in relationship to whatever we were talking about that night.

This model, using current movies as examples of different aspects of the screenwriting process, became a viable way of illustrating the craft of the writer. I wanted people to take a look at what they were doing when they wrote their scripts. After a few sessions, I came up with the idea that if everyone in class saw the same movie, we could discuss it together.

With that in mind, I started going over several films I thought would work as teaching examples. Whatever I showed, I wanted it to be a good film, a film we could learn from, so after some consideration, I chose for our first example Robert Rossen's *The Hustler*, a movie I had always liked. I think Rossen is one of those forgotten geniuses of Hollywood; *Body and Soul*, *All the King's Men* and *Lilith* are only a few of his films. *The Hustler*, written by Rossen and Sidney Carroll from the novel by Walter Tevis, and starring Paul Newman, Piper Laurie and George C. Scott, was made in 1961 and had been nominated for several Academy Awards.

Paul Newman plays Fast Eddie Felson, a pool shark from Oakland, who hustles his way across the country in order to challenge the unbeatable Minnesota Fats, brilliantly played by Jackie Gleason. In a wonderfully choreographed cinematic pool game, he beats Fats, only to defeat himself by drinking too much booze and succumbing to his own ego. In short, he's a winner who's a loser.

When I showed the film to the class, I really didn't know what their reaction would be. I didn't have to worry: they loved it. As I watched it in that first screening, I began to really see the intricate nooks and crannies of telling a story with pictures.

What I saw as the story unfolded was a series of movements, very musical in origin. Since I was becoming aware of the importance of setting up the story from the very beginning of the screenplay, I studied the opening of the film very carefully. In the first scene, Fast Eddie and his "manager," Charlie (Myron McCormick), set up their "hustle" in a small-town bar. What was so striking was the way it was done: Fast Eddie is shooting pool, and it's obvious he's had too much to drink. As the money begins piling up on the table, he makes a "lucky shot," and Charlie bets he can't make the same shot again. People take the bet; they think he's too drunk to make it again. The hustle is on.

With the money on the table, we hear the sound of the cue striking a pool ball, then we cut outside as a smiling Eddie holds up a fistful of money. It's a beautiful little sequence and revealed to me everything I needed to know about Fast Eddie's character—who he is, what he does and the behavior that exposes his weakness, his inner flaw. In other words, it sets up the characters and the story.

While discussing the film in class, I realized that those first few pages of the screenplay are important because they set up not only the main character but everything that follows as well. Those first few minutes of *The Hustler* show Fast Eddie's desire to win "ten grand" in one night, and how he plans to do it by defeating the legendary, unbeatable Minnesota Fats. That's his motivation, his dramatic need, and his pride becomes the source of his downfall.

I managed to get ahold of the screenplay at an old cinema bookshop, and discovered that one of the things which makes the film so interesting is the way the story unfolds. Each scene is placed in the context of an emotional and psychological progression, and those individual scenes keep the story moving like movements in a symphony.

After the credits, the story begins with almost ritualistic precision. Eddie walks into the Ames pool hall and calls it the "Church of the Good Hustler." The game is on. The rack is broken by Minnesota Fats, and the Fat Man goes on a spree. We see why he's "the best there is." Then it's Eddie's turn; he wins game after game. The stakes keep getting higher and higher. At that point, Bert (George C. Scott), Fats's manager, starts watching the game, while drinking milk. Eddie, knowing he's got a sure thing, begins drinking, confident in his prowess. He wins every game; his dream of winning ten thousand dollars in one night has been achieved. Drinking too much, Eddie drunkenly challenges Minnesota Fats to one more game, winner take all. Charlie walks out, pissed. Fats looks to Bert;

Bert looks at Eddie and tells Minnesota Fats, "Take the bet; the guy's a loser."

Eddie is shocked, but too drunk to do anything about it. And this was another illustration for me that action is character; what a person does is who he or she is. I watched as the Fat Man prepares for this final game by performing an elaborate ritual: he takes off his coat, washes his hands, pours talcum powder on his hands, puts his jacket back on and steps forward, ready to play. Eddie laughs, not understanding the significance of the action. But I saw in that one action that Minnesota Fats has more character and class than Eddie has in his entire body. It's not the lack of talent that beats Eddie; it's the lack of character. Bert Gordon's prophecy turns out to be true: Fast Eddie Felson is a loser.

What's the difference between being a winner and a loser? That's the question that haunts Eddie as he wanders to the bus station to store his bags. This, I saw, is where the true story of Fast Eddie Felson really begins.

As I read and reread the script, I began to see that it has a definite form, a definite structure. I thought that if I broke the movie down into each of these different movements, I could find a way of defining some of the qualities that make it work.

The first time I showed the film I showed it in its entirety, then discussed with the class what we liked or disliked. The more we talked about it, the more I was able to define the movements of the story. In order to set up the transformation of Eddie's character from loser to winner, I saw, it was necessary to show him first as a loser; then I could chart his emotional journey to becoming a winner.

What I realized later was that as I was preparing to teach *The Hustler*, I was expanding my skills of reading. I was still reading my two or three screenplays a day, but now when I read the first few pages, I was looking for the elements that set up the story. I was looking for movements of unfolding action. If I didn't find them I felt I was under no obligation to read further than the first thirty pages. If it didn't work by then, it wasn't going to work at all.

One night after work, I was having a drink with a screenwriter and was sharing my experience about what I was learning teaching the screenwriting course at Sherwood Oaks. As I talked about it, I had a "bright" idea: why not show only a portion of the movie, then discuss that in relation to the whole? The writer thought it was a great idea, because he himself was having difficulty setting up the story in a new screenplay he was writing. I thought that if I isolated the elements of that first act, then showed that portion of the film, I could lead a discussion of what goes into setting up a good movie.

In the next class, I showed only the first thirty minutes, what I termed "the first movement," of *The Hustler*. In these early scenes, we see Eddie in action, hustling at a small-time pool hall; we see him playing Minnesota Fats at the height of his pool prowess; and then we watch him, through a haze of booze and ego, plunge into the abyss of the loser. When he leaves his partner Charlie, he is broke and alone. From Eddie's point of view, it's a new beginning; now the story can begin.

People loved the class. I didn't get to leave until almost eleven-thirty, and as I made my way through the gauntlet of street people on Hollywood Boulevard, I felt I was really onto something.

Several days later, as Fouad, Eddie and I were driving to a meeting, I was telling them about the class when Fouad casually mentioned that if I was going to be teaching, I should teach the whammo chart.

Thinking about Fouad's comment, I realized that if I had showed the first act of *The Hustler*, maybe I should show the second act as well. I reread the script, only this time I focused on the relationship between Fast Eddie and Sarah, his girlfriend, played by Piper Laurie.

I knew where the first act ended—with Eddie losing everything he had won. That was my start point. In class, we talked about how it was clear at this stage that Eddie didn't know where he was going or what he was going to do. What was so interesting for me was the locale of the next scene: a bus station. When I raised the question as to whether the location might reflect the emotional state of the character, it dawned on me that a bus station is a place of new beginnings, a place where people come and go, a place of transition. Emotionally, he's at ground zero, a point of departure, the point of new beginnings.

In the next class, I suggested that the bus station scene really marks the true beginning of the story. When Eddie arrives at the station, he sees an attractive woman sitting alone, drinking coffee, reading. Their eyes meet, then she turns away. "There is a suggestion of tired wakefulness, of self-sufficiency, about her," the stage directions read. Eddie tries to hustle her, but Sarah keeps him in his place. He drifts off to sleep, and when he wakes, she's gone. He leaves, heads for a nearby bar and is surprised to find Sarah sitting at a table. They talk and he makes a pass at her—"Let's you and me get a bottle," he says. She thinks carefully about it for a long moment, then accepts. As they get up to leave, we see she's lame.

Does that tell us anything about her character? I wondered. I recalled what Peckinpah did in *The Wild Bunch* when he gave Pike Bishop, the William Holden character, a limp. That reflected an emotional state of mind. Could it be the same here? Sarah is lame, a cripple. It's very clear, I saw, that she has very little self-respect or self-worth. She drinks too much and has no sense of purpose in life, and her limp underscores her emotional qualities in a visual way.

Eddie's relationship with Sarah unfolds like a symphonic movement through the course of the second act. About halfway through this unit of action, Sarah says, "We never talk about anything—we stay here in this room, and we drink, and we make love. We're strangers. What happens when the liquor and the money run out, Eddie?"

This is the next story point: Sarah's remark moves the story forward. A few scenes later, Eddie's money does run out, and Bert Gordon offers him a deal. He'll stake Eddie in pool, but the split will be 75/25. "Who do you think you are, General Motors?" Eddie asks. "How much do you think you're worth these days?" Bert asks. "You think I can lose?" Eddie asks. "I never saw you do anything else," Bert replies.

Pissed, his pride affronted, Eddie storms out, and finds himself in a shabby pool hall in a game with another hustler. As I shared with the class, it's this behavior that reveals Eddie's tendencies as a loser. Eddie, incensed at these small-time pool hustlers, angrily loses control and rashly shows them what real pool playing is all about. When the game is over, Eddie tries to collect his winnings, but the players declare they don't like "pool sharks" and drag him into the men's room. We don't see anything except his silhouette, as they beat him mercilessly. Then we hear Eddie scream. Silence, then another scream, as they break both his thumbs.

This scene, I now understood, is really the centerpiece of the movie. Eddie starts high, loses control and crashes to rock bottom. There's nowhere else to go except up. Eddie stumbles back to Sarah's apartment, broken in body, mind and spirit. As Sarah cares for him over the next few weeks, we see a change in her behavior: the apartment is clean, she stops drinking and she studies industriously for her college courses. Eddie changes too: he begins to open up to Sarah and share his true feelings.

The next scene has Eddie and Sarah on a picnic and is pivotal in terms of the story's progression. With both thumbs still in casts, Eddie asks Sarah if he's really a loser. Reading the script again, I felt this scene embodies the essence of his character. Eddie shares with Sarah what Bert Gordon told him: "Some people want to lose, and are always looking for an excuse to lose." Sarah asks if Bert is a winner. Yes, Eddie answers. What makes a winner? she asks. In frustration, he holds up his broken hands and says, "Why did I do it? I coulda beat that guy, I coulda beat him cold. He never woulda known. But I just had to show 'em, I just had to show those creeps and those punks what the game is like when it's great, when it's really great . . . like all of a sudden I got oil in my arm. The pool cue is a part of me . . . [it's] got nerves in it. It's a piece of wood but it's got nerves in it. You can feel the roll of those balls. You don't have to look. You just know. You make shots that nobody's ever made before. And you play that game the way nobody ever played it before."

"You're not a loser, Eddie," she says. "You're a winner. Some men never get to feel that way about anything." And she confesses that she loves him. Eddie's response is simple: "You need the words?" "Yes," she replies, "but if you ever say them I'll never let you take them back."

I saw this as the beginning of Eddie's transformation, because it moves the story forward to the next level. At this moment Eddie undergoes a change in character; it is the first step in his shift from being a loser to being a winner, and it begins the next movement. With his thumbs healed, Eddie tracks down Bert and admits he's "not such a high-class piece of property right now. And a twenty-five percent slice of something big is better than a hundred percent slice of nothing." Eddie knows that in order to rise above his situation, he must first acknowledge the truth about it.

At this point I began to understand that each story "movement" has a specific dramatic function. When I went back and reexamined the film, movement by movement, I saw that Eddie's character is set up through his behavior in Act I. The second movement deals with his self-destructive behavior; he is broken both physically and spiritually. Only when he can confront the truth of who he is can he begin healing and thus initiate his transformation. The third movement completes that transformation.

As I was studying the script in preparation for the next class, I focused on the third and final movement of the film, and realized that the picnic scene between Eddie and Sarah spins the story around into the resolution of the film. The night before Eddie leaves for Kentucky with Bert, he takes Sarah out to dinner and tells her he's leaving the next morning; Bert is staking him. She does not bear it well: "If you were going to come back you wouldn't have taken me out tonight. You're hustling me, Eddie. You never stopped hustling me." He tells her it's not true, that he's coming back. "What do you want me to do?" she says. "Just sit here and wait? Faithful little Sarah. Pull the shades down and sit." "What's your idea of love? Chains?" Eddie replies. She breaks down and confesses she's scared because "I wanted you to be real, Eddie."

Caught between his feelings of love and guilt, he agrees to take her with him. The next morning Eddie arrives with Sarah at the train, something Bert does not appreciate. As the train pulls away from the station, I saw that the train is a symbol of transition; in this case, it takes us into the third movement.

Arriving in Kentucky, Eddie plays his first match. He loses game after game and Bert wants to call it a night. "I still think you're a loser," Bert tells him. Eddie literally begs Bert for the chance to play another game as Sarah tells him not to beg. Eddie responds by playing with his own money, and loses again. He tells Sarah to go back to the hotel, and she tells him that if he keeps playing for Bert "he'll break your heart, your guts." Bert finally gives in and lets Eddie play. The game lasts all night and finally Eddie wins, redeeming himself in his own eyes. But the price he pays is very high.

When he returns to the hotel, he learns that Bert had seduced Sarah, and that Sarah committed suicide. Eddie stares, disbelieving, and looks at Bert, who turns away. It was then that I understood that Sarah was the sacrifice necessary for Eddie to complete his transformation. In the final scene, Eddie returns to challenge Minnesota Fats.

Eddie seems different—poised, confident. It's a fast game. Eddie wins everything in sight. Fats finally quits; "I can't beat you, Eddie," he says. Bert decides he should get half of what Eddie has won. "What happens if I don't pay?" Eddie asks him. "You're gonna get your thumbs broken; your fingers, too," Bert replies.

Eddie confesses to Bert that he loved Sarah, and "traded her in on a pool game. . . . You don't know what winnin' is, Bert. You're a loser. 'Cause you're dead inside, and you can't live unless you make everything else dead around you. . . . The price is too high. . . . You tell your boys they better kill me, Bert. They better go all the way with me. Because if they just bust me up, I'll put all those pieces back together and so help me, so help me God, Bert . . . I'm gonna come back here and I'm gonna kill you."

Eddie turns his back on Bert and pays homage to Fats: "Fat Man, you shoot a great game of pool." Eddie takes his cue case, takes a last look around, and walks out.

Fade-out. The end.

When this session of the class ended, I started thinking about what had worked in the film and what didn't. Breaking *The Hustler* into units of dramatic action and presenting it in terms of different movements, I think, was significant. Not only did I learn to analyze film in a new and effective way, but teaching it in this way actually supported and expanded my reading experience at Cinemobile. Only then did it dawn on me that in the process of teaching others I was really teaching myself.

When I could acknowledge this to myself, I had a deep-seated feeling that I was on the verge of gaining a new insight into my understanding of the movies. It didn't matter whether I was teaching, writing or reading, I just knew I was on the verge of something. I didn't know what it was, I didn't know what it looked like and I certainly didn't know how to explain it; all I knew was that I had to be patient and wait for it to be revealed. It wasn't a question of "if" or "how" or "what"; it was a question of when.

12

Chinatown

Jake: "I'll tell you the unwritten law, you dumb son of a bitch. You gotta be rich to kill somebody, anybody, and get away with it. You think you got that kind of dough, you think you got that kind of class?"
—JAKE GITTES (Jack Nicholson) TO CURLY (Burt Young),
omitted lines from a scene in the film
Chinatown (Robert Towne)

It was in the early fall of 1973, and a light rain was falling as I pulled into the Paramount lot, parked the car and made my way to the screening room. As I walked through the dampness, I knew I did not want to be there. It had been an extremely full and stressful day. I had read my usual quota of scripts, attended my usual quota of meetings, had a large and late lunch with a writer and drank a little too much wine. My throat was raw, and I felt I was coming down with a cold. Nothing would be better, I thought, than soaking in a long hot bath, having a nice cup of hot tea and crawling into bed. But that's not the way it was; as Fouad left the office, he handed me an invitation to a special screening of *China-town* and told me to go because he and Eddie had a dinner meeting.

The buzz around town was that *Chinatown* was really a hot film. Directed by Roman Polanski, the young cinematic virtuoso of *Knife in the Water* and *Rosemary's Baby,* "the word" was that Jack Nicholson had given a truly extraordinary, Academy Award–

winning performance and that Faye Dunaway and John Huston were masterful. But no matter what the hype was, or how great the film might be, I knew as I walked into that screening room and said my hellos to various people in the industry, I wanted to be somewhere else.

The film began, the tickle in my throat became very noticeable and I kept asking myself, Why am I here? As the story unfolded, my critical mind kicked in and I started complaining about the movie. I thought it was flat, the characters dull and one-dimensional. Before I knew it, I nodded off. I don't know how much of the film I missed, I just knew it was one of those evenings where my body was in the screening room, but I certainly was not.

When I heard the last lines of the film, "Forget it, Jake. . . . It's Chinatown," that's exactly what I wanted to do. By the time I got home I had already forgotten about it. When Fouad asked about it the next day, I told him it was okay, nothing more; about a "7."

Over the next few days, when people asked how I liked the movie I replied it was all hype and no substance. The film went into release soon after, received great critical reviews, did well financially and that was that.

So much for my introduction to *Chinatown*.

I've written a lot about my experience of *Chinatown*, both in *Screenplay* and *The Screenwriter's Workbook*, and as I would soon realize, the film is perhaps *the* classic movie of the 1970s. It is a film that works on every level: story, characters, historical perspective and visual dynamic. A mystery-thriller in the style and tradition of Raymond Chandler, *Chinatown* took an infamous water scandal that occurred shortly after the turn of the century and used it as the canvas for a personal story line. Robert Towne used the Owens Valley scandal as the dramatic backdrop for a story about a private detective uncovering a major crime, but updated the action from the turn of the century to Los Angeles in 1937. In this way, Towne achieved the same revolutionary shift in filmmaking as did the Flemish painters of the fifteenth and sixteenth centuries, who placed the portraits of their patrons against the backdrop of Italian landscapes, a move which changed the course of art history.

After that initial screening I didn't think about *Chinatown* too much, I simply did my job and taught another class at Sherwood Oaks, something I was beginning to enjoy. And that's the way it stayed until about six months later. I had just started a new eight-week class called "The Foundations of Screenwriting" when Gary called me at work one day and told me Robert Towne had agreed to be a guest speaker at the next class, and I would have the privilege of interviewing him.

The next week, I met Towne during the class break at Sherwood Oaks and told him we had been discussing the creation of character. When the class resumed, I started our question-and-answer period by asking Towne about his background. He told us he had grown up in San Pedro, just south of L.A., then moved to Brentwood.

When we started talking about *Chinatown*, I asked him how he went about creating his characters, especially how he'd conceived Jake Gittes, the Jack Nicholson character. He replied that first he asks himself, What is this character afraid of? In other words, what is his or her deepest fear? Gittes, a private detective specializing in "discreet investigation," has a certain reputation to uphold, so he does everything to make a good impression. He dresses immaculately, has his shoes shined every day and has his own code of ethics. Gittes's deepest fear is not being taken seriously.

When I asked about the genesis of the movie, Towne replied that he wanted to incorporate the famous Owens Valley scandal into a Raymond Chandler–like movie. He didn't go into any detail and I didn't pursue it, not knowing anything about the scandal myself. When the class ended, I felt it had been a great session and that I, personally, had picked up an incredible amount of information about the craft of screenwriting. All in all, it was a very revealing evening.

As Towne and I walked out to the parking lot together through the array of Hollywood Boulevard's finest, I mentioned that one of my neighbors was the producer Harry Gittes, and asked if that's where he got the name for the Jack Nicholson character. He smiled and told me he'd known Harry for years.

I was very impressed with Bob Towne, both by what he said and how he said it. He was open, insightful, articulate, engaging and extremely literate, qualities I genuinely admire. I was so impressed that I decided to see *Chinatown* again. I wanted to see if I'd be able to catch those little nuances of character and story that Towne had talked about during the class.

The theater was only partially full as I settled into my seat, and as I munched my popcorn I was truly looking forward to seeing the film again. The lights dimmed, the curtains parted and the titles played over music inspired by those classic film noirs of the forties. This time, watching the story unfold was literally an act of discovery; this was not the same film I'd seen at that first screening at Paramount. This was a film where each little episode or event, no matter how apparently insignificant, was connected with Gittes's gradual uncovering of the water scandal. The story was built solidly, piece by piece, incident by incident; it was structured much differently than the sweeping symphonic movements of *The Hustler*. Fascinated, I followed the film's unusual progression like bread crumbs through the forest.

By the end of the film, when Evelyn Mulwray is killed in Chinatown, the innocent victim of the entire affair, I felt I had seen the movie for the first time. When I heard that familiar last line, "For-get it, Jake. . . . It's Chinatown," I was touched, moved and inspired. But I still felt I was missing something; the film seemed to unfold in an almost monotonic way, with no real highs or lows, the most dramatic moment being the famous slap scene, when Gittes slaps Evelyn Mulwray until she reveals that "the girl" is both "my daugh-ter *and* my sister." The film lingered with me over the next few days as various scenes kept coming back. Curious, I wanted to check it out further, so I got a copy of the screenplay.

I still recall the excitement and mesmerizing awe I experienced while reading the screenplay. I remembered Towne saying in class that his intention in the script was to show that "some crimes are punished because they can be punished. If you kill somebody, rob or rape somebody, you'll be caught and thrown into jail. But crimes against an entire community you can't really punish, so you end up rewarding them. You know, those people who get their names on streets and plaques at City Hall. And that's the basic point of view of the story."

For me, *Chinatown* was literally a voyage of discovery. Against the backdrop of the Owens Valley water scandal, we follow Gittes as he uncovers the puzzle one piece at a time. That's why it's such a great film. We learn what's going on at the same time Jake Gittes does. Audience and character are linked together as they connect these bits and pieces of seemingly unrelated information, like assembling a giant jigsaw puzzle.

More important, it was while reading and rereading the screen-play that I began to develop an understanding about the nature of dramatic structure. Studying and teaching *The Hustler* had allowed me to follow the movements of a story that led to its dramatic reso-lution. But as I watched, reread and taught the script of *Chinatown*,

I began to grasp something more. I began to see a certain *form* to the story line, in the way it unfolded and the relationship between the story points that powered the tale forward.

As I studied the screenplay I noted that it was definitely a story told in pictures. The very first image on screen is a series of photographs showing a man and woman having sex in a park. Over these pictures, we hear the moans and groans of Curly, the husband of the woman, played by Burt Young. I asked myself, What does this show? The answer was immediate: it shows what Jake Gittes, the main character, does for a living. He's a private detective specializing in divorces, unfaithful spouses and "going through other people's dirty linen," as one of the characters remarks. It's his "métier."

I also discovered who Jake is by what he does; when he offers Curly a drink, he chooses the most inexpensive whiskey because Curly hasn't paid his bill yet. By the same token, he wouldn't take Curly's last dime; "What kind of guy do you think I am," he says. And throughout the movie he proclaims to Escobar, the police lieutenant and his former partner in Chinatown, that he's not the kind of cop who would "extort nobody." I saw what kind of a character he is by what he does, by his actions.

Towne sets up the story in the very first scene. When the phony Mrs. Mulwray (Diane Ladd) hires him to find out who her husband is having an affair with, he begins his surveillance of Hollis Mulwray. Here, the audience and character are connected; we learn what Gittes learns. He follows Mulwray to City Hall, hears Mulwray defy the City Council by saying he will not build a dam that will fail, like the Van der Lip dam, which had collapsed several years before, killing hundreds of people. He will not make the same mistake twice, he says. Moments later, a farmer drives a herd of sheep into the council chambers; the man accuses Mulwray of stealing the water from the valley, thus ruining the grazing and starving the livestock, and then asks the question that drives the entire film: "Who's paying you to do that, Mr. Mulwray?"

After the council scene, Gittes follows Mulwray to the dried-out Los Angeles River bed, then to the ocean, where Gittes's long surveillance is rewarded when he witnesses water being dumped into the ocean. Several hours later, when Gittes gets back to his car, he picks up a leaflet off the windshield declaring, "Our city is dying of thirst!" and "Save our city."

I had not been aware of this theme of water until I read the screenplay several times. But as I began tracing the connection I felt like Gittes when Noah Cross (John Huston) tells him, "You may think you know what's going on, but believe me, you don't."

The next morning, after Gittes finds "the girl" and closes the case, he sees the pictures he had taken on the front page of the newspaper. The headlines read "scandal," and when he returns to his office, he finds a woman waiting for him: Faye Dunaway. She asks if he knows her and he says no, he would have remembered. She tells him that if they've never met, how could she have hired him to find out who her husband is having an affair with? "You see, my name is Mrs. Evelyn Mulwray."

This was definitely a key incident in the movie. If Faye Dunaway is the real Mrs. Mulwray, who is the Diane Ladd character who hired Gittes, claiming she was Mrs. Mulwray? And who hired her? And why? That's the question that shocks Gittes into action.

Taking another look at this first unit of dramatic action, I saw it took about twenty-five pages to set up the entire story. The relationship between these scenes of seemingly unrelated information is like a prologue, because it establishes the story by posing the question of who set up Gittes. "L.A.'s a small town," he says, "and I'm not supposed to be the one caught with my pants down." This entire unit of dramatic action serves to establish three things: who the characters are, what the story is about and what the dramatic situation is, the circumstances surrounding the action—that is, "L.A. is dying of thirst." What I had learned from studying the first movement of *The Hustler* was substantiated by this first movement in *Chinatown*. Was there a connection? Are all good screenplays like this? I wondered.

When I viewed *Chinatown* again, I focused on this first unit of dramatic action, which I now called Act I, and confirmed that it had a definite form. It is a self-contained unit of dramatic action which sets up the basic elements of the story line. Every scene, every piece of information, no matter what, reveals something about the story and leads to that moment when the real Evelyn Mulwray shows up. That moment is the turning point that hooks into the action and pushes the story into Act II. These events are literally strung together on the story line, and one night in class I started calling this the skeleton of the story. After a while, I felt silly calling it the skeleton, and as I thought about it some more I realized it was really the structure of the story.

As an English major at Berkeley, I had a hard time with definitions; I don't think I ever "got" words like plot, theme, premise, protagonist, antagonist, denouement, style or structure. I knew if I really wanted to communicate my understanding of the screenplay, I would have to rely on those definitions, which I found vague and had never really understood. Either that, or create my own. The more I thought about it, the more I felt like I wanted to create a definition of structure that would be applicable to the screenplay.

What is structure? How do I define it? In the dictionary, I found several definitions, but two seemed to fit the requirements of what I was trying to put into words. One was *"to build,* or *put something together,"* like a building, table or chair; the second definition was the *"relationship between the parts and the whole."*

In *Chinatown*, I could see that each scene in Act I was a part of the whole, and that each scene was built, or constructed, in such a way that it was related to the whole. When I understood that, a lot of things fell into place. I saw, for example, that good structure in a screenplay should be almost invisible. If it draws attention to itself, I was learning through my reading experience, it doesn't work. Is there any way to separate the color green from a leaf, or heat from fire? They're related to each other, part and parcel of the whole. The same way with an ice cube and water. An ice cube has a definite crystalline structure, and water has a definite molecular structure. When the ice cube melts, is it possible to separate the molecules that were the ice cube and the ones that were the water? Ain't no way.

Reading *Chinatown* again, I began to see how each scene and sequence is related to the whole. Once I understood this relationship, I saw there has to be a context to hold everything in place. I knew from teaching *The Hustler* and *Chinatown* that the first act was all about setting up the story and characters; that must, I realized, be the context that holds it together. I thought I was onto something, I just didn't know what; but when I went into work each day I was actually looking forward to reading the scripts piled on my desk. I looked at every screenplay as a potential learning experience. When I had meetings, or met with writers, we ended up talking about the craft of screenwriting. I tried to relate what I read in their work to what I was discovering about the structure of a screenplay. It was a very exciting and informative time. The more I talked, the more I taught, the more I began to see there must be some kind of dramatic context which holds the story in place.

Context, the dictionary says, is the space that holds something in place. If I take an empty glass, for example, I see there's a space inside that holds the liquid, or content, in place. It doesn't matter what kind of liquid it is; the content could be water, tea, orange juice, cola, beer, coffee or ice-blended mocha. The space inside doesn't change; only the content changes. If I was looking for some kind of context for the screenplay, I could see that this first unit of dramatic action, Act I, would be to set up the story, introduce the characters and establish the dramatic premise. In other words, Act I is a unit of dramatic action which is held together by its context of the Set-Up.

It's very clear in *Chinatown* that the main character is Jake Gittes. That's established on page one. When the phony Mrs. Mulwray hires him to find out who Mr. Mulwray is having an affair with, that's the dramatic premise, because the answer to that question leads Gittes to uncover the water scandal. L.A. in a drought provides the dramatic situation. The Set-Up is really the key to the story, because it establishes what we learn later to be the motivation of Noah Cross, Mulwray's former partner, who owned the Water Department.

But what happens then? That's just the Set-Up. There's got to be a point, I thought, some kind of incident, episode or event that moves the story from Act I into Act II. One night, while I was talking about the film in class, it dawned on me that the key scene that moves the story into Act II is the one in which the real Mrs. Mulwray shows up. Her presence causes Gittes to run the risk of losing his detective's license. If Faye Dunaway is the real Mrs. Mulwray, who was the woman who claimed to be Mrs. Mulwray; and who was the person who hired her, and why? That's what Gittes has to find out. That scene, I felt, is definitely crucial to the movement of the story line.

When I checked this out with some of the screenplays I read at work, I found that the good ones all had some kind of scene that was instrumental in moving the story forward into this next unit of dramatic action, Act II. When I went to the movies, I started watching the first twenty or thirty minutes of the film very carefully. About twenty or twenty-five minutes into the film, I noticed that an event usually happened that shifted the story line into Act II.

That told me what most writers intuitively knew: after the first twenty or thirty pages of their screenplays it was time to move the story up a level, into the next stage of dramatic action. I went back to some of the films that inspired me, to *L'Avventura*, *The Wild Bunch*, *La Grande Illusion*, and found the same thing: there was a scene at the end of Act I that moved the story into Act II. And, if this scene or sequence happened at the end of Act I, there must be a similar event that happens at the end of Act II, some kind of turning point that moves the story into Act III. When I checked that out in the screenplays I read and the movies I saw, I found there was such a scene and that it moved the story from Act II into Act III. If that was really true, if all good screenplays have a key scene at the end of Acts I and II, it would confirm a conceptual consistency of screenplay form; in other words, all well-written screenplays would have this event, no matter whether comedy, drama or period piece.

Once I determined the consistency of the form, I knew I was on the right track. The next step was to define that particular incident or event that happened at the end of Act I or Act II.

It so happened that at that time in my life I used to play touch football on weekends. It was a pickup game and for the most part, the same guys came almost every week. Many of them were ex-jocks, guys who had formerly played college or pro ball, and most of the others were in the entertainment business. The games were fun but exhausting, and afterward I would climb into the bathtub and soak in hot water. I found the bathtub a great place to meditate. I could let my mind wander, thinking about work, about what I would teach in my next class, about what worked and what didn't in the screenplays I had read, about a plan for the coming week.

It was during one of these "sessions" in the tub, after a physically intense game of touch football, that I wondered whether I could define those events occurring at the end of Acts I and II. At first I called it a turning point, but I felt that this was way too general. I wanted a term that would label it clearly as a major point in the plot that moved the story forward. After some deliberation, I decided to call it a Plot Point. I knew from occupying both sides of the desk, as a writer and story executive, that one of the things missing between the writer and the executive was a commonality of language. Plot Point I and Plot Point II, I decided, would be easily understood by everyone.

Once I decided on the name, I needed to create a definition. Soaking in the tub, I was on the verge of falling asleep when a thought raced across my mind. I sat up, wide awake. This scene or sequence, I knew, is part of the plot because it moves the story forward. It's also a specific point in the story that moves the action forward. And that's when the definition came: after playing around with the words, I wrote that a Plot Point is "any incident, episode or event that hooks into the action and spins it around into another direction." It was a definition that worked, for it incorporated both Plot Points, the one at the end of Act I as well as the one at the end of Act II.

With this new context, I sat down to reread *Chinatown* again. I had already seen the movie at least four or five times, and read the screenplay I don't know how many times. I knew Plot Point I was when the real Mrs. Mulwray shows up, and I thought Plot Point II might be the scene after Gittes and Evelyn Mulwray make love, when she receives a phone call and he follows her to the house in Echo Park where he thinks the girl is being held prisoner. But I was wrong. A few years later I determined it was the scene where Gittes finds the bifocal glasses in the saltwater pond and learns they did not belong to Hollis Mulwray. If the glasses did not belong to Mulwray, whom did they belong to? It could only be one person—the person who killed him. And that would be Plot Point II.

When Evelyn tells him that Mulwray didn't wear bifocals, Gittes knows the person responsible must be Noah Cross, the John Huston character, and that's when everything clicked into place. The reason Cross wants Gittes to find "the girl" is because she's his daughter. He's the person behind the water scandal, the man responsible for the death of Hollis Mulwray and Ida Sessions, the phony Mrs. Mulwray; but Jake has to prove it. And that's what leads to the death of Evelyn Mulwray. When Gittes left Chinatown, he tells Evelyn in an earlier scene, he tried to keep someone from being hurt "and actually ended up making sure they were hurt." Full-circle turn. His personal history had repeated itself.

If the context of Act I is the Set-Up, then what, I asked, is the context of Act II? As I began reading and rereading Act II, I noticed some obvious things. First, Act II is a longer unit of dramatic action; more happens here than in either Act I or Act III. It's twice as long.

As I was thinking about this late one afternoon, I recalled a lesson from one of my courses in English literature; namely, all drama is conflict. Conflict is certainly what Jake Gittes experiences in Act II. Gittes's dramatic need is to find out what's going on and who's behind it. But all he encounters are obstacles; no one is telling him the truth about what's going on, and he has to learn it for himself. I thought that if conflict drives the action of Act II, then the dramatic context must be *Confrontation*. In this middle section of the film, the main character is forced to confront obstacle after obstacle in order to achieve his or her dramatic need.

When I established that, I traced the story line from the point at which Gittes comes to understand that the same person who set him up must be responsible for Hollis Mulwray's murder. I recalled we'd already seen the photographs of Mulwray and Noah Cross having a heated argument in front of the Pig n' Whistle, and though we didn't know it at the time, it told us everything.

When Gittes goes looking for Mulwray at the Oak Pass Reservoir, he meets Lieutenant Escobar, a man he used to work with in Chinatown. Some boys swimming in the reservoir had discovered Mulwray's body.

"Ain't it something," the Coroner says to Gittes, "in the middle of a drought and the water commissioner drowns. Only in L.A." But later, Gittes learns they found salt water in his lungs. Water again. I began to see that each story point, no matter how trivial or seemingly insignificant, becomes an obstacle for Gittes as he follows this trail of understanding. Once again, we learn what's happening at the same time Gittes does.

These story points are the glue that holds the story together and drives it to its resolution. And yet, as I watched, taught and explained the film, I still had the feeling I was missing something. During one of my classes at Sherwood Oaks, I suddenly got that the context of the entire movie deals with uncovering the water scandal. That event is always hovering in the background and laces through the action. In my interview with Towne, I recalled he had based *Chinatown* on the Owens Valley scandal, and while I had heard about it, I really didn't know anything about it. What was the scandal? When did it happen? I decided that if I wanted to get a clearer understanding of the film, I would have to understand the forces working on, and behind, the story. That meant understanding the water scandal that Bob Towne based the movie on, "the Rape of the Owens Valley." So I went to the library and researched Bob Towne's research. And here's what I found.

As Gittes sits in the City Council chambers at the beginning of the story, the Mayor makes the point that "Los Angeles is really a desert community. Beneath this building, beneath every street, there's a desert. Without water the dust will rise up and cover us as though we'd never existed. Los Angeles is right next door to the Pacific Ocean. We can swim in it, fish in it, sail on it, but you can't drink it, you can't water your lawns with it, and you can't irrigate an orange grove with it."

I went to the index file, found some books and articles on the Owens Valley scandal, sat down and started reading. I learned that in 1900, Los Angeles was growing so fast it was literally running out of water. If the city was to survive, it had to find another source. So a group of wealthy and enterprising businessmen, all upstanding patrons of the city, joined forces and conspired a scheme that was so daring and so brazen that it ranks as one of the biggest scandals of the twentieth century.

The nearest water source to L.A. was the Owens River, located in the Owens Valley, a fertile and green area located some two-hundred-plus miles northeast of Los Angeles. These wealthy businessmen—"men of vision," they called themselves—figured that if Los Angeles had a steady flow of water, it would become an oasis. So they conspired to buy up the rights to the Owens River, by force if necessary, then buy up the worthless land in the area now known as the San Fernando Valley. Once they had the land rights, they would place a bond issue on the ballot that would have the taxpayers of Los Angeles fund the building of a major aqueduct stemming from the Owens Valley and crossing some 250 miles of blazing desert and jagged foothills before reaching the San Fernando Valley. The businessmen would then turn around and sell this oasis of "fertile" land, now with a steady water supply, to the City of Los Angeles for an enormous sum of money: approximately $300 million. In the early 1900s, this would have made each one of them extremely wealthy.

That was the plan. The government knew about it, the newspapers knew about it, the local politicians knew about it. When the time was right, the authorities would "influence" the people of Los Angeles to pass the proposed bond issue and build the Owens Valley pipeline.

A few years later, in 1906, a severe drought fell upon Los Angeles. Things got bad, then worse. People were forbidden to wash their cars or water their lawns; they couldn't flush their toilets more than a few times a day. The city dried up; flowers died, lawns turned brown and scare headlines declared "Los Angeles is dying of thirst!" To underscore the drastic need for water and make certain the citizens passed the bond issue, the Department of Water and Power started dumping thousands of gallons of water into the ocean. This, in the middle of a severe drought.

When it came time for the people of Los Angeles to vote for the funding of the aqueduct, the bond issue passed easily. The Owens Valley pipeline took several years to build, and these "men of vision" who now owned the San Fernando Valley made a fortune. When it was finished William Mulholland, then head of the Department of Water and Power, turned the water over to the city: "There it is," he said. "Take it."

Los Angeles flourished and grew like wildfire; the Owens Valley withered and died. No wonder it was called "the Rape of the Owens Valley." "Either you bring the water to L.A., or you bring L.A. to the water," Noah Cross says to Jake Gittes.

Understanding the background of the Owens Valley scandal absolutely magnified my understanding of the movie. It was the last piece of the jigsaw puzzle. I saw so clearly how all the pieces fit together as a single unit of dramatic action.

When I saw the film after I had done my research, it just blew me away; the water scandal is woven through the story like a strand of gold woven through a fifteenth-century tapestry, and Gittes manages to unravel it one piece at a time. That's why it's such a great film. Audience and character are linked together in a journey of discovery and understanding.

One night in my class at Sherwood Oaks, as I was in the middle of a discussion about *Chinatown*, a woman raised her hand and asked a totally unrelated question: "What is a screenplay?" The question took me by surprise. I had no answer, so I just kept talking. As I was going through the story's progression, talking about Plot Points I and II, I had a sudden flash of inspiration, literally an epiphany, and an image etched itself across my mind.

I turned to the woman who had asked the question and said, "You want to know what a screenplay is? This is what it is." I drew a long horizontal line on the board, then bisected it with two shorter, vertical lines. "This is the beginning, this is the middle and this is the end," I said. Then I drew a little *x* next to the first vertical line and said, "This particular incident, when the real Mrs. Mulwray shows up, takes us from the beginning to the middle, from Act I into Act II, and is the true beginning of the story." Then I drew a second *x* next to the second vertical line and said, "Here Gittes learns Noah Cross must be the man responsible for the murders and the scandal, and this scene takes us from the middle to the end." Here's the diagram I drew on the board that night:

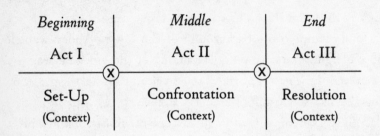

This simple illustration, I realized, is an illustration of screenplay structure; this is what a screenplay would look like if it were a painting hanging on the wall. There is a definite beginning, middle and end, and a point at which the beginning turns into the middle plus one at which the middle turns into the end.

It is form, not formula.

I really didn't understand the significance of what I had drawn on the board, or the concept I had uncovered. The only thing I knew was that I had a diagram I could use to illustrate the conceptual form of dramatic structure in a screenplay.

I wasn't sure whether this diagram was valid only for *Chinatown* or whether it could be used as a model for all screenplays.

But I was determined to find out.

13

The Paradigm

Alvy: *"That's essentially how I feel about life—full of lone-liness, misery, suffering and unhappiness and it's all over much too quickly. . . . Annie and I broke up . . . I still can't get my mind around that . . . I keep sifting the pieces of the relationship through my mind and examining my life and trying to figure out where the screw-up came. A year ago Annie and I were in love. . . ."*

—ALVY SINGER (Woody Allen)
in the opening monologue
Annie Hall (Woody Allen, Marshall Brickman)

Over the next few months, I set a goal for myself: I wanted to determine whether the screenplays I read, or the movies I saw, followed the structural form I found in *Chinatown* and *The Hustler*. If they did, I knew I would have some kind of measuring tool to gauge the accuracy of my opinions. If they did not, then I wanted to find out how they differed, and what the exceptions were.

I recalled something one of my physics professors once said regarding Newton's Law of Gravity, the famous apple-bonking-him-on-the-head episode. He said Newton didn't really discover gravity, he only uncovered what was already there. That made quite an impression on me, and I brought it to bear on all the discussions and arguments about screenplay structure I encountered during my classes at Sherwood Oaks. I knew I was swimming upstream with this one, standing alone in the face of no agreement, but I found the more I talked about the nature of dramatic structure, the clearer and more succinct my ideas became.

As I read the seemingly unending stack of screenplays at Cinemobile, I wondered whether my ideas about structure were valid or whether they were singular in nature, applying only to a few films. Had I, in fact, uncovered something which had been there since the time of Aristotle, or was I trying to impose my own systems and beliefs on the screenplay?

I honestly didn't know, but now, when I was reading a screenplay, I found I could make a preliminary evaluation after reading the first ten pages. After thirty pages I felt I could make a decision about whether I should continue reading or put it in the "out box," the wastebasket. Most of the time I was pretty accurate. I found that if the script was set up properly, if the characters and dramatic premise had been articulated and defined early on, I kept reading. After all, as I shared with my class, the job of the screenwriter is to keep the reader turning pages. When I found a well-written script, all the elements seemed to be in place. Whether I rated it a 7 or an 8—or maybe even one of those rare 9s—on our hot sheet, I began to see a commonality of structure. It was as though the screenwriters were digging into the vaults of the collective unconscious and intuitively knew that after a certain point a particular event is needed to push the story forward, either into Act II or Act III.

The more screenwriters I met and talked with, both at work or at the many weekend seminars I was asked to moderate at Sherwood Oaks, the more I believed I was articulating what everybody knew, either on a conscious or unconscious level,. I knew I wasn't teaching anybody anything they didn't already know. They just didn't know they knew it.

Talking about the craft of screenwriting, and how to approach the actual process of writing, I broke things down into the structural form I uncovered in *Chinatown* and *The Hustler*. But even then, there was a lot of discussion about that; people didn't necessarily believe they could write a screenplay the way I was describing it. People would support, deny and discuss the merits of the three-act structure or Plot Points I and II, but it seemed no one was yet ready to embrace these ideas fully.

Personally, I've always found the most exciting part of the creative process to be the moment that lies somewhere between confusion and clarity; and indeed, what I was searching for was slightly out of focus. "A man's reach should exceed his grasp" is the way the poet puts it. For myself, I was trying to be patient, willing to be in an "I don't know" position, simply asking myself questions, soaking up information and letting it "cook." It is a state I've learned to trust and surrender to completely.

Every screenplay I read, every movie I saw, I used as an exercise; I would try to analyze its form and uncover its structure. I would see a movie like *Network* (Paddy Chayefsky), for example, or *Barry Lyndon*, or *The Godfather*, or *Three Days of the Condor* (Lorenzo Semple, David Rayfiel), or the "first edition" of *Close Encounters of the Third Kind*, or *Annie Hall* (Woody Allen), and dive deep inside looking for clues, trying to isolate and define those key incidents that held the film together.

I was trying to find a form, or a model, that was consistent in expression and which embodied the underlying foundations of structure. I didn't think I was doing it to prove myself "right," or prove some kind of point; I was doing it because I wanted to explore, expand and broaden my own reading and writing experience. I felt if I could find a "form," something that would help me understand, organize and structure my own screenplays, I would be the one who most benefited.

I began to carry a little notepad with me when I went to the movies. First, I would sit in the audience and just let the movie "wash" over me. Afterward, I would make notes about what I remembered, events that could possibly be the Plot Points at the end of Acts I and II, then go over the film in my mind, trying to put the pieces together. A few days later, I would go back and see the film again, only this time I would make notes while I was watching it. Whenever a particular incident, episode or event spun the story around into another direction, I would look at my watch, time it and notate it on the diagram. Was that really the Plot Point at the end of Act I, or was it just another scene? What about Plot Point II?

When I got home, I would read my notes, then draw up my graphic representation (I still had no name for it) and start breaking it down into beginning, middle and end, trying to determine at what point the story changed, or shifted into the next story progression.

So here was *the question*: did all films, no matter what genre, whether drama, thriller, action-adventure, western, love story, mystery, etc., fall within the parameters of the sketchy diagram I had uncovered that night in class?

To help me find the answer, I decided to create a *definition of structure*, based on my study of *Chinatown* and *The Hustler*. I asked myself what a good definition of dramatic structure would be. It is a story told in pictures, with dialogue and description, that's true, but that definition didn't account for the narrative line of action which is the foundation of every story, movie and screenplay. So what did I want to define? A story? A story always has the same components—beginning, middle and end (although not necessarily in that order, as Jean-Luc Godard says)—but that doesn't define the line of dramatic or comedic action. I knew that when I started to build a story, I had to create specific events, then link them together in scenes and sequences that would be contained in individual units of dramatic action.

That was my start point. Before I went to sleep each night, I went over the films I had seen and the screenplays I had read, and clarified, refined and reduced my question to its simplest components: what are the key elements needed to define dramatic structure?

I thought about this question for several days, and then, about a week or two later, on a late Sunday afternoon, I was soaking in a hot tub and thinking about *Three Days of the Condor* when I finally found an answer.

Released in 1975, written by Lorenzo Semple and David Rayfiel, directed by Sydney Pollack and starring Robert Redford and Faye Dunaway, the film is a taut political thriller that tries to capture the CIA paranoia that swept the country after the Watergate scandal. It had a definite line of dramatic action, a linear story line, and as I was soaking in the tub, mulling over certain scenes, I suddenly "got" the connection I was looking for. What is dramatic structure but a linear arrangement of related incidents, episodes and events? And those incidents, of course, lead to the end, the resolution of the story line. It didn't matter whether it was a linear or nonlinear story line. Structure is the strand that holds the story in place, like a string holding pearls.

Finally, I had the definition I was looking for: if the word "structure" means "to build, or put something together," or the "relationship between the parts and the whole," then dramatic structure for the screenplay must be *a linear arrangement of related incidents, episodes or events leading to a dramatic resolution.*

So simple, so obvious; I don't know why I hadn't seen it before. I mean, all stories have a beginning, middle and end, and it's those pieces, the scenes and sequences of the story line, which are assembled and built into a story line that goes from the beginning, point A, to the end, point Z.

It was a definition that worked within the context of the movies I had studied, whether it was a linear story line like *Chinatown*, *The Hustler* or *Three Days of the Condor* or a nonlinear film like *Annie Hall*; *Last Year at Marienbad*; *Citizen Kane*; *Hiroshima, Mon Amour* or *Midnight Cowboy*. There's always going to be a beginning, middle and end, and a particular point where the beginning turns into the middle and the middle into the end. Beginning, middle and end; Set-Up, Confrontation, Resolution. That's what connects all stories—whether myths, fables, epics, poems, plays, dreams, movies or novels—everything that's ever been written or performed since the beginning of time.

Great in theory, but now I wanted to see if this definition worked on all films, regardless of genre. I decided to study two more films to see if they followed the ideas of structure I was attempting to define, two films as different as night and day. One would be *Three Days of the Condor* (based on the book *Six Days of the Condor*, by James Grady), the other *Annie Hall*.

In *Three Days of the Condor*, Robert Redford plays a man who works at the "American Literary Historical Society," a reading cell of the CIA. The employees read books, searching for word combinations that might be linked to various spy activities. Redford's character is bright, intelligent, likable; the first words out of his mouth when he arrives at work are "Anything in the pouch for me?" It's only later that we learn he's uncovered some strange references in several novels from the Middle East that raise his suspicions.

Before the story begins, he has sent a query to CIA headquarters in Langley, Virginia, to check it out.

As Redford ducks and weaves through the back alleys of Manhattan to get lunch for his coworkers, a mailman walks to the door of the office to deliver a package. When the CIA workers open the door to let him in, two other men step inside, pull out automatic weapons and proceed to kill everyone in the office. When Redford returns, food in hand, he finds everyone dead, brutally murdered. Plot Point I. It happens about twenty-three minutes into the film.

Redford doesn't have much time to think. But it dawns on him that only because he was "out to lunch" is he still alive. If someone went to the trouble to kill everyone in this CIA office, he knows he must be next on the hit list.

The killings hook into the action and "spin" it around into another direction: Act II. At this point, Redford does the only thing he can do—he flees the office for the safety of the street. His escape to the street marks the true beginning of the movie.

Who murdered Redford's coworkers? And why? As in *Chinatown*, the audience learns what's going on at the same time the main character does. At the beginning of Act II, he's lost and alone, wandering the streets, where every person might be a potential killer. He calls the CIA looking for help and is told to avoid all the places he's known, especially his home. He doesn't know where to go, what to do or whom to trust.

Lorenzo Semple and David Rayfiel have set up the story line in the following way: Act I establishes that Redford has uncovered some kind of conspiracy developing within the CIA, but he, and we, don't know what it is. Before the movie begins, in what I termed the *back story*, he has sent a query to CIA headquarters about it. The answer to that question results in the killing of the entire staff at Redford's office by a high-ranking official, the leader of the secret CIA. All he knows now is that his friends and coworkers have been murdered and he's going to be next.

So far, the narrative line of dramatic action is established by an integrated series of events. When Redford phones Cliff Robertson, the head of his section at the CIA, Robertson convinces him that his friend Sam, also in the CIA, will meet him behind a hotel and bring him safely into headquarters. But when he goes to meet Sam, his friend is killed by the CIA man who is with him, and the murder is blamed on Redford.

Completely alone, Redford hides in a store, and when Faye Dunaway picks up her dry cleaning, he forces her at gunpoint to take him to her apartment. He wants to rest, collect his thoughts, find out what action to take.

The form I was seeking to establish fit. The dramatic context for Act II is *Confrontation*, and Redford encounters obstacles everywhere. Out of dramatic necessity he kidnaps Faye Dunaway. All the way through the first part of the second act, Redford is a victim, hunted by the hired assassin, Max von Sydow.

Now, I found this very interesting. In film, the main character has to be active; that is, he or she causes things to happen, and is not always reacting to things that happen. It's Newton's Third Law of Motion: for every action, there's an equal and opposite reaction. Same thing in the movies. So, if Redford is constantly reacting, he becomes a passive character, and will no longer be in the foreground of the story.

When I studied the film again from this perspective, I saw that when Redford stumbles from the CIA office, leaving his dead coworkers behind, into Act II, he doesn't know what, or why, this is happening. All he knows is that he must be the next person on the hit list. He needs to get his bearings and seek a sanctuary. Hiding in the cleaners, and kidnapping the Faye Dunaway character, is an active event; for the first time since the murders, he's taking matters into his own hands and causing something to happen. Which leads to the next stage of the story.

Once he's with Dunaway, he's safe, at least for the time being, and we begin to hear his side of the story. While his relationship with her is guarded, she gradually begins to trust him, so much so that she agrees to help. But when Redford is attacked in Dunaway's apartment by the mailman killer, he realizes he's got to do something. He's got to turn the situation around; instead of being a victim, he's got to become the aggressor. In other words, he's got to be active. And there's that primary requisite in writing a screenplay again. Action is character; what a person does determines who he or she is. Film is behavior.

As I analyzed the film and read the screenplay, I saw that the form of my graphic representation worked. I began to see that structure is really the foundation of the screenplay, and that its specific purpose is to hold the story in place, the same way gravity keeps the planets anchored in alignment. Act I sets up Redford and the story; Plot Point I is the killing of his coworkers. In Act II he confronts obstacle after obstacle, and Plot Point II is when he takes action and kidnaps the Cliff Robertson character with the help of Faye Dunaway. Act III resolves the story when Redford breaks into the house of the leader of the secret CIA, who then is killed by the hired assassin, Max von Sydow.

It wasn't long before I began to incorporate my analysis of the movies I was seeing and the screenplays I was reading into my pitches at work. If I read a screenplay I liked, an 8 or above, and recommended it to Eddie and Fouad as something we should pursue,

I broke it down and put in on the whammo chart, labeling Act I, II and III, the Set-Up, Confrontation and Resolution, as well as identifying the Plot Points at the end of Acts I and II.

In my quest to document the form, I began timing various movies and checking out the page numbers of the good screenplays I read at Cinemobile. That's when I began to notice a consistency of form. The average screenplay *Set-Up* took approximately twenty-five to thirty pages, or about twenty-five to thirty minutes. Plot Point I usually occurred around pages twenty-five or thirty, or about twenty-five or thirty minutes into the film. Act II, the *Confrontation*, where the characters encounter conflict and obstacles, was approximately sixty pages in length, or about sixty minutes long. Plot Point II occurred between pages eighty-five and ninety, or about eighty-five or ninety minutes into the film, and Act III, the *Resolution*, was anywhere from twenty-two to thirty pages in length. These page numbers were only approximations, and simply embodied the *form* of the screenplay. It was not, as many people think, "writing by the numbers."

While all this looked and sounded good, I was still a little uncertain about whether it worked for all films, especially comedies. And what about those nonlinear films, where past and present intersect with the use of flashbacks during the story?

I didn't have any answers for that, but I was patient and pretty certain I would find a way to check it out, and that's what happened. A few months later I found the second film I chose to study. After Fouad returned from a trip to New York, he told me to check out Woody Allen's new film, *Annie Hall*. It hadn't been released yet, but there was going to be a special screening and Fouad wanted me to go. Needless to say, I was more than a little curious. I had seen several of Allen's films — *Take the Money and Run*, *Bananas*, *Sleeper* — and thought they were extremely funny and original.

When I walked out of the screening room, I thought *Annie Hall*, subtitled a "nervous romance," was one of the funniest movies I had ever seen. The structure itself is unique; from the first minute of the opening monologue, when Woody Allen wonders what went wrong in his relationship with Annie Hall, I was totally hooked. I noticed that while the film begins in present time with Alvy's whining for his lost relationship, bits and pieces of that relationship are shown. The story, while set up in present time, moves backward to some hysterical scenes of Alvy's early childhood. He grew up under a roller coaster, he says, which is why he tends to be a little nervous. The film flashes back to his two marriages—based, we see, on sex rather than love—and we share some of his memories with Annie, then flash back to his initial encounter with her when they first meet on the tennis court.

As I began to analyze the structure of the movie in relation to my diagram, a question arose that hit me with the weight of a sledgehammer. It was this: had I really uncovered a structural form that worked, or once more was I just trying to force or impose my will, or system, on something that wasn't really there? In my analysis of *Annie Hall*, was I trying to force a square peg into a round hole?

At that moment, I questioned and doubted everything I had learned and understood about structure. I crawled into my bathtub and didn't come out for hours. But after a few days, I realized I was simply running from something I did not want to deal with. I knew I had to start over, rethink my ideas.

Through Eddie, I obtained a copy of the screenplay. I read it and tried to break it down into the structure I'd used for *The Hustler*, *Chinatown* and *Three Days of the Condor*, but it didn't work. I didn't understand how *Annie Hall* was put together. So I started over, from the beginning. Was it possible, I wondered, to separate character from structure? To structure a story line around the growth and change of a character? This concept, I thought, was a major component of *Annie Hall*; Alvy is a person who refuses to change, whereas Annie Hall is a person who changes and grows constantly. Is it possible for a screenplay told mostly in flashback to be structured by the dramatic need of the character?

With that in mind, once I read the first page, I saw the genius of Woody Allen. He set up his character's point of view immediately, from page one, word one, through the monologue. As I continued turning pages I saw that Act I set up Alvy's present situation and past relationships. Everything Alvy refers to relates back to the time when he and Annie were together.

This was an interesting insight for me. Alvy's character, as set up in Act I, goes from present time to past time. Act II deals with Alvy and Annie's relationship, re-creating their first stirrings of passion (including that glorious subtext scene on the balcony) to their final separation. In the last part of the movie, Alvy unsuccessfully tries to re-create his relationship with Annie with other women.

Woody Allen is brilliant at setting up characters, then getting inside their heads. Alvy explains his point of view, how he sees life, in the opening monologue: "A lot of suffering, pain, anxiety and problems—and it's all over much too quickly." He tells a joke, attributed to Groucho Marx, that reveals how he feels about himself: "I would never belong to any club that would have someone like me for a member. That's the key joke of my adult life in terms of my relationships with women." And that's what the film shows us: his relationships with women, focusing on Annie Hall.

I went back to the definition of structure and asked myself if character could reflect "the relationship between the parts and the whole." If the "whole" is the screenplay, then one of the "parts" would definitely be the character. If I explored the movie from Alvy's point of view, I thought, I could possibly define structure from the character's perspective. "Point of view" is defined as "the way a person sees the world." And Alvy certainly "sees" his world in a bizarre and unusual way.

And here's where my background in English literature came into play. In one of my English lit classes at Berkeley I had studied Henry James, the great American novelist. James was a renowned literary theorist who explored the craft of the novel and built up a body of critical essays analyzing the elements that make up great novels. In one of his essays, *The Art of Fiction*, he formulated a theory about character that sparked a new understanding.

The question he raised was this: *"What is character but the determination of incident, and what is incident but the illumination of character."* When I examined his statement within the larger context of creating characters for the screen, I saw something I had not seen before.

The key word was *"incident."* In all my reading and movie analysis, I was becoming aware of the idea that most good movies focus on the unfolding of a specific incident or event, which then becomes the engine that powers the story to its completion.

Approaching the movie from this point of view opened a whole new vista in terms of understanding the relationship between story and structure. In *Annie Hall*, the key incident that drives the story forward is Alvy's relationship with Annie Hall. That's a no-brainer. In the opening monologue, within the first two minutes of the film, Alvy says, "I keep sifting the pieces of the relationship through my mind and examining my life and trying to figure out where the screw-up came." Since the film is told in an odd structural dynamic, the incident, the relationship with Annie, provides the "pieces" that tell the story.

The first act, after the monologue, shows us Alvy's early school years as he grew up under the roller coaster at Coney Island, leading to his tendency toward anxiety and depression. It not only shows us his dysfunctional childhood but also illustrates his relationship with women, starting with his mother, who's always trying to change his father. It illustrates Alvy's early obsession with sex and his belief that sex is the predominant drive in a relationship, the fantasy source and wellspring of all happiness.

And that, for me, is the key to the film: Alvy's search for happiness. Alvy believes Annie Hall will be the key that unlocks the happiness he knows is inside him. He thinks that the source of happiness is to be found outside himself, through another person, or by having a lot of money or a powerful job, or through drugs and alcohol, or through eating great food—anything, in short, that will fill up the empty hole of loneliness and unhappiness that so many people feel inside. Like Gatsby searching for the green light, Alvy's search for a woman becomes a mirror of his quest for happiness. What gets in the way is his unrealistic idealism, which becomes the source of his breakup with Annie Hall. You know, "*I Love You, You're Perfect, Now Change.*" Alvy's quest to make Annie into his own image is the very reason the relationship fails. Alvy is not able to accept Annie for who she is, because he wants her to conform to his image of who she is and what she should be. Unconditional love, it ain't.

In Act II, we watch the relationship begin to unravel when Alvy suggests that Annie take adult education classes, then criticizes her when she quotes her teacher. He sulks when she expresses herself by singing in a nightclub, and is totally jealous when Tony Lacy (Paul Simon) takes an interest in her and invites them to a little gathering after the show. Alvy, of course, declines. We know where this relationship is going—down the tubes.

Near the end of Act II, almost at the end of their relationship, there's a marvelous scene done in split screen, where Annie and Alvy are both seen in therapy sessions; Alvy lies on a couch, Annie sits in a chair. Both lament the fact that their feelings have changed toward each other, but it's how they see the same thing that brings the humor out. Both psychiatrists ask, "Do you have sex often?" Alvy replies, "Hardly ever. Maybe three times a week." And Annie replies: "Constantly! I'd say three times a week. . . ." It's a perfect illustration of *the world is as you see it*, as the ancient scripture puts it.

Just before Plot Point II, when Alvy is invited to give an award on a TV show in L.A., they fly out but Alvy gets sick, naturally, and can't present the award. Later, they end up at a party at Tony Lacy's house, where he renews his interest in Annie. Alvy sees just how different they are; though he's the one who has given her the opportunity to grow and change, he can't deal with it. On the flight home, the two of them are immersed in their own thoughts, each knowing the relationship is over. Annie turns to him and says: "You know, I don't think our relationship is working." And Alvy replies, "A relationship, I think . . . is like a shark. . . . It has to constantly move forward or it dies. . . . And I think what we've got on our hands . . . is a dead shark." The truth at last.

The relationship ends not with a bang but a whimper. Soon after they return to New York, Annie moves to L.A. to be with Tony Lacy, and Alvy tries to re-create some of his experiences with Annie with other women, but it's not the same. It doesn't work because no one can step into the same river twice. Their breakup, Plot Point II, "spins" the action into Act III, the Resolution.

Once I analyzed the film from the perspective of character, I understood Alvy's dramatic need, and only then did the structure ring true. It didn't matter that the film is told in flashback—the structure was still clear. Alvy sets up what's going through his mind in the opening monologue. He sets up his disjointed childhood and how he relates to women with visual "excerpts" of his two brief marriages. At that point he cuts to the flashback of his first meeting with Annie at the tennis club. That incident sets up the relationship and leads us into Act II.

When I reviewed the film again, it became evident that there was a definite relationship between story, character and structure. They are part and parcel of the same thing. There was no way I could separate them. That's when I learned that good structure does not create a good story, but rather that a good story is what creates structure.

At this point I felt I finally had some tangible concepts about the structure and form of the screenplay. The only thing I didn't have was a name for my graphic representation, my diagram. I wanted the name to reflect its nature of a model, or example, of what a screenplay is, wanted a name that could encompass its many attributes.

I thought about it for weeks, and then one day, reading a George Leonard book about the psychological shifts we go through in terms of behavior, I came across the term referred to as a *paradigm shift*. When I looked up the word "paradigm," I found it meant "a model, example or conceptual scheme." That's what my graphic representation was—a model, or an example. If I could hang a screenplay on a wall like a painting, I could find its true nature, and it would look like my graphic representation.

After thinking about it for a while, I decided to call it the *Paradigm*. Little did I know how accurate that would be.

14

Second Time Around

"*You don't write because
you want to say something; you write
because you've got something to say.*"
—F. SCOTT FITZGERALD
The Crack-Up

When I started discussing the *Paradigm* in my class at Sherwood Oaks, most of the people had a hard time accepting it. Some thought it was too "formulaic," others thought it was simply a number system and maintained, rightly, that there ain't no way you can write a screenplay "by the numbers." That's the truth.

But I kept talking about how the *Paradigm* embodies screenplay form, referencing it to current movies, and soon, people started listening. When I related it to the movies they were seeing, they began to understand. And once they understood the dynamics of screenplay structure, they began to approach the craft of screenwriting with more awareness. The result was a deeper appreciation and enjoyment of the movie experience.

After class, people often asked if I could recommend any good books on screenwriting. I couldn't. When I went into bookstores, I could find only a few books about screenwriting, the best being Lajos Egri's *The Art of Dramatic Writing*, but it focused on plays and playwriting, had been in print for more than thirty years and was a very hard read. There wasn't much else around.

During the latter part of 1975, I began to feel the constraints of my job. I had been at Cinemobile for a little over two years, and I was getting tired of the endless circle of meetings and deals. Sometimes, I woke up in the middle of the night with a current crisis at Cinemobile on the edge of my consciousness. More and more I found myself thinking about the possibility of going back to writing screenplays. I had to accept the inevitable truth: it was time for a change.

Coincidentally, rumors began surfacing that Fouad was going to sell the company to Taft Broadcasting, but nobody knew exactly what that would mean. Not even Eddie was privileged to that information. Little gossip items had run in the trade papers, and I was finding many producers and agents reluctant to send material to a company that might be in the process of being sold. But selling the company was never mentioned in the office. Only one thing was certain: Fouad was traveling a lot to Taft headquarters in Ohio. But, despite our speculation, it was still business as usual.

One day, while all this was going on, Fouad called me into his office and informed me that he had just hired two assistants to help read all the scripts being submitted. I was thrilled, because during the last several months screenplay submissions had almost doubled.

I liked having two assistants to share the load. Both were knowledgeable and informed. One, Bill Blaylock, was a graduate of the University of Southern California School of Business. The other was Bruce Gilbert, a friend and associate of Jane Fonda's and her then-husband, political activist Tom Hayden. Bruce had been involved in Tom Hayden's political career and had worked with Jane Fonda for a while, and was helping to develop a story about a

Marine wife who falls in love with an outspoken Vietnam veteran confined to a wheelchair. At that time in the mid-seventies, the subject of Vietnam was an extremely hard sell, but Fonda, Bruce and producer Jerome Hellman were passionate about making the movie and would not give up until they brought it to the screen.

With Bill and Bruce now on board, I went about organizing the Story Department. I created a system by which screenplays were logged in, with date, person submitting them and any elements which might be attached, like stars, directors or producers, etc. Then the script would be read by any one of the three of us. Any screenplays regarded as 8 or above had to be read by all three of us before it went to Eddie. Once the system was in place, I created a reader's report (known as coverage) and, over the course of several meetings with my new assistants, explained how the reader's coverage should be written. I explained the *Paradigm*, drawing it out and showing them how it worked and how to use it as an analytical tool. I even had them see *Chinatown* and *Annie Hall*.

One night, Bruce and I went out for a drink after work, and he asked if I would read the first draft of the screenplay he was helping develop. The script, *Coming Home*, was written by Nancy Dowd, and I found that while the story was strong and powerful, and the subject matter fierce, it seemed to wander and lose focus in many places. That made the script, even though fueled by a powerful subject, "soft" and "fuzzy." Bruce told me that after much debate they had finally decided to bring in another writer and take a new approach with the material. That writer was Waldo Salt, the great screenwriter who had so eloquently adapted *Midnight Cowboy* from the novel by James Leo Herlihy.

It was not too long after that that Gary asked me to moderate a panel of screenwriters at a daylong Sherwood Oaks Screenwriting Conference. One of the writers on the panel was Waldo Salt.

Before the morning session, I introduced myself to him, told him Bruce and I were working together and was immediately impressed by his friendliness, his directness, his honesty, his openness. That was his style. He reminded me of Jean Renoir to a certain degree.

Waldo Salt. Short and dynamic, with a shock of dark, wavy hair, now mostly gray, he spoke with a kind of raspy voice, a carryover, I think, from all his years of smoking. What struck me most about him, I think, were his eyes: dark and penetrating, watery, as if he were always on the edge of tears.

The only thing I knew about Waldo Salt as a screenwriter was that he had written *Serpico*, won the Academy Award for *Midnight Cowboy* and was now rewriting *Coming Home*. I loved *Midnight Cowboy*, and told him I had read the Nancy Dowd draft of *Coming Home* and had met his daughter, Jennifer, several times. It wasn't too long before we started talking abut the industry, and the craft of screenwriting.

When I think about courage, I think about the life and career of Waldo Salt; it's a story of passion, dedication, persistence, inspiration, genius and outspoken integrity. After writing several notable films during the forties, Waldo, like so many other writers and filmmakers of the time, became a member of the Communist Party, mainly, he told me, because he believed it was for the common man and against fascism. During the HUAC hearings in the early fifties, he was blacklisted, and for many, many years was unable to get any kind of work under his own name. He moved to New York eventually, and started writing television shows under a pseudonym.

Other blacklisted writers, known as the Hollywood Ten, served time in prison or were forced to go to other countries to live and work. I knew a lot about the blacklist at that time, as I was then in a relationship with Kate Lardner, Ring Lardner Jr.'s daughter. Ring was one of the Hollywood Ten, an Academy Award winner for *Woman of the Year* and *M*A*S*H* who had been forced to serve a year in prison for refusing to name names to the committee.

The blacklist period was a horrific time for everyone, and it was during those years, Waldo told me, that he was forced to confront the facts of his life; everything he had believed in up to that time, his personal as well as political beliefs, had crumbled away like sand, and he was forced to reinvent himself, both as a person and as a writer. It was either that, he said, or suicide.

After several years, when he was finally released from the bondage of the blacklist, he was able to put his name on the films he had written. The first two films he wrote under his own name were *Taras Bulba* and *Flight from Ashiya*, and they were just awful. He went into a deep depression, until he came to understand that if he was going to fail, he'd better do it on his own terms. So he made an agreement with himself that any film which had his name on it must be the best job he could do, no matter how long it took. He had suffered too much for it to be any other way. His scripts honor that commitment.

After the panel we went out for coffee, and I asked him what changes he was thinking about making in the rewrite of *Coming Home*. He replied that he didn't know yet, as he was still collecting information. I told him about my days of making documentaries for David Wolper, of working with Renoir, of hanging out with Peckinpah, and that I was thinking of going back to writing. Almost as an afterthought, he warned me not to be too hard on myself, that it had taken him a few years to reinvent himself as a writer.

As I recall, it was during this conversation with Waldo that he said something highly significant: he believed that the character's need in the story determines the dramatic structure. I told him that

I had recently come to the same understanding as I was analyzing *Annie Hall*. It was a wonderful moment of shared insight for both of us.

Afterward, we had a long and passionate discussion about capturing "the truth of the human condition" in a screenplay. The key to a successful screenplay, he emphasized, was preparing the material. Dialogue, he said, is "perishable," because the actor can always improvise lines to make it work. But, he added forcefully, the character's dramatic need is sacrosanct. That cannot be changed, because it holds the entire story in place. Putting words down on paper, he said, was the easiest part of the screenwriting process; it was the visual conception of the story that took so long. And he quoted Picasso: "Art is the elimination of the unnecessary."

After we parted, our conversation stayed with me for several days. I reflected on how inspiring Waldo was, how he'd stood firm in the face of his struggle, not giving in until he came to a personal understanding about who he was and the way he wanted to live his life. And I wondered if I had the courage to live the way Waldo did, or whether in a similar situation I would give in and ultimately go against my own integrity. That would be the worst sin, I thought— giving up my own principles just to make somebody else a lot of money.

A few months later, we learned Fouad had sold Cinemobile to the Taft Broadcasting Company, and shortly thereafter the entire staff of Cine Artists, including Fouad, Eddie, Bernie Weitzman and myself, were fired. I was getting the opportunity to pursue my wish, whether I liked it or not. At the moment I didn't feel too bad about it. I had made many contacts and felt, deep down, that if I wanted to get another job, I could do so fairly easily. Or maybe I would fulfill my wish and go back to writing.

Our last day came and went at Cinemobile; we shared our "last supper" together, then went our separate ways. I remember waking up the next morning, getting out of bed, thinking I had to go to work, then realizing I didn't. I joyfully crawled back into bed, cup of coffee in hand and the morning paper spread out all over the bed. Over the next few months I had interviews with companies I knew I didn't want to work for, and started enjoying the freedom of not having to go to the office every day.

I had been away from the writing experience for a little more than two years, and though I missed it, in truth, I was a little frightened to go back to it. The first time around had been a rewarding, but painful, experience. On the one hand, I missed the satisfaction of bringing an idea or character into existence, of reaching inside myself to investigate different situations or emotions. On the other hand, I had experienced a lot of pain and loneliness writing and remembered how I used to "hit my head against the typewriter" until something came out. If I was going to resume my writing experience after this hiatus, I knew I would have to reinvent myself as a writer, the way Waldo Salt had. I was determined that the second time around was not going to be a duplication of the first.

As I went back over my past writing experience, I knew I had to make some distinctions. One of the things that had made it so difficult for me was that I wanted what I'd written to be "perfect." My teaching experience had taught me that it's okay to lay shitty pages down, because I could always go back and rework them later. I'd learned I couldn't change something from nothing; I had to have something to change.

The next step was asking myself what kind of experience I wanted to create for myself. When I faced the blank sheet of paper, I decided, I wanted to create a positive, successful and enjoyable experience. When I sat down at my desk I wanted it to be an adventure. I never knew what was going to come out, and I understood I couldn't write "perfect" pages. Renoir had told me "Perfection exists only in the mind, not in reality," and that if he ever wrote anything he thought was perfect, he would never write again. It was a lesson I wanted to follow. If I wasn't going to enjoy myself, why write? What would be the point?

Discipline had always been a biggie for me; sometimes I had it, sometimes I didn't. If I was going to jump back into the writing experience, I had to address two things: when I was going to write—that is, the actual time of day or night—and how many pages I wanted to write before I could feel it was okay to stop. At Cinemobile, I'd met too many writers who felt they had to work all day, morning to night, thirteen or fourteen hours a day. And what they told me was that their best work occurred within the first few hours.

So I set strong goals for myself: I wanted to write five or six days a week, three or four hours a day, and I would not leave the desk until I had finished at least three or more pages a day, knowing that some days would be better than others. I remembered what the great English novelist W. Somerset Maugham had said about writing. As a writer, he worked five days a week, three hours a day, writing three pages a day. A reporter once asked him what he did when he was stuck and nothing was coming out; did he get up and walk away or did he just sit in front of the typewriter? And he replied that if nothing was happening at the typewriter on a given day, he simply typed his name for three hours.

My new parameters now defined and articulated, I chose what I would do as my first project: I was going to rewrite my *Balinger* script, which had been in negotiation with the Robert Aldrich Company. Aldrich was the noted director of *The Big Knife*, *The Dirty Dozen*, *Ulzana's Raid* and *Kiss Me Deadly*, among other films.

While the deal was never formalized, I had enough input from him to make changes that I thought would enhance the material.

Armed with my intention to create a positive and successful writing experience, I sat down at the typewriter to begin the rewrite. Immediately, old "stuff" came up again. Every word I put down on paper, I judged, evaluated and crossed out; then I started over, got angry and abruptly shoved my chair back and walked away. In less than an hour my mood had shifted from one of joyous optimism to one of dark despair. I left my desk, changed the sheets on the beds and again tried to go back to work.

It was only then that I remembered Waldo's words: I had to support myself, be compassionate with myself, for in truth, I certainly couldn't judge what I had written after such a long absence. After all, I hadn't used these writing "muscles" in a couple of years, so I at least owed myself a few months to try and loosen up and get back into the flow of things.

For the next few weeks, every time I sat down to work I confronted these feelings of resistance. I was very productive: I washed and cleaned the kitchen walls, floors and ceiling; went shopping; cleaned the refrigerator (twice in one day); made phone calls; sharpened all my pencils; set up various lunch meetings; and did all the things I needed to do so I could avoid facing the blank sheet of paper.

One day, in the midst of all this strain and pain, I was listening to some music when the needle got stuck in a groove and the same refrain kept repeating itself, over and over again. When I went to fix it, I thought, How appropriate a symbol this is; my life is the same way right now. I'm stuck in an old groove. I keep repeating old patterns over and over again, and I can't seem to break out. That thought sparked a response, and I suddenly felt a wave of insight and understanding surge through me.

Many years before, I had taken a psychology course and heard about "the groove" theory of behavior. According to this theory, when we do something for the first time, and it makes us feel good, that feeling creates a "groove" in our consciousness. We like what it does, whether it's beneficial or not. If we continue with whatever it is that gives us pleasure—whether it be cigarettes, food, sugar, caffeine, sex, whatever—the more ingrained the habit becomes, the deeper the "groove" gets. When we want to stop, it's extremely difficult because, according to this theory, the groove has become so ingrained in our consciousness that we can't change it. The only way to alter the habit is to create a new groove, a new habit.

The more I thought about the groove theory, the more sense it made. Working at the typewriter, I realized, seemed to be the source of my frustration. If I wanted to create a new groove, I would have to create a new habit. I could work at a different time, for example, either late afternoon or night; I could work with a partner; or, I suddenly realized, I could find another way to put words on paper—I could write in longhand.

So I went out and bought several legal pads and a lot of pens and started organizing myself to begin this new writing experience. It was difficult at first; I didn't have much stamina writing longhand for extended periods, plus my mind sometimes went so fast I couldn't get all the words down. And then there were those times I couldn't read my own handwriting. But I persisted.

I spent the next several months working on various projects: I finished the rewrite on *Balinger*, wrote an original script (my first in longhand) called *The Run* for Douglas Trumbull, the special-effects wizard, about a man who sets out to break the water-speed record, specifically designing it for his new filmic process called "Showscan." I was hired to write some openings and closings for Sam

Peckinpah's TV show, *The Westerner*, then being sold in syndication, and wrote the narration for a documentary about the members of a Native American tribe called *Chosa: The Divided Trail*, later nominated for an Academy Award.

At that point I felt very comfortable writing longhand, so I decided to write about what was currently going on in my life. I remembered all those requests I'd received for a book on screenwriting, and I thought it might be a good time to actually do something about it. I outlined the course I was teaching at Sherwood Oaks, focusing on the *Paradigm* as the foundation of screenwriting. Never having written a proposal before, I was told by a friend that I should write an introduction, along with the first three chapters, followed by chapter outlines for the rest of the book.

But as I sat down to write the introduction, I found myself slipping back into an old negative groove. Once again, I hit the familiar wall of resistance. It was déjà vu all over again: the harder I worked, the worse it got. Every morning, I went to my desk and started scribbling, but it felt forced, contrived and much too dry and intellectual; it just wasn't working. I would bounce up and rush off to clean the kitchen, make the beds, scrub the walls or vacuum the rugs.

What do I do now? I wondered.

Once again, I went back to the beginning. What kind of a writing experience did I want to create for myself? What did I hope to accomplish with it? What was my intention? Knowing it was the writer's job to keep the reader turning pages, what could I do to make that happen?

The next day, I sat down at my desk and started free-associating. What did I want to do? The answer came immediately: communicate the foundations of screenwriting by illustrating the nature of dramatic structure using examples of several contemporary movies.

I wanted to show how the context of the *Paradigm* worked. But how would I do that?

A few days later, as I was sitting quietly, eyes closed in a meditative state, mulling over what I wanted to accomplish, I was startled to hear a voice welling up from inside me that said, quite clearly, "Write from your own experience." The voice was loud, almost insistent. At first, I thought I was imagining things, but I heard the voice again, and it said the same thing: "Write from your own experience." Somehow, I knew with an intuitive, mystical certainty that this was the voice of my "creative self," that aspect of myself that is called by many different names: "instinct," "the muse," "intuition," "God," the "Inner Self." To me, it's all the same. It's that part of myself that resides beyond the mind, beyond personality, beyond any thoughts, feelings or emotions, beyond all those doubts and fears that make up my daily life.

Over the next several days, I focused on my experience as a screenwriter, a reader and a teacher. I recalled incidents and events that happened to me while teaching at Sherwood Oaks and reading scripts at Cinemobile. I played through these experiences again and again, as if I were watching a movie move across the landscape of my mind.

At this stage, I didn't feel obligated to sit down and write. I was content to remain in this reflective state and wait for the words to come. Then, one night, about 3 A.M., I awoke with a start and became aware of thoughts racing across my mind in a river of words. As I became awake the thoughts grew stronger, more insistent, and it was then that I realized the words were forming the opening sentences of the introduction to the book: "As a writer-producer for David L. Wolper Productions, a freelance screenwriter and head of the Story Department at Cinemobile Systems, I spent several years writing and reading screenplays."

I had the feeling these words were just the tip of the iceberg. So I reached for the pad of paper on my nightstand, grabbed a pen, lit the candle next to the bed and started writing. A torrent of words came gushing out, as if they had already been written and I was simply catching them and throwing them down on paper. There seemed to be no separation between me, my thoughts, the pen and paper. It was all one.

Without being aware of time, I kept writing, and the words kept flowing, filling sheet after sheet of paper. I finished around 5:30 A.M., and when I looked back over what I had written, I saw it was the first draft of the introduction to the book, which now had a title—*Screenplay: The Foundations of Screenwriting*.

I made a big pot of coffee, got my son off to school and started looking back over what I had written during the middle of the night. It was rough, and some of it was illegible, but basically it was all there; I had to polish and hone it, rearrange some paragraphs and sentences, but I knew I had broken through the wall of resistance which had confronted me over the past weeks.

I felt energized, elated, filled with a sense of joy and accomplishment. I had written from my own experience; I had taken incidents, episodes and events from my own reading, writing and teaching experience and incorporated them into the body of the material. I had "pushed my mind" out of the way, and hadn't paid any attention to what my critical mind had been saying.

That experience was so powerful that it became the origin of an exercise which I called "the critic's page." As I sat down to rework the introduction I took out an extra sheet of paper and titled it "the critic's page." I started writing, and it wasn't long before I became aware of the critical voice at the back of my mind. I hadn't been conscious of it when I was writing in the middle of the night, but now my mind was extremely active, judging and evaluating what I was writing. Now I just wrote the criticisms down on the critic's page. Whatever they were—"These pages are no good," "Boring," "I've read this before," "No one's going to read this," "Who are you kidding," "This will never sell," etc., etc., etc.—I simply said to myself, "So what?" and continued writing.

That took the energy off of writing "perfect" words. And when I read over the critic's pages a few days later, I saw I had written the same negative comments over and over again. My comments were always the same. I couldn't believe it.

The more I continued to do this exercise, the freer I became. And then an amazing shift occurred: as I became aware of the critical mind making its judgments and evaluations, I didn't have the urge to respond anymore. I was totally detached. The words "So what?" became my guiding light. I just continued writing, going back and honing and polishing and rewriting the material until I was satisfied with it.

Not only had I created a "new groove," I'd learned a whole new way of working. Rather than writing "perfect words" on the page, I was throwing down words and ideas without even thinking about how good or bad they were. That led me to a new, natural style of working.

Writing fast, throwing words and ideas down on the page, not letting any of my critical thoughts, comments or doubts get in the way, was like a breath of fresh air. I wasn't paying attention to the critical mind. That, to me, was liberation. When I went back and read the material again, I changed a lot, adding words and paragraphs, rewriting about 80 percent of what I had written. I worked the way Jean Renoir always told me to work, from beginning to end, beginning to end. In that way, the material is always fresh, always new.

A few days later, when I sat down to continue working on the book, I had a new outlook and a new perspective on the craft of writing. I had a rule to follow: whatever works, works, and whatever doesn't, doesn't. That's when the realization hit: it doesn't matter *how* you write, it just matters *that* you write.

Over the next few months, I wrote the presentation for *Screenplay*. It consisted of the Introduction, the first three chapters and chapter outlines for the rest of the book. I read it over and over again, changing a little here, a little there, but I knew I had done the best job I could do. When I finished, I felt a great deal of satisfaction.

I called an agent friend of mine in New York whom I had met through my job at Cinemobile and asked if she would take a look at it. She did, told me she could sell it, and within six weeks it was bought by a major publisher on a "whim." I got a small advance, and started writing, knowing I had found my own way of working that incorporated my experience and the movies which had so inspired me.

And that made it all worthwhile.

Finding
the Mid-Point

*"Writing a screenplay is in many ways similar to executing
a piece of carpentry. If you take some wood and nails and
glue and make a bookcase, only to find when you're done
that it topples over when you try to stand it upright, you
may have created something really very beautiful, but it
won't work as a bookcase."*

—WILLIAM GOLDMAN
Adventures in the Screen Trade

When *Screenplay: The Foundations of Screenwriting* was first
published in 1979, it surprised everyone by becoming an
immediate best-seller. There were three printings within the first
six months of publication, and it wasn't long before many of the
major colleges and universities across the land were using it as a
text. The publisher was astonished. So was I.

A few months after publication, I started a new class at Sherwood Oaks. Word of mouth had apparently spread, and my
screenwriting course suddenly became very popular. For this new
eight-week session, so many people had signed up that my class
had to be moved into the main room. Almost two hundred people
jammed into the room, braving the rigors of that run-down, tat-
tered dream factory on Hollywood Boulevard.

I learned that screenwriters made up only a small percentage of the people attending. People came from all over, from within the industry and without; there were production executives; working, recognizable actors from both film and television; novelists; playwrights; journalists; businessmen and businesswomen; and nonprofessionals. All of them, it seemed, were deeply immersed in the world of the movies, motivated by a desire to learn more about the art and craft of screenwriting. I used several teaching films during this period: *Chinatown*, *Annie Hall*, *Manhattan* (Woody Allen), *Body Heat* (Larry Kasdan) and *Absence of Malice* (Kurt Luedtke).

One night, at the end of the evening's class, Gary took me aside and told me a lot of people were interested in a workshop that would focus on the actual writing of the screenplay, and wondered whether I would teach it. I told him I'd think about it, and over the next few days decided it might be a good opportunity to expand my teaching experience.

I had never taught an actual writing workshop, and wanted to design a course in which participants could achieve a specific writing goal. Gradually, the form of the class began to take shape in my head. I decided that during the eight-week session material would be presented and a writing assignment given that would be handed in and read at the next week's class. That way, we could all learn from each other.

What did I want the writer to accomplish in this class? As I thought about it I realized that writing Act I was totally doable during this eight-week session and would give the writers the experience of actually writing their screenplays. I conceived the course so it would begin with an overview of the preparation the writer needed to do before he or she could start writing. I knew from my own experience that a writer doesn't just sit down and start writing. The actual writing process includes examining ideas from all sides, and there are questions that must be asked and answered before one word can be written on the page.

Where does the writer begin? How does a writer go about choosing a story? How is the idea prepared and structured into a definite story line? What's the best way to go about creating characters? Those were the questions I wanted to focus on. My personal goal was clear and simple: I wanted the writer to walk away from this class with the screenplay prepared and the first act of the screenplay written.

With this in mind, I designed and laid out the class; we would begin by isolating and defining the writer's idea, then articulate it into a specific action and character. Once the writer put into words what and who the story was about, he or she would have a start point on which to build and then expand the material. The next step would be creating the characters, followed by laying out the story progression, and then the process of building the incidents, episodes and events that make up the action of the screenplay could begin. At that point, the writers would start writing Act I.

But how was I going to teach the class? I vividly recalled my first teaching experience at Sherwood Oaks, and I certainly didn't want to repeat it. I remembered the one and only creative writing class I had taken in college. The writer's material was read silently by the entire class and the pages were then judged and criticized by classmates and instructor. Then we made whatever changes were suggested and brought the revised pages back to class. What was so frustrating for me, and I'm sure for everyone else in the class, was that I did not end up writing what I wanted to write. I ended up writing a watered-down version of what everybody else thought my idea should be. It was awful. I swore I would never let this happen again.

My intention for this newly created workshop was to let the writers explore their own ideas so they could expand their knowledge of the craft. I was very clear on the fact that I wasn't going to "teach" them anything they didn't know. In truth, they were going to teach themselves, and that's why I wanted them to take risks and expand their personal reach. If that meant writing shitty pages to get to the "good stuff," so be it.

I realized that if I wanted this to happen, I would have to create a "safe space," an environment where people would feel free to try things that might not work without any fear of failure or embarrassment, without fear of censure or the varied opinions of their classmates. It didn't matter how good their pages were; what was more important was for them to get their story down on paper. "Just tell the story" became my motto. What I most wanted the writer to take away from this class was the understanding that the writing experience is a journey of exploration, a journey influenced by the ebb and flow of dramatic necessity.

When the course began, the first thing we did was articulate our individual goals; what did each person want to accomplish during the eight weeks we spent together? Then we made an agreement that nobody would share anybody else's ideas outside the classroom. Students could talk about what I said, or the material I gave them, but people's ideas were "safe," off limits, outside of class. At that point, I heard everybody's ideas and had the writers determine their endings, their beginnings and Plot Points I and II. Many people had doubts about their endings. Can't we let the ending grow out of the story? they asked. I answered, Of course, but it's essential to begin somewhere; it might as well be with the ending. After all, they didn't plan a vacation by going to the airport and seeing what flights were available to what destination, did they? Of course not. They planned where they were going, then organized their trip. In the same way, they had only 120 pages to tell their story.

During the next session, we created the characters. I had students trace the life of their character from birth up until the time the story begins. This was an exercise in free association and automatic writing. It's a very liberating exercise, because it gives the character a voice and helps form his or her personal history. I first started doing this exercise as an actor at Berkeley. In the third session, we structured the screenplay on cards, outlining the scenes and sequences, and formed the overall content of the story line. Then we started writing pages.

We began simply, building each module of story line based on the exercises I assigned so that we moved through the eight-week course easily. There were a few glitches, to be sure, but nothing really serious. After the first few classes people felt comfortable, and safe, and started sharing ideas freely with each other.

When the first eight-week session was complete, I was gratified to see that all fifteen people in class had completed writing the first act of their screenplay. All of them liked the writing process so much they did not want to stop after writing Act I; they wanted to continue on, writing Acts II and III. So we took a two-week break, then resumed a new eight-week session to work on Act II.

When our second session began, I discovered that most of the class had continued to write during the break. They told me they didn't want to lose the discipline and creative energy they had built up during the initial eight-week class, so they had begun writing the first part of Act II. When I read the pages they had written during their time off, I was astonished. Generally speaking, they were awful. The characters were dull and uninteresting, and there seemed to be no trace of an organic story line, no progression and certainly no line of development. The conflict was either minimal or nonexistent. When it came to writing the second act, I felt, they were like blind men in a rainstorm: they didn't know where they were going and they were all wet.

Why did this happen? They had laid out and set up their story line in Act I, so why was Act II such a mess?

Writing Act II is much different from writing Act I. First of all, it's a much longer unit of dramatic action than either Act I or Act III. In my writing experience, Act II was always the most difficult, because jumping into the void of what I termed the "sixty blank sheets of paper" without any sense of guidance or direction is a formidable challenge. When I was writing Act II, I found it easy to get lost in the maze of my own creation. In Act II, I always had to know where I was and where I was going. Which is easier said than done.

Was there some way, I asked myself, that the screenwriter could approach writing Act II without getting lost and floundering in uncertainty? It sounded nice when I thought about it, but in truth I had no idea how to do it. So I posed the question to myself and, in a test of patience, waited for an answer, and one day while jogging I remembered a conversation I had had with Paul Schrader a few months earlier. He told me that when he writes a screenplay "something happens" around page 60.

That really intrigued me. When I got home, I immediately took another look at the *Paradigm*. It leaped off the page at me: page 60. I hadn't thought too much about it at the time, but I suddenly got that page 60 is halfway through the second act. It grabbed my attention. Once again, I recalled what Peckinpah had told me— that when he started writing his scripts, he aimed for the "center-piece." I wondered if there was something, some kind of incident or event, that happens around the same time in other screenplays.

Perhaps there was a way to break Act II down into two distinct units of dramatic action, separated by an event that occurred around page 60. If there *was* such an event, it would move the story forward, kicking it up to another level. Peckinpah used to structure his scripts pointing toward the centerpiece, like the train robbery in *The Wild Bunch*, and if I could identify such an event in the middle of Act II, then it might be a useful tool that would serve the writer in preparing and writing the second act.

So I went searching for an event that occurred somewhere around the middle of Act II, an event that would be a Plot Point, yes, but more important, a definite story point that would keep the action moving toward the Plot Point at the end of Act II.

It was about this time that Paul Mazursky, the writer-director-actor, was invited to speak and show his latest film, *An Unmarried Woman*, at Sherwood Oaks. The film, starring Jill Clayburgh and Alan Bates, was about a woman whose husband leaves her for a younger woman after many years of marriage. When the screening ended, I moderated the question-and-answer session with Mazursky. I really liked the film, especially the idea of the character's quest for her own personal identity, freedom and independence. It was, I realized, a story of self-discovery, as well as a relevant, topical and meaningful dramatization of the issues confronting an entire generation of women.

I found myself thinking about the film for several days after, a sure sign there was something I wanted to learn from it. I responded to the shifts in the character's behavior, the personal arc of transformation that the Jill Clayburgh character, Erica, experiences as she lets go of an old way of life to enter a new phase of self-worth and self-sufficiency.

I got a copy of the screenplay and started reading. Immediately, I saw how the first thirty pages clearly set up the story and the overall structure of the film. Act I sets up the marriage of Erica and her husband, played by Michael Murphy. The movie opens with them jogging together before work; they arrive home, enjoy a "quickie" and see their teenage girl off to school, then he takes off for work. Nothing much there, just a day in the life of the main character. She joins her friends at their weekly "consciousness-raising group" at a fashionable restaurant, and we're privy to their discussions of sex, love and marriage. It's clear that most of her friends are divorced, separated, unhappy, dissatisfied and cynical about men. Erica, it seems, has the marriage the rest of them all strive for.

When she arrives home, her husband mauls her, seeking sex. It's easy to see he's on edge, and it appears he's in some sort of midlife crisis. The next day, we see Erica at her part-time job at an art gallery, being "hustled" by Charlie the painter (Cliff Gorman), and later, we see her meet her husband for lunch.

So far, so good. It seems the perfect marriage—essentially satisfying, with those few occasional bumps in the road. Over lunch, she's discussing their upcoming summer plans, but it's obvious that he's distracted, distant. They leave the restaurant and are walking along the street when her husband suddenly breaks down and starts to cry. She asks what's wrong, and he blurts out: "I'm in love with another woman," someone he met at Bloomingdale's, a teacher. In shock, she staggers down the street, trying to comprehend what has just happened. That's Plot Point I, the event that spins the story around into Act II. It occurs about twenty-five minutes into the film.

So much for seventeen years of marriage. It is a major life change for Erica, and acts as the true beginning of the story. Act II starts with her feelings of anger, resentment and betrayal surfacing as she expresses her hostility toward men—all men. She finds it difficult adjusting to her new life as an unmarried woman. It's almost seven weeks before she can even take off her wedding ring and trash it, along with some of her husband's personal objects.

Unhappy, dissatisfied, angry, she enters therapy, and in the course of time learns how to be a single parent to her fifteen-year-old daughter. Finally, at the insistence of one of her friends, she agrees to go on a blind date. Needless to say, it's a disaster. Paul Mazursky plays a minor role in this little sequence, which takes place in a Chinese restaurant. During lunch, Erica meets an old friend, who tells her how sorry she is about her plight. Disgusted with her "new life" as an unmarried woman, Erica leaves. Her date insists on taking her home, and on the way makes a ridiculous pass at her; Erica's so pissed she throws him out of the cab in the middle of East River Drive.

When Erica shares this experience with her therapist, the woman tells her that maybe it's time to give up her anger at men, because all men are not to blame for her current condition; it's her husband who is the cause of her situation. When Erica asks what she should do, the therapist replies, "I can't tell you what to do, but I can tell you what I would do—I'd go out and get laid."

Which is what Erica does. Halfway through the second act, about sixty minutes into the film, sixty pages into the screenplay, she begins to experiment with her sexuality. She goes to a bar, meets a friend, sees Charlie the painter and blindly agrees to go to bed with him. It is less than a satisfying sexual encounter (she's had sex with only one man, her husband, for the last seventeen years), but she's finally broken free of the self-imposed mental chains of marital fidelity. She is now free to be "an unmarried woman," ready to explore her femininity.

At the end of Act II, she meets Saul Kaplan, an artist, played by Alan Bates. In a beautiful scene illustrating the strength and brevity of great screenwriting, Saul is in the gallery hanging paintings for his new show. When Erica joins him, he asks her whether the painting should be hung higher or lower. She answers,

"Higher," and he responds with "I think I'll keep it where it is." At which point we cut to his loft, where they've just finished having sex. He confesses that he likes her and wants to see her again, but she refuses, saying she's still experimenting and doesn't want to enter into anything serious. "Nothing personal," she adds.

A short time later, they meet at a party. They talk, enjoy each other's company, decide to leave the party together and soon begin seeing each other.

Act III develops the relationship between Erica and Saul. When he asks her to come with him to Vermont, where he's going to work on a new show, she declines. She's thinking of moving into a new apartment, has her daughter to care for and is hesitant to jump into a committed relationship. He doesn't force the issue, but we can see he's disappointed. We can also see that Erica has truly become a single person, able to choose for herself what she needs and wants, regardless of any man in her life. And this is the key to her transformation.

In the last scene of the film, his bags packed, Saul lowers a large painting to the street, then asks her to hold it for him. When she does, he gets into his car and drives off. If she's such an independent, free-spirited person, the scene seems to say, she can manage on her own.

That's how we leave her, buffeted by the wind and carrying this huge canvas as she makes her way through the city. She's gained her freedom, her independence, but what she'll do with it remains to be seen. For me, it's the perfect ending.

As I started identifying the emotional movements of the story, I saw that Erica's growth, her transformation, actually takes place during Act II. Act I sets up her marriage. Act II establishes her as an unmarried woman, and in Act III she is a single person. Looking at it more closely, I saw that Erica's change occurs in two parts.

In the first part she is reacting to her new situation; in the second part she is exploring her sexuality. The shift in her development is sparked by the therapist's telling her to give up her anger at men and go out and get laid. Erica's night with Charlie the painter literally breaks Act II into two separate units of dramatic action. Wanting to confirm this, I started rereading a few of the current screenplays I was using as teaching films in class, *Body Heat* and *Manhattan*.

In *Body Heat*, Ned Racine (William Hurt) is a man looking for a quick score. When he meets the married Matty Walker (Kathleen Turner) and begins an intense sexual relationship with her, she casually mentions that she wishes her husband were dead so the two of them could be together. "It's what I want the most," she tells him. For Ned, it's the quick score he's been dreaming of: "The man's gonna die for no reason but we want him dead."

Ned plans and executes the murder of Matty's husband around the middle of Act II, around page 60, an action that seals his fate. The murder sequence is the event which links the first half of Act II with the second half of Act II. Looking at it in a story overview, Ned and Matty meet in Act I; at Plot Point I, they have sex. The first part of Act II builds their relationship, sexually, and the seed for murder is planted. When the murder occurs, the police investigate. Plot Point II occurs when Ned tells his friend, the detective in charge of the murder investigation, that he's going to continue seeing Matty. Act III shows Matty setting him up for having committed the crime. The murder is the key event that leads the story to its conclusion.

In Woody Allen's *Manhattan*, when Ike (Allen) and Mary (Diane Keaton) first meet, they don't like each other. She's having an affair with his best friend, Yale (Michael Murphy), a married man, and he finds her to be a pseudo-intellectual, a phony. He goes his way, she goes hers. Then they meet again by accident at the museum one night and discover they like each other. They spend the night walking and talking about everything and nothing. Several days later, on a lonely Sunday afternoon, Mary calls Ike and they spend the afternoon together. Their friendship intensifies, and they end up having sex. It happens right around page 60.

Three films where an event happens in the middle of Act II, an event that holds the story together and moves it forward simultaneously. Just to be sure, I went back to *Chinatown* to see if I could find a similar story point occurring in the middle of Act II. As I reread the script from this perspective, I saw that when Jake Gittes learns Evelyn Mulwray has married her father's business partner, it is a major story point. It pushes the story forward, because Gittes has now established a motive that could possibly help explain the murder of Hollis Mulwray.

I began to see the relationship between these stories: they all had some event happening in the middle of Act II, like a link in the chain of dramatic action. If the screenwriter could establish a story point in the middle of Act II, he or she could prepare, organize and structure the material into two basic units of dramatic action. In that way, the writer could control the story line and not get lost during the actual writing.

Wanting to verify that I was on the right track, I went and looked at other films. In *Annie Hall*, Alvy and Annie meet at Plot Point I, and in the middle of Act II they move in together, which becomes the catalyst that exposes the basic weakness of their relationship. Same thing in *Three Days of the Condor*; after Redford kidnaps Faye Dunaway, he convinces her of his innocence around page 60 and she agrees to help him. He has been a victim during the first half of Act II, and the "rules" of dramatic story progression demand that he become active during the second half.

When I started using this concept of a "middle point" in the Act II workshop, it worked extremely well. It gave the writers a way to develop this sixty-page unit of dramatic action. During two different workshops, I had the writers structure Act II around an event that takes place about page 60. If they knew the Plot Point at the end of Act I and the Plot Point at the end of Act II, they could determine this middle point.

I was amazed at the results. Once my students understood what they had to do, I saw they had a firm grasp on Act II; for the first time, they could control it. No longer would they have to dive into sixty blank pages, struggling to find their way to Plot Point II. They didn't get lost. They knew where they were going and how to get there.

That's when I had a sudden insight: when you're *in* the *Paradigm*, you can't *see* the *Paradigm*. I understood that watching a movie and writing a screenplay have the same relationship as an apple and an orange. When I'm watching a good movie, I'm sitting in my seat, eyes glued to the screen, emotionally wired to what's happening in the story. It's really the screenwriter who's leading us through the story. And if the writer doesn't know what's happening, who does? Developing this middle point, I saw, could become a tool, a technique, to help keep screenwriters on track so they're able to build their story with maximum dramatic value.

I used this new awareness in my workshops after that and confirmed how effective it is in preparing and writing Act II. I wanted to give it a name. After a lot of debate and input from my students, I decided to call it the *Mid-Point*, because this particular event occurs in the middle of Act II. It could either be a dramatic sequence, like the murder in *Body Heat*, or a simple action or line or two of dialogue. But the function remains the same: the Mid-Point is an event that moves the story forward, shifting the action from the First Half of Act II into the Second Half of Act II. Not only does it help the writer structure and write Act II, it's also a great help in preparing the material. Once again, it confirmed the importance of dramatic structure in preparing and writing a screenplay.

When I drew the *Paradigm* of *An Unmarried Woman*, it looked like this:

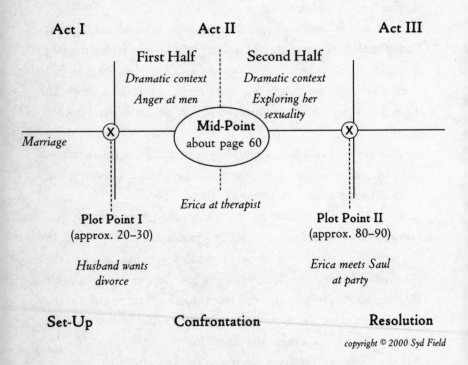

I went back to the definition of what a screenplay is: a story told with pictures, in dialogue and description, held together by the context of dramatic structure. Screenplays are all about structure, while movies are all about story. You can't have one without the other. Without structure, there is only a random progression of events leading nowhere, like two parallel lines moving toward infinity. With structure, there is clarity, insight and understanding.

With my new understanding of the Mid-Point, my awareness and approach to screenwriting changed. I understood that structure is not something rigid and inflexible. It's more like a tree that bends in the wind but doesn't break. It is a fluid construct, like gravity; it holds the screenplay, and the movie, in place.

From that moment on, the nature of dramatic structure became the focus of my teaching. It underscored and heightened my enjoyment of going to the movies. Looking at, studying and analyzing *An Unmarried Woman* was the key that opened me up to the secret of writing Act II.

No matter what the evolution of movie storytelling might be, or might become, no matter how many different ways the language of film may be articulated in the future, certain truths remain. One of them is that in every story, there will always be a beginning, middle and end, though not necessarily in that order.

Of that, I was sure.

16

Time Past,
Time Present

*"Form follows structure;
structure doesn't follow form."*
—I. M. PEI
Architect

It was a late afternoon in January when I stepped off the plane in Oslo, Norway, and I was immediately engulfed with a blast of icy air that took my breath away. It was the early eighties, and *Screenplay* had exploded in terms of popularity, and as a result I had been invited to lecture and teach at universities across the country. Foreign governments were also inviting me to speak and conduct workshops so that I could illustrate how dramatic structure was related to the global evolution currently going on in the movies. Over and over again, filmmakers from various countries were sharing with me how they felt that something was going on in American film, and they wanted to find out what that "something" was. They wanted to understand what was not working in their movies. While they didn't necessarily "like" the American movie in terms of content, they liked the form, the seamless qualities, of our films.

I had been invited to Oslo as a guest of the Norwegian government to give a series of screenwriting workshops for the national film industry. Someone from the Ministry of Culture was there to greet me at the gate, and I was whisked through Customs and into the warm car that was waiting. The sun was bright, the shadows stark and the cold intense as we drove through the picturesque city. I thought about one of my literary idols, the great Norwegian playwright Henrik Ibsen, and how his plays like *Hedda Gabler*, *The Wild Duck*, *Enemy of the People*, *Ghosts* and many others had revolutionized and shaped world theater and changed the face and nature of modern drama.

I checked into the hotel, washed up and was met in the lobby by my hosts, the minister and deputy minister of culture, along with a well-known Norwegian producer, John Jacobsen, the man who had originally contacted me in Los Angeles. I was welcomed with great hospitality and friendliness and taken to a fine restaurant that Ibsen himself had frequented; there was even a plaque on the wall commemorating the fact. How ironic, I thought; during his lifetime Ibsen had been dismissed in his native land as being too radical, too revolutionary, and it was only in his declining years that he was able to see one of his plays produced in Norway. Only after the world had acknowledged and acclaimed him as a Master of Theater had his own country accepted him. Sitting in this restaurant where the great Ibsen may have conceived and written some of his masterpieces put me in a state of gratitude and bliss; it was almost like sitting in a shrine. Either that, or I was totally zonked from the champagne and jet lag.

That first weekend, I conducted a screenwriting seminar for about a hundred Norwegian writers, discussing current movies and the changes taking place in international cinema. During the two-day session, I talked abut the nature of screenplay structure, introduced the *Paradigm* and discussed the many different ways of creating character, using *Chinatown* as my teaching film. After lunch we screened it and I analyzed it in terms of structure and character. A few days later, I gave the same workshop for a group of producers, directors, actors, readers and executives who had been selected by the National Film Commission, but in this course, the emphasis was on reading and evaluating the screenplay rather than on writing it. This, it was explained to me, was the real purpose of my visit: to put the writer and the reader on the same page; to instill a comprehensive understanding of the form, craft and dramatic structure of the modern film. The Norwegians know the value of having an international film success, and since the country had, at the time, sizable national funds available for film production, they wanted to capitalize on it.

After these two workshops, I was taken to the mountains and ensconced in a small, five-star hotel at a famous ski resort, where I had been invited to conduct a weeklong screenwriting course for about twenty prestigious Norwegian screenwriters, playwrights and novelists, along with a few directors and producers. Cloistered in this beautiful forest hotel, we spent the week talking, reading, watching movies and exploring the art and craft of screenwriting. The time together allowed us to break down the barriers of language and culture, and the forest environment was the perfect backdrop.

In the beginning, we focused on the distinctions between film, TV, stage and the novel and how to adapt from one form into another. Our start point was simple: what made the screenplay, as an art form, different from the play or novel? We also talked extensively about the distinctions between the European film and the Hollywood film. I illustrated dramatic structure by explaining the *Paradigm*, and stated that a screenplay is different from a novel or play because it's *a story told with pictures*. As screenwriters, we had to identify our ideas, find the "pictures" to illustrate those ideas, then build a story around them.

One night after dinner, a few of us went for a walk which was to be followed by one of those famous invigorating Scandinavian saunas. I donned my newly purchased winter gear and joined the others outside. As we followed the trails the sky was blazing with stars, so clear and bright it seemed I could almost touch them.

I don't remember exactly how it happened, but we started talking about time and its relationship to plays, movies and screenplays. I shared my opinion that the best scripts generally follow an incident or an event that is resolved over a short period of time—a few hours, a few days, sometimes a few months. As we continued our walk and conversation I looked into the night sky and was reminded of the phenomenon astronomers call "look-back time," the time it takes for the light of a distant star to reach the earth, measured in "light-years." In most cases, it takes many millions of light-years before the light of a distant star reaches us. So, as we stand in present time gazing at the light emitted from stars in the night sky, the light we see could be millions of years old. In essence, we're looking back into time.

We all agreed that we measure time in different ways. We walked in silence for a few moments, listening to the crunch of our boots in the freshly fallen snow. One of the writers, a well-known novelist, said the only constants of the universe are time, space and gravity, and he shared his new insight that the *Paradigm* is a lot like gravity because it's the unseen structure that holds the story in place. Another writer commented that he found the *Paradigm* valid in terms of writing for television. He was writing a six-hour miniseries for television and only now understood that he could structure the entire six hours on the *Paradigm* and then structure each of the three two-hour episodes individually with their own *Paradigm*.

Another writer wondered aloud whether the *Paradigm* would be applicable to stories told in "flashbacks." "Of course," I replied. "You just have to be careful how you use it." But when asked how I would structure a movie that cuts back and forth between time, I didn't have a ready answer.

We walked back to the hotel, spent a glorious time in the sauna and had a nightcap together. When I left, the others were still in a lively discussion about structure and the *Paradigm*. That night, as I crawled into bed, I realized I had no answers for writing a film based on flashbacks—or any kind of nonlinear film, for that matter. But the conversation had planted a seed that was soon going to blossom.

Over the next few days, as we discussed movies and the craft of screenwriting, we focused on the challenge of writing flashbacks. Flashbacks, I knew, can be one of the parts of a linear film or the basis of an entire film. Either way, their function is to move the story forward or to reveal information about the main character. I recalled something Waldo Salt had told me a few years earlier. He said that when he was writing *Midnight Cowboy*, he never thought in terms of flashbacks, only in terms of the *flashpresent*. Flashbacks, he said, are those visual moments that show the character recalling a particular incident or event in the past that is related to a situation in present time. Like Alvy remembering those "pieces of relationship" with Annie Hall. Similarly, in *The Wild Bunch*, when Pike Bishop and Deke Thornton remember those days and nights in prison, the scenes show us the past relationship between the two men and help shed light on the present situation.

Waldo believed that most flashbacks occur within the present moment, and that's why he categorized them as flashpresents, rather than flash*backs*. Would it be possible to structure a movie using the concept of a flashpresent? What would happen if a film cut back and forth between past time and present time? Would the *Paradigm* still apply? We talked about the importance of a character's memory through the flashpresent during the rest of the week, and though we raised many valuable questions, we came up with no answers.

When the Norwegian workshop was over and we were enjoying our last meal together, one of the writers, a famous Norwegian novelist, told me he had been working on a novel for almost two years and that when the workshop began, he had been stuck, unable to move forward. He confessed that he really hadn't known how to fix it. As a last resort, he continued, he had come to the workshop, thinking he would put the novel aside and start working on a screenplay. Then he confided to me that during our discussions of the *Paradigm*, he suddenly found the solution he had been seeking. Only now did he understand what he had to do to fix his novel, and he wanted to thank me for showing him the way.

I never saw him again, but a few years later I received his book, along with a note telling me his novel was currently one of the top-selling books in Norway. "I owe you one," he said.

My experience in Norway had demonstrated to me that the writer could use the *Paradigm* as an effective means to navigate, or chart, the story line in any narrative and visual form. The *Paradigm* was relevant not only for the feature-length screenplay but was equally applicable to short films, television miniseries, novels and plays. There's always a beginning, middle and end, and a certain point at which the beginning turns into the middle and the middle into the end.

Several months after the Norwegian workshop, I was invited by the Belgian government to teach a screenwriting workshop in Brussels. In the Norwegian workshop, I'd learned that most European movies are about ninety minutes in length. The Belgian workshop, also composed of writers, actors, producers and directors, wanted to address how the European approach to writing a screenplay differed from the Hollywood approach. Specifically, the participants wanted to know how I would structure a European film that is nonlinear. Does the idea of the movie influence its structure? they asked. Of course, I replied. Film is a universal language. While the two styles may differ, they are still the same in the sense of telling a story with pictures. I knew, for instance, that European culture is steeped in the tradition of literature and that European filmmakers approach their filmmaking from this same tradition. Therefore, the idea behind the film is often more important than the story, whereas in the American movie the idea is developed into a story and then dramatized into a story line.

When I expressed this idea at the next session, I was greeted with howls of derision, and we started an intense dialogue about the distinctions between the American and European film. As I was questioned, doubted and argued with, I tried to illustrate my point of view with two different examples, both dealing with the construct of time.

One of the most fascinating directors for me was Alain Resnais, the brilliant creator of *Hiroshima, Mon Amour, Night and Fog* and many other great movies. In particular, I had always been fascinated with his *Last Year at Marienbad* (Alain Robbe-Grillet). The whole movie is about the subjective context of time, steeped, as it were, in fantasy and alienation. Four characters (they have no names) meet at a plush estate, where a man, X, tries to convince a woman, A, they had met last year at a resort, perhaps Marienbad, and she had promised to run away with him this year. That's his point of view. We don't know if they really met, or whether it's simply a fantasy, wishful thinking or a figment of his imagination. The element of time past, time present and time future collide within the subjective reality of their characters. In the world of our imagination, Resnais says, time has no linear relevance; there is no past, no future, only now.

I wondered how an American movie would handle this idea of time. As I was thinking about this, one of my favorite romantic movies, *An Affair to Remember* (Delmer Daves, Leo McCarey), popped into my head. To even think about comparing these two films is really stretching things a bit. But the more I thought about it, the more I began to see a connection, a link of time. *Last Year at Marienbad* is subjective, *An Affair to Remember* sentimental and objective, a story about unfulfilled love, not about the landscape of time and memory. But *An Affair to Remember* is a movie that uses the device of time as an essential part of the story, as opposed to *Last Year at Marienbad*, which dramatizes the idea of the subjective reality of time.

The story of *An Affair to Remember* is simple: Cary Grant and Deborah Kerr meet on an ocean liner, have an intense affair and, even though she's betrothed to another, agree to meet a year later if they still feel the same, at a certain time and place. Cut to a year later. She races to meet him, is hit by a car, and obviously the two miss their appointment with destiny. The only distinction between the two movies is their approach; one is based on an intellectual idea, the other is simply the basis of a romantic story. Seeing it put in this context, the Belgian writers began to understand one of the major distinctions in how the Americans and the Europeans approach their stories.

When I returned home from the Brussels workshop, I found myself thinking more and more about the concept of linear and nonlinear structure. That's when I began to understand that if the story line is laid out from beginning to end, then it could be shuffled and rearranged at will. While I was working on *Hollywood and the*

Stars, I remembered this kind of structure from the opening sequence of *Beau Geste* (Robert Carson). Made in 1939, it is one of the early adventure films; from the very first moment that we see the fort standing isolated in the desert against the distant skyline, there is mystery, suspense, tension.

The film opens with a mounted unit of the Foreign Legion arriving at an abandoned fort in the desert. Dead men, armed with rifles, are propped up in the turrets. When the bugler volunteers to investigate, we watch him scale the wall and follow him inside as he finds the fort littered with dead bodies. We cut back outside the fort, to the officer in charge, and suddenly hear gunshots. Who fired them? Why? The bugler does not respond, so the officer in charge investigates. He finds nothing except dead bodies. What happened? Suddenly the fort bursts into flame. Who started the fire? What happened to the bugler after he entered the fort? Questions, questions, questions.

I love that opening. If the purpose of the first ten minutes of a movie is to grab the audience's attention, then *Beau Geste* succeeds totally on that score. The story had dictated the structure of the opening. That's when I confirmed that if I wanted to tell a story in which time plays a prominent part, I would first have to structure it as a linear story, from beginning to end, point A to point Z. The opening of the film poses the question of what happened at the fort. That sets up the story, so the rest of the film flashes back to show us what happened, and the story ends where it began. If I wanted to write a nonlinear story, I had to first lay it out in a linear fashion, from beginning to end. Once I knew where the story was going, I could go back and chop it up into pieces like a jigsaw puzzle, then structure the pieces any way I wanted them. Just like *Last Year at Marienbad* and *The English Patient* (Anthony Minghella, based on the novel by Michael Ondaatje).

How could I express this in my screenwriting workshops? The answer was obvious. I needed an example to illustrate the nonlinear structure, a movie that allowed me to explore the element of time as an integral part of the story line. Once again, I had no answers, only questions.

One day, I was talking with a friend of mine, Jack Hill, the noted writer-director of several classic low-budget, hip seventies films like *Switchblade Sisters, Spider Baby* and *The Big Doll House*, to name a few. He has an extraordinary mind when it comes to movies, and I guess that's why Quentin Tarantino calls him his mentor. When I mentioned I was looking for a film that dealt with the idea of time, Jack immediately recommended *The Killing*, written by Stanley Kubrick with Jim Thompson. He told me it probably had everything I was looking for. Now, I had not seen *The Killing* for many years, but as I recalled, it had been structured like a jigsaw puzzle.

I started calling around to see how I could get a copy of the Stanley Kubrick film. I found out James Harris had coproduced it with Kubrick, and I'd recently had the opportunity of spending time with Harris when he was teaching a class at Sherwood Oaks. I called James and asked whether it would be possible to see the movie. By coincidence, he said, they had just completed screening a trial video version, and if I didn't mind its not being a finished product, I could borrow a copy. I drove over to his office, picked up a copy, took it home, sat down and watched.

The movie, made in 1956, is considered one of the last films made in the classic film noir tradition of the forties, but as usual, Kubrick added his own unique touch. Based on the Lionel White novel *Clean Break*, the story is about a racetrack robbery, but the simple linear story line is broken down into a nonlinear presentation.

Powered by the intricate details that go into the planning of a major heist, the story moves backward and forward through time. Time is revealed through the characters' actions, structured in a novelistic, nonlinear story line.

The robbery coincides with the running of the seventh race, and the very first images we see on screen are the horses moving onto the track. Several times during the course of the film we see this same shot of the horses leaving the stables and entering the track. Robbing the racetrack in and of itself is not very significant, either in terms of action or character, but it's the way the story's told that makes it so noteworthy. Kubrick notes, "It was the handling of time that may have made this more than just a good crime film."

As the film begins, we watch Marvin Unger (Jay C. Flippen) walk into the betting area and, as the narrator states in a voice-over commentary, bets on all the horses in the race. So begins the introduction of the scheme conceived by Johnny Clay (Sterling Hayden), a small-time ex-con. The narrator sets up the action and the characters, tells us their background and the part they play in the robbery.

Once the characters are set up, Johnny brings them together and they go over the heist, detail by detail, down to the last minute. This scene, I saw, was the Plot Point at the end of Act I. At this juncture of the story, we know what they're going to do, we just don't know how they're going to do it. Character and audience are connected by the line of action.

On the day of the robbery, the tension mounts immediately as we see how the little things of life often spoil the most elaborate schemes. The heist itself begins halfway through the movie, at Mid-Point, and Kubrick follows each separate strand of the robbery from each character's point of view, doubling back in time, flashing forward to the next element of the plan. Each time he presents another character's point of view, he moves the clock backward or forward.

The narrator bridges the action: "Earlier that afternoon, Maurice the wrestler started for the track. He was to be there by 4 P.M.," he says in the voice-over. As Maurice moves to the bar, we see Johnny nonchalantly standing by the employee entrance. As per his instructions, the wrestler starts a fight with the bartender, and it takes the entire security force to get him under control. It is 4:23 P.M. before Maurice is finally overwhelmed. And while this is happening, Johnny, unobserved, slips through the track staff's door, which has been left unlocked.

Next, the film cuts back to 2:15 P.M. and we see the robbery from Johnny's point of view. We watch again as Maurice takes on the security force, then see Johnny slip inside the employee entrance. He goes into the employee dressing room, puts on a clown face, takes out a gun stored in a locker and forces his way into the cashier's office. There, he has a cashier dump a cool two million into a large bag. The whole thing takes a little over a minute.

Johnny rips off his mask, hat and jacket, stuffs them into a laundry bag, then heaves it out the window. Now, dressed in a suit and tie, he casually makes his way into the crowd through the commotion in the betting area. We watch as a policeman, a member of the gang, puts the laundry bag into a car and drives away, then drops the bag off in a predesignated motel room. The robbery is successful. Plot Point II.

Though the incidents of the movie are told moving back and forth through time, the context of action is simple: preparing the robbery is the first half of the film, executing the robbery is the second half, and the action keeps these elements firmly in place. I saw that once the structural integrity of a script is established, it's no problem to cut back and forth through time, because the dramatic context of the story has been clearly stated.

The resolution, Act III, begins in present time as the group waits for Johnny to bring the loot. Because of the confusion caused by the robbery, traffic is snarled and Johnny is delayed. The gang sits nervously drinking, listening to the radio reports of the "daring holdup." Suddenly, the door bursts open and two mobsters break in. Shots are fired, and in the ensuing shoot-out everyone is killed except George (Elisha Cook Jr.), who now knows that his wife has betrayed him. Injured, he staggers out of the building as Johnny pulls up with the money, and watches him climb into his car. Then, as George enters his apartment, he sees his wife packing. "Why did you do it?" he asks, and shoots her. He collapses to the floor, knocking over the little birdcage, the symbol of his own limited existence.

Next, we flash back to Johnny watching George staggering into his car. Johnny, knowing something terrible has gone wrong, then drives away, and on the way to the airport stops and buys the largest suitcase he can find and stuffs the money inside. At the airport, he insists on taking the large suitcase with him as a carry-on, but the clerk tells him it's against the rules. Reluctantly, he checks the bag through to Boston. We follow the bag as it's hurled onto the conveyor belt, piled on top of the luggage cart and started on its way to the plane. At this point, we know something is going to happen, we just don't know what.

An older woman stands at the gate cradling her small dog, waiting for her husband to arrive. As the luggage cart moves toward the plane, the dog leaps from the woman's arms and races onto the tarmac. The luggage truck, Johnny's suitcase prominently perched on top, swerves to avoid hitting the dog, and the suitcase topples over, spilling its contents of two million in cash to the winds. Johnny looks on horrified, numb with shock and disbelief. "The best-laid plans of mice and men go oft astray," the poet says, illustrating one of Kubrick's favorite themes.

"Make a run for it," Johnny's girlfriend tells him, but he mumbles, "What's the difference" and, resigned to his fate, turns around to face the two FBI agents advancing toward him, guns drawn. Fade-out. The end.

After analyzing the structural components of *The Killing*, I knew that there's no real difference in preparing a linear and a nonlinear film. Whether it's a story told in a straight line, from beginning to end, or a story that's not told in a straight line, the *Paradigm* works.

More important, I knew now, without a doubt, that the form of the screenplay is constant. Like gravity, it is structure that holds everything together, regardless of whether it's in a linear or nonlinear form.

17

New Voices,
New Visions

"PULP (pulp) n. 1. A soft, moist, shapeless mass of matter.

2. A magazine or book containing lurid subject matter and being characteristically printed on rough, unfinished paper."

—QUENTIN TARANTINO, ROGER AVARY
Preface to *Pulp Fiction*

It was the middle of the afternoon on New Year's Eve day of 1989 when I stuffed the manuscript of *Selling a Screenplay* into a large FedEx envelope, got into my car and drove down to the post office to send it off to New York. I knew my editor wouldn't read it until after the holidays, but I didn't care. The book was finished. I could usher in the New Year with a sense of satisfaction and relief.

Selling a Screenplay seemed like the culmination of the eighties for me. I had spent more than two years writing the book, had watched it grow and evolve through several permutations before it reached its final form, and I was very pleased with the result. My objective was to give a voice to the buyer, "the other side of the desk."

In Hollywood, everyone is either a buyer or a seller. What does the buyer look for? When a writer writes a screenplay, he or she has to sell it to an agent. The agent has to sell it to a production company or studio. Then the executive has to sell it to his or her boss. The boss then has to sell it to upper management, the head of the studio. If it's a large-budget movie, the studio head has to sell it to the CEO, who then has to sell it to the board. And so on and so on. That's just the way it works.

I presented the buyer's point of view because I wanted to illustrate the process that all pitches go through before a penny is spent in buying, optioning or developing a screenplay. I went all over Hollywood, interviewing readers, producers, executives and heads of studios. In addition, I included interviews with writers Oliver Stone, Alvin Sargent, Anna Hamilton Phelan, James L. Brooks, Douglas Day Stewart, Earl Wallace, Bill Kelley and Dan Petrie Jr., who shared their screenwriting process and confided how some of their scripts sometimes had to wait ten or more years before they got the green light for production.

When I returned home from the post office, I was surprised to find a message from my editor on the answering machine. He wished me a happy New Year and hoped I had the same success with *Selling a Screenplay* that I'd had with *The Screenwriter's Workbook*.

Published in 1984, *The Screenwriter's Workbook* was received with great enthusiasm and popularity and went into three printings within the first year. Colleges and universities around the country picked it up and started using it as a text in their creative writing classes. The success of the book resulted in my traveling extensively, both in the U.S. and foreign countries.

Meanwhile, Sherwood Oaks was finding it difficult to compete with major colleges and universities, who were now offering their own continuing education courses in film, and was in the process of shutting down. During this time, many people asked if I would be willing to teach writing workshops in their homes. So, once or twice a week, I started teaching intimate workshops for ten or twelve students. I carried a small whiteboard under my arm, propped it up against a chair in the living room and started guiding people through the process of writing a screenplay.

In this way I taught many professional writers, directors, development people, advertising executives, actors, attorneys, housewives, doctors, physicists, set designers and production managers, some famous, some not so famous. I was invited to teach a group of elite journalists, including the editors of the two major Los Angeles newspapers and feature writers for several prominent national magazines.

During the middle to late eighties, I spent several years participating as a final judge in the prestigious Nissan screenwriting competition and was invited to become a member of the prominent Filmic Writing Advisory Board at the University of Southern California's School of Cinema/Television, then joined the school's film faculty. I taught, gave lectures and workshops at UCLA and at UC Berkeley, Santa Barbara, Davis and San Diego and was invited as guest lecturer to Harvard, Stanford, NYU, Columbia and several other prominent universities. I spent the better part of two years traveling to various cities on weekends, crisscrossing the country every few weeks under the auspices of the American Film Institute. I became an adviser to the NEA in Washington, reading grants and proposals, and had been elected to chair the Academic Liaison Committee at the Writers Guild of America West, where I had the opportunity of introducing several programs which are still functioning today.

I read thousands of screenplays and was asked to be an expert legal witness for several copyright infringement cases for clients like Steven Spielberg, Universal Pictures, United Artists, Sylvester Stallone and many, many other individuals and companies. I was a screenwriting consultant for the entire Animation Department at Disney, working on *Oliver!* and *The Little Mermaid*, gave special courses for the story departments at 20th Century Fox and Universal Pictures, was a screenplay consultant to Tri-Star Pictures and was called in as a consultant on several major films, including *Wall Street*, *White Palace*, *Broadcast News* and others.

During the eighties, I traveled extensively throughout Europe presenting workshops, seminars and lectures. Norway, then Brussels, had only been the beginning. From there it was on to Toronto, Edmonton and Montreal, then Berlin, Zurich, Paris, Amsterdam, Rome, back again to Oslo, Madrid, Berlin and several times London. I started using new teaching films; instead of *Chinatown* I used *Witness* (Earl Wallace, Bill Kelley); *The Big Easy* (Dan Petrie Jr.); *Broadcast News* (James L. Brooks); *Gorillas in the Mist*, written by one of my students, Anna Hamilton Phelan; and *Ordinary People* (Alvin Sargent).

As the dawn of the nineties approached I was getting burned out from the constant traveling. Once again, I started feeling that the end of one thing is always the beginning of something else. I thought about writing a new book, but had no clear vision of it.

As I wondered what the new decade might have in store for me, I attended a Writers Guild screening of a newly released film called *Dances With Wolves*, written by Michael Blake and directed by Kevin Costner. I loved it; the epic, visual sweep of the story reminded me of classic westerns like *Red River* and *The Searchers*. *Dances With Wolves* was a story about a man on a spiritual quest, and I was struck by its originality and point of view. For me, the film poignantly captured the "passing of the way," a change of life in which the old gives rise to the new. The Native Americans were richly portrayed, unlike the stereotypical white soldiers, and expressed a sacred worldview affirming the relationship between all living things, what modern physicists now term the Gaia Principle. It was unlike any western I had ever seen. Yes, it said, we are one planet, one world.

A few weeks later, I was conducting a workshop in Vienna and found myself talking about the film. I didn't remember it in all its detail, but what had moved me so much was the spiritual dynamic it expressed. It captured the Native American belief that all life is sacred, all life is related: the trees, the animals, the stones, the earth and the sky. The earth is just one giant, wondrous, living organism, and every living thing on this planet is connected to the life force. We are all the same, and we must honor and respect ourselves and each other, whether human, creatures and plants, or things.

It was around this time that I had a vague notion about writing a book analyzing the relationship between the screenplay and the movie. The more I thought about it, the more attracted I became to the idea. I could choose three or four films, analyze them in terms of character and action, include excerpts from the screenplays and add interviews with the screenwriters. I could show the distinctions between what's on the page and what's on the screen and create the kind of a book that I personally would like to read.

After seeing *Dances With Wolves*, I felt the idea had a lot of merit, but I needed some other films to analyze and write about. I started viewing movies with the purpose of using them in the book.

A short time later, I saw *Terminator 2: Judgment Day* (James Cameron, William Wisher). Putting it mildly, the film was a revelation; it absolutely blew me away. As I sat perched on the edge of my seat, totally mesmerized by the visual pyrotechnics, I knew this movie *was* the future. I had seen *Terminator* years earlier, and thought the idea behind the film was incredible, but nothing prepared me for what I was now seeing on the screen.

If I asked myself what the future of film would look like in terms of special effects and computer technology, it would be *Terminator 2*. Special effects fused into an active, dynamic story line, expanding and heightening the moviegoing experience. When I watched the T-1000 morph out of the linoleum tile into the holographic form of the night watchman, I was knocked breathless, totally awestruck by what I was seeing.

I walked out of the film with my pulse pounding and images flooding my mind. I couldn't get the movie out of my head. I was emotionally struck by the Terminator's sacrificing his "life" at the end. When the Terminator, a cyborg, a robot, sacrifices his life for the good of humankind, I thought about Joseph Campbell's statement that a hero "is someone who has given his or her life to something bigger than oneself." And, in the very last shot, we hear Sarah Conner (Linda Hamilton) telling us in a voice-over narration, "If a machine can learn the value of a human life, then maybe we can, too." All this in a shoot-'em-up action movie.

Was there some kind of new direction in film emerging? Some kind of shift in our collective unconscious, a new trend, in terms of themes and ideas? For days, I was caught in swirling thoughts of a new evolutionary force that might be emerging in Hollywood. When I told my editor in New York about it, and added that I wanted to base my next book on an in-depth analysis of modern screenplays like *Dances With Wolves* and *Terminator 2*, he said he liked the idea very much and suggested I add two more films. Did I have any ideas? I mentioned two movies that were popular at the time, but which I hadn't seen: *Thelma & Louise* (Callie Khouri), and *Silence of the Lambs* (Ted Tally). My editor liked the idea well enough to tell me to just go ahead and start writing.

I chose those two films for a couple of reasons. The first was that I had followed the turbulent and stormy tribulations of MGM and the Italian financier who was accused of defrauding the studio. *Thelma & Louise* had been caught in the legal struggle that ensued, but when it finally reached the screens it was an instant hit; everyone, it seemed, had an opinion about it. Second, *Silence of the Lambs* had been released a few months earlier, and the character of Hannibal Lecter was turning out to be *the* hot topic on late-night TV. I felt that gave both films a lot of merit. And all four movies had been released within six months of each other, in '90 and '91, right at the beginning of the new decade. I found that quite interesting.

Looking more closely at the four films, I saw they reflected, at least from my point of view, four different aspects of movies in the nineties. *Thelma & Louise* represented a new, more complex form of the "buddy movie." In this original screenplay, the two main characters were women, which was a significant departure. More important, I found that this was only the outer shell of the story line; the heart of the movie was the journey to insight and self-discovery both women took. *Silence of the Lambs* was the absolute horror movie. What made it so horrific was that Hannibal Lecter could easily have been my next-door neighbor. An adaptation from a Thomas Harris novel, Ted Tally's screenplay was extraordinary. *Dances With Wolves* was the author's adaptation from his own novel, and *Terminator 2: Judgment Day* was the sequel to an original screenplay that had taken more than seven years to get made.

As I was preparing the book I began to see four very different themes emerge. *Dances With Wolves* had a spiritual theme woven throughout the journey of John Dunbar's search for himself; *Thelma & Louise* reflected the journey of self-discovery and enlightenment; *Silence of the Lambs*, a story about letting go of the past, took the horror film to a new level; and *Terminator 2: Judgment Day* was, I felt, both prophetic and revolutionary in terms of expanding the technology of film.

To my mind, James Cameron single-handedly oversaw the creation of the new "morphing" computer technology for *Terminator 2: Judgment Day*. And if we hadn't had *T2*, we wouldn't have had the technology to create *Jurassic Park*, *Forrest Gump*, *Toy Story* or even *Titanic*.

For each of these four movies, I illustrated these themes as I analyzed the screenplay in relation to the movie, augmented by the writers' perspectives in their candid and revealing interviews. The result was *Four Screenplays*. Published in the fall of 1994, it was extremely well received, and as of this writing is being used as a text in history, English and philosophy courses in colleges around the country, and has been made available in several different languages.

Shortly after the publication of the book, I was invited to speak at a screenwriting seminar at the Mill Valley Film Festival in California. Mill Valley has a very special place in my heart because it was there, after *Screenplay* was first published, that I conducted my very first two-day screenwriting seminar, which I called "The Screenwriter's Workshop."

Mill Valley is a dedicated, intimate and avant-garde film festival screening a variety of films that are individual in taste, style and vision. During the morning presentation, I spoke about the journey of self-discovery in *Thelma & Louise*, the technological advancement of computer graphics in *Terminator 2: Judgment Day*, the spiritual themes of *Dances With Wolves* and the use of flashbacks in *Silence of the Lambs*. Along the way I incorporated some of Joseph Campbell's ideas and the new cinematic themes I saw taking hold in the nineties. During my talk I casually mentioned that from my perspective, we were in the middle of a revolution—at which point someone raised his hand and asked if I included *Pulp Fiction* as a part of that revolution.

I had a lot of mixed feelings about *Pulp Fiction*. When I had first seen it a few months earlier it was storming across the country, creating an avalanche of opinion. People either loved it or hated it. When I walked out of the screening, I was one of those who hated it. I felt it was way too long, had much too much gratuitous violence and was too talky. Basically, I thought, it was a B movie—shallow, exploitative, the epitome of everything I don't like in the movies. Influential maybe, significant maybe, but in no way revolutionary, at least as I was defining the term.

When I asked the person what he liked about the film he replied that it represented a totally new structure and that he was curious to hear my opinion. Now, I had heard this before; several people had confronted me with the film's structure and "dared" me to analyze it in terms of the *Paradigm*. As far as everybody was concerned it seemed like *Pulp Fiction* was *it*—innovative in thought, concept and execution, everything a revolutionary film should be.

I replied that *Pulp Fiction* might be influential and striking in form, but to my mind it was a still a B movie, and because of that I would not classify it as revolutionary. After I finished the seminar and was preparing to leave, I was approached by a man who was intrigued by my evaluation of *Pulp Fiction* and invited me to be a guest on the local National Public Radio station.

The next day at the NPR station, the interviewer asked me what kind of an impact I thought *Pulp Fiction* might have on young, emerging filmmakers. Was it a landmark film? It was a huge topic, to be sure, and I tried to answer it by saying *Pulp Fiction* seemed to spark a new awareness in the filmgoer's consciousness. Yes, I added, we were riding a wave of change, and while technology would definitely affect the movies, the real "revolution" was going to manifest itself more in terms of form than content—that is, *what* you show and *how* you show it. *Pulp Fiction*, I said, was definitely a part of that.

"Why?" he asked. I explained that Hollywood was in a period of change comparable to the late twenties when sound was introduced. At that time, through audiences' desire to hear actors "speak," the camera was imprisoned inside a refrigerator, and as a result we lost all the movement and fluidity of the camera we had attained during the Silent Era. Scenes had to be staged around the microphone. The actors entered the camera's frame, spoke their lines and exited from the camera's frame; the actors, the writers, the cameramen, became the prisoners of sound.

The screenwriters of the Silent Era did not know much about writing dialogue; their forte was telling stories with pictures, so Hollywood brought in Broadway playwrights to help them tell their stories in words, not pictures. That's a theme F. Scott Fitzgerald touches on in his final novel, *The Last Tycoon*. Since that time, we've remained in a state of technological flux: from black and white to Technicolor, standard screen size to CinemaScope, 35mm to 70mm—and now, computer graphics and digital technology. It's the screenwriters who have really become the artisans of change, because they must learn to adapt this new hi-tech awareness to their screenplays.

"What do you think makes *Pulp Fiction* so influential?" the interviewer asked. I told him I had asked myself that same question many times and had no real answer. I concluded the interview by saying *Pulp Fiction* is definitely an influential film, and may even be revolutionary, and left it at that. Because the movie was such a hot topic of conversation, I thought I needed to look at it more closely.

When I returned home from Mill Valley, I got ahold of the screenplay. When I opened it, I read on the title page that *Pulp Fiction* was really "three stories . . . about one story." I turned the page and read two dictionary definitions of *Pulp*: "A soft, moist, shapeless mass of matter," and "A magazine or book containing lurid subject matter and being characteristically printed on rough, unfinished paper." That's certainly an accurate description of the film. But on the third page, I was surprised to find a Table of Contents. That was odd, I thought; who writes a Table of Contents for a screenplay? I saw that the film was broken down into five individual parts: Part I was the *Prologue*; Part II, *Vincent Vega and Marcellus Wallace's Wife*; Part III, *The Gold Watch*; Part IV, *The Bonnie Situation*; and Part V, the *Epilogue*.

As I studied the script, I saw that all three stories bounce off the inciting incident of Jules and Vinnie retrieving Marcellus Wallace's briefcase from the four kids. This one incident became the hub of all three stories, and I noticed that each story is structured as a whole, in linear fashion; it starts at the beginning of the action, goes into the middle, then proceeds to the end. Each section is like a short story, presented from a different character's point of view.

I remembered Henry James's literary question: *What is character but the determination of incident? And what is incident but the illumination of character?* If this key incident is the hub of the story, as I now understood it, then everything in the film, whether actions, reactions, thoughts, memories or flashbacks, is tethered to this one incident.

Suddenly, it all made sense. Understanding that *Pulp Fiction* is "three stories about one story" allowed me to see the film as one unified whole. The movie is three stories surrounded by a prologue and epilogue, what screenwriters call a "bookend" technique, as in *The Bridges of Madison County* (Richard LaGravenese), *Sunset Boulevard* or *Saving Private Ryan* (Robert Rodat).

Now I began to see how the film was put together. The *Prologue* sets up Pumpkin and Honey Bunny (Tim Roth and Amanda

Plummer) in a coffee shop discussing various types of small-time robbery. When they finish their meal, they pull their guns and rob the place. The film freezes and we cut to the main titles. Then we cut into the middle of a conversation between Jules (Samuel L. Jackson) and Vinnie (John Travolta), who are having an enlightening discussion about the relative merits of a Big Mac here and abroad.

That sets up the entire film and tells us everything we need to know: the two men are killers working for Marcellus Wallace (Ving Rhames); their job, their dramatic need, is to retrieve the briefcase. That's the true beginning of the story. In Part I, Jules and Vinnie arrive, state their position and kill the three guys, and it's only by the grace of God they're not killed themselves. Vinnie takes Mia (Uma Thurman) out to dinner, and after she almost accidentally overdoses, they say good night. Part II is about Butch (Bruce Willis) and his Gold Watch and what happens when he wins the fight instead of losing it as he had agreed to do. Part III deals with cleaning up Marvin's remains, which are splattered all over the car, a continuation of Part I. That's followed by the *Epilogue*, in which Jules talks about his transformation and the significance of Divine Intervention and then Pumpkin and Honey Bunny resume the holdup that began the film in the Prologue.

It became crystal clear to me that no matter what kind of story is being told, whether told in a straight line or not, the story requirements remain the same. No matter what the form of the film, whether linear or nonlinear, there is always going to be a beginning, a middle and an end. A film like *Courage Under Fire* (Patrick Sheane Duncan), for example, or *Groundhog Day* (Danny Rubin, Harold Ramis), or *The Usual Suspects* (Chrisopher McQuarrie), or *The English Patient*, or *Sliding Doors* (Peter Howitt) are all structured around a specific, inciting incident; only when that incident is shown does the story line split off into different directions. To build a nonlinear movie means to define the parts, then structure each part from beginning to end, at which point the screenwriter can put them in any order he or she desires.

I saw that *Pulp Fiction* was indeed a new departure, a kind of beacon leading us into the future, just like Gatsby's green light, because it presents a new way of looking at things. It's as revolutionary in its own way as *Terminator 2: Judgment Day* was.

A few months later, I was in Mexico City conducting a screenwriting workshop for the Mexican government when I was invited to see a new film by the noted Mexican director Jorge Fons called *El Callejón de los Milagros* (*Midaq Alley*) with Salma Hayek, in one of her first major film roles before she became an international star. Released a short time after *Pulp Fiction*, this film seemed more novelistic than cinematic. There were four stories in the film, each one revolving around four or five different characters, all living, working and loving on the same street and linked by an incident that shatters a father-son relationship. This incident affects all the characters in some way, and is woven into the film's structure as characters and events sometimes fold back on themselves novelistically. The film, though high in melodrama, is unique, striking, in terms of concept and execution.

Comparing these two films, *Pulp Fiction* and *El Callejón de los Milagros*, so different in context and culture, yet so similar in form and execution, I began to understand the many different ways a story can be told. When I saw *The English Patient* I liked it very much. I didn't think it was mere coincidence that all these films had emerged at the same time. I thought there might be something larger going on, a new consciousness and awareness in approaching the craft of screenwriting. When I read the screenplay of *The English Patient* I saw there were really two stories entwined between time past and time present. One story, the past, has Almásy (Ralph

Fiennes) and Katherine (Kristin Scott Thomas) meeting and falling in love, and is shown through the memories and flashpresent sequences of the English Patient recalling his memories in present time. Even though the end is the beginning, and the beginning is the end, the two stories move forward in a linear fashion; it's through the brilliant transitions of sight, sound and image that the movie moves so fluidly, illuminating both past and present in an emotional movie experience.

Using this new awareness, I started having my students focus and define the key incident of their stories, then showed them how to fuse the characters and the events into a structural whole. It didn't matter whether it was a linear or nonlinear story line; I wanted my students to understand that screenplay structure is not something embedded in concrete, but flexible, like a tree that bends in the wind but doesn't break. This would allow their stories to be told more visually, with more action than explanation.

To my mind, this is a shift in the craft of screenwriting, because it wasn't too long ago that movie characters needed to explain who they were, what their background was and what their motivation or purpose was. Things were explained through the characters' dialogue. But as a new generation grew up having watched television, it became pretty obvious that their visual sense had been heightened; their stories became more visual, unfolding with clarity and simplicity. It was a clear sign of evolution at work: Steven Spielberg, George Lucas, Francis Ford Coppola, Robert Zemeckis, James Cameron, Terry Malick, Frank Darabont and others had discovered that words of explanation held back the visual line and forward thrust of the visual action.

I saw this same evolutionary force happening after *Pulp Fiction;* the style and personality of Tarantino's voice and vision was beginning to influence filmmakers around the world. The more I traveled, conducting workshops and seeing many different films, the more I understood I had acquired a new way of understanding movies, thanks to *Pulp Fiction*.

As the decade came to a close, I found the influence of *Pulp Fiction* to be a major inspiration for filmmakers, not only in Hollywood, but also in England, Germany, Argentina, Brazil, Mexico and other countries. This new generation of moviemakers is exploring the innovative ground of cinematic territory and is "pushing the envelope" in terms of film form. But no matter how fragmented these artists' stories may be, they follow the same model: beginning, middle and end. Only when the key incident or situation is set up does the story line splinter into different directions, crosscutting between time past and time present.

I think the German film *Run Lola Run*, written and directed by Tom Tykwer, is heavily influenced by *Pulp Fiction*. Fusing animation and special effects into what I call a "one-line movie," the film is not so much a story as an idea, one action told with three different possibilities. Tykwer said in an interview, "Everyone has experienced the feeling of wishing he or she could turn the clock back just twenty minutes and do something differently. You can actually do that in a film." And that's the governing principle behind this movie.

The film tells three stories distinguished by the different choices the main character makes. Lola has twenty minutes to find a bag containing $100,000 that her criminal boyfriend left on the subway; otherwise he's going to be killed. She can't find the bag, so she sets out to raise $100,000. Three different realities are dramatized. In the first one, she runs to her unsympathetic father, who works in a bank, and asks for the money. He says no. She decides to rob the bank, and somehow manages to get away with it, only to be shot and killed by a nervous policeman. That solution is unacceptable.

The second story re-creates the first, except she's delayed by a minute or so, and thus has a different choice to make in order to obtain the money. This time she manages to get the money, but in the end her boyfriend is killed. This, too, is unacceptable, so the film creates a third reality, and this time, after she receives the phone call from her boyfriend, Lola goes to the casino, wins $100,000, makes it to their rendezvous in time, delivers the money safely and they live "happily ever after."

The film moves like the speed of light. Tykwer says, "You can only beat time in movies. In reality, we all know we're victims of time—it's going on, going on, going on, and we can't stop it. Every second we come closer to our own death." Lola manages to beat time only "with the weapon of the movies," he says. Which brings me back to the point that we're in the middle of a cinematic revolution, a revolution accentuated not only by technology but by form.

I look at the movies as an indication of where we are as a society, and since we're a culture of moviegoers, the times are certainly changing. The way filmmakers are telling their stories today is evolving right in front of our eyes. Novelistic in structure, either linear or nonlinear in form, function and design, the movies are pushing all boundaries of visual storytelling. Whether shot digitally or on tape, whether shown in theaters, on television or on the Internet, movies are forging new pathways, leading to an expanded visual experience heralding the sounds and sights of new voices and new visions.

Which is what going to the movies is all about.

18

On Going
to the Movies

"The book says that we may be through with the past,
but the past may not be through with us."
—PAUL THOMAS ANDERSON
Magnolia

Not too long ago, I was invited to an evening at the Writers Guild of America to attend a program with a renowned Academy Award–winning screenwriter-director. A number of writers, directors, producers and guests had also been invited, as well as several film students. The evening began with a screening of the writer-director's latest film, followed by a question-and-answer session. The writer spoke about the genesis of the film and some of the problems he had while writing the screenplay.

Toward the end of the evening, one of the students stood up and asked the filmmaker whether he thought the traditional three-act structure was still relevant. The filmmaker thought for a moment, then replied, "You've got to get beyond all that; you've got to find new ways of telling your story."

I found his remark interesting, because this particular filmmaker, noted for both his writing and directorial talents, has always worked within the framework of a "traditional" three-act structure. As a director, he's known for his straightforward narrative films. While he uses many different filmmaking techniques—like voice-over narration, flashbacks and crosscutting—to tell his stories, his films have always been well structured.

As I was driving home that night I thought a lot about the filmmaker's comment. Many filmmakers today insist the narrative story line is passé, out of date, not "part of the scene" anymore. They loudly proclaim that the three-act structure is dead and no longer pertinent to the modern movie. One filmmaker even went on record to state, "The Hollywood narrative film is in its death throes right now and people are looking for something else. The whole school of Act I/Act II/Act III is destructive to a thriving, growing cinema."

Since *Pulp Fiction* there have been many films that illustrate this approach in fracturing the form, though more for shock value, I think, than for anything else; *Fight Club, Body Shots, Go* and *Best Laid Plans* are just a few examples. These films don't necessarily illustrate a particular intellectual idea, like Alain Resnais did in *Last Year at Marienbad*; they simply seem obligated to break the form for what they term "artistic reasons."

It seems pretty clear that the social and cultural forces working on the "Gen X" and "PlayStation Generation" are actually changing the way we see things. *Run Lola Run* reflects this really well. The movie unfolds like a video game. Every time Lola fails to get the $100,000 to save her boyfriend, guess what? The game's over. She goes back to the beginning and plays another game until she wins.

It's also true that filmmakers are indeed searching for new ways of telling their stories: *Being John Malkovich, The Matrix* (Andy and Larry Wachowski), *Magnolia* (Paul Thomas Anderson), *The Sixth Sense* (M. Night Shyamalan), *Wonder Boys* (Steve Kloves), *American Beauty* (Alan Ball), *Traffic* (Stephen Gaghan) and *Gladiator* (David

Franzoni) push the form both in style and content. At first glance these films may *seem* to be in rebellion against the narrative film, but the truth is they're as traditional as their predecessors.

I agree it's time to push the form. The traditional way of "seeing things" has changed, and we need to be open to the sights and sounds of new voices and new visions. Because of the advance of film technology, many of our movies look great, slick as waxed apples in the supermarket, but they're geared more for the disposable market than anything else. Just look at *Mission Impossible: 2* and *The Perfect Storm*. Both, in cinematic terms, are dazzling, but they're like cotton candy, nothing more than sugar and water. There's no content. As Gertrude Stein once remarked about Oakland, "There ain't no there when you get there."

Movies are a source of both entertainment and enlightenment. So, when I read some of the comments of these filmmakers about pushing the form to another level, I'm a little confused. I love their passion, love their take on things, but when I see what they declare to be their "forward-looking" films, it seems obvious they don't understand the distinction between form and formula.

To me, film is a language that speaks directly to the heart. When I see a movie I like, I can talk endlessly about the visual brilliance of the director, the great acting of the actors, the broad sweep of the photography, the poetry of the editing or the ingeniousness of the special effects. But when I get right down to it, there's only one thing that holds the whole thing together.

And that's the story.

Ideas, concepts, jargon, analytical comments, don't really mean a thing. Whether the movie proceeds in a straight line or a circle, or is fractured and splintered into little pieces, doesn't make a bit of difference. Movies are all about story. No matter who we are, or where we live, or what generation we may belong to, the singular aspects of storytelling remain the same. It's been that way since Plato created stories out of shadows on the wall. The art of telling a story with pictures exists beyond time, culture and language. Walk into the Elmira caves in Spain and look at the rock paintings, or into the Accademia Museum in Venice, and gaze upon those magnificent panels depicting the twelve stations of the cross, and you enter the grand view of visual storytelling.

When I walk into a darkened movie theater and wait for the lights to dim and watch those flickering images of the title sequence unfold, it is a moment of magic. And it's no different now than it was for Shakespeare in sixteenth-century Elizabethan England. Shakespeare knew there were two ways to grab the attention of the audience. The groundlings, as they (the common man) were known, watched the performance standing in the pit, the large open area directly in front of the stage. The majority of the audience were heavy drinkers, and it's well documented that they were not afraid to vocalize their likes and dislikes by throwing rotten eggs or tomatoes at the players if they didn't like what they were seeing. Shakespeare had to grab their attention immediately.

One of the ways he grabbed the audience's attention was by beginning the play with a dynamic action sequence, like the ghost walking the parapet in *Hamlet* or the three witches huddling over the cauldron prophesying the future of Macbeth. The second way was opening with a character scene; in *Romeo and Juliet*, for example, the chorus comes onstage and declares this to be a story about two "star-crossed lovers." We do this in our films today, but instead of the chorus we use a voice-over narrator and he or she tells us what we need to know. Lester, the Kevin Spacey character in *American Beauty*, does this; the movie opens with him telling us, "My name is Lester Burnham. I'm forty-two years old. In less than a year, I'll be dead. . . . In a way, I'm dead already."

The Green Mile (Frank Darabont) uses the "bookend" approach; the opening has the Tom Hanks character, now an old man, reflecting on an incident he experienced while working as a prison guard many years before. The film concludes with him as an old man who has shared his experience with us. Spielberg also does this in *Saving Private Ryan*, when the Matt Damon character revisits the cemetery at the Normandy beachhead and then we flash back into the story. When the story has been told, it ends back at the beginning again, in present time, with the Matt Damon character asking his wife and children if his life has been worth the lives that were lost saving him. It's a strong, character-driven opening.

An action film grabs the attention of the audience immediately. When I first saw *The Matrix*, I had the same feeling I had when I saw *Terminator 2: Judgment Day*. I walked out of the theater knowing "this is the future." *The Matrix* is an incredible blend of mind-grabbing content and dynamic visual execution. The seeds of its origins may be the comic books, but it still incorporates mythological figures who are larger than life. So to say this is a "traditional" or "conventional" film may seem bizarre, but it happens to be true.

The opening scene is no ordinary action sequence of flying fists, fired shots and a few explosions. This is a totally unique ass-grabbing sequence; it pits Trinity (Carrie-Ann Moss), a lone woman, against several armed policemen, all wearing bullet-proof vests. Right before our eyes, in the most amazing physical feats, whether suspended in midair or walking on walls and ceilings, Trinity escapes. We see her leaping from rooftop to rooftop, building to building, totally disregarding gravity as she flies through the air to reach the other side. From there, it's a race against the huge garbage truck to reach the ringing telephone. She makes it in the nick of time and answers the phone just as the truck slams into the telephone booth.

Whoa . . . If that's not a grabber, I don't know what is. In terms of information, we don't know who Trinity is, whether she's a "good guy" or a "bad guy," nor do we know what the story's about, or how she managed to escape the way she did. But it's an opening that certainly grabs our attention.

At this point, I want to know *what* the story is about, and *who* it's about. In dramatic terms, exposition is defined as *the necessary information needed to move the story forward*, and that's exactly what we get next. Neo, the main character (Keanu Reeves), asks Trinity about the Matrix. But she doesn't explain anything; she only warns him that he's in danger because "they're watching you." And, she stresses, "The truth is out there, Neo, and it's looking for you and will find you, if you want it to." Then she's gone.

What is the Matrix? Morpheus explains later that we're inhabiting a parallel universe and that the Matrix is a state of virtual reality, an illusion, maya, and we've all been programmed to accept it *as real*. The truth, the "real" world, has been destroyed and re-created by a race of machines, artificial intelligence and the computers into a form of virtual reality.

So begins the hero's journey. Morpheus (Laurence Fishburne), the rebel leader, is dedicated to waging war against the Matrix to reveal "the truth," thus liberating humanity from the bondage of the machines. Morpheus believes in the prophecy that the rebels' only hope of winning is by finding "the One," a human being endowed with godlike powers who will lead them in their war of liberation. And he believes Neo is "the One." As Morpheus tells Neo, the mind and body are entwined with each other even though they are separate entities; therefore, Morpheus says, if you can control your mind, you can control reality, and thus your destiny.

I love that. An ancient teaching brought into a contemporary situation, futuristic in thought and execution. Neo, like Hamlet, or the warrior Arjuna in the classic Indian tale the Bhagavad Gita, must choose his own destiny. I found this theme of choice to be a recurring motif throughout the film. This is illustrated when Neo receives a package and a cell phone pops out, ringing. Morpheus is on the line. He tells Neo, "They're after you. There are only two ways for you to leave the building; either you choose to leave by the scaffolding hanging outside the window, or you choose to leave as a prisoner." Like Hamlet and Arjuna, Neo embodies the stance of the reluctant hero, and before he can rise to another, higher level of consciousness, he must accept himself and his own destiny.

This fusion of the ancient and futuristic is embodied in the various names used in *The Matrix*. I confess I didn't know what most of the names meant, so I explored their origins. I found the names to be derived from ancient history and mythology. The rebel ship, the *Nebuchadnezzar*, is named after the famed fifth-century-B.C. Babylonian king who's credited with tearing down and rebuilding the ancient temples, so he's both a destroyer and a builder. The name fits the ship's destiny, for it houses the small rebel band determined to destroy and rebuild the Matrix. In Greek mythology *Morpheus* is the god of sleep, responsible for building and weaving the fabric of our dreams in the deep-sleep state. *Neo*, of course, means "new," and *Trinity* has several religious implications. These mythological echoes are simply a way of adding more insight and dimension to the story line.

At this point, the story progresses by action and explanation. Only when Neo can accept being "the One" can he really *be* "the One." In other words, what we believe to be true *is* true. At Plot Point I, during the meeting with Morpheus, Neo is offered a choice: take the blue pill and get ordinary reality, or take the red pill and get the truth. Neo doesn't hesitate—he takes the red one. Reality distorts as he falls between the corridors of virtual reality and the netherworld. In a sequence as bizarre and evocative as a Geiger painting, Neo is reborn as a man freed from the restraints of his limited mind. As the embryo of himself, Neo must retrain both his body and his mind until he is capable of exploring the untapped resources of his unlimited self, as seen in martial arts contests with Morpheus.

Neo's encounter with the Oracle is the Mid-Point of the story. She's a great character. I expected an old, old man, extremely wise, with white hair and possibly a long straggly beard. Instead, I was delightfully surprised to discover a middle-aged woman baking cookies. When she casually asks if he believes he's "the One," Neo shakes his head and says, "I'm just an ordinary guy." Once again, his belief systems, the limitations of his own mind, imprison him. Too bad, she says. Why? he asks. "Because Morpheus believes in you, Neo, and no one, not even you or me, can convince him otherwise," she says. "He believes it so blindly that he's going to sacrifice his life for you. You're going to have to make a choice. On one hand, you'll have Morpheus's life . . . and on the other hand, you'll have your own. . . . One of you is going to die. . . . Which one will be up to you."

She is his "mirror," reflecting what he believes, telling him what she sees within him. His struggle guides him to the understanding that he can wear the mantle of "the One" only if he chooses to. Only when we can give up the concepts of our limited self can we attain enlightenment and liberation. The reluctant hero must accept the challenge of being who he or she really is, in much the same way that Hamlet and Arjuna must choose to accept their own destiny. Whether he likes it or not, Neo is "the One" who has been chosen to "set the times right."

At Plot Point II, Neo makes his decision to rescue Morpheus. "The Oracle told me this would happen," Neo says. "She told me I would have to make a choice. . . ." He pauses, and in one of the earlier drafts of the script says, "I may not be what Morpheus thinks I am, but if I don't try to help him, then I'm not even what I think I am . . . I'm going in after him." When he declares himself in this fashion, it is the first step in accepting himself as "the One." At this juncture, I remembered that moment at Plot Point I when Morpheus asks Neo if he believes in fate. No, Neo replies, "because I don't like the idea that I'm not in control of my life." Whether he believes it or not, whether he knows it or not, he's now in the hands of his fate, his destiny.

After rescuing Morpheus, Neo doesn't make it out of the Matrix in time, and in a tremendous fight scene dies at the hands of Agent Smith. As Trinity stands over Neo's inert body, she shares what the Oracle has told her—that she would fall in love with the man who was "the One." Even though Neo's dead, she believes with all her heart that love is stronger than the physical body. She kisses him, then demands that he "get up." Neo's eyes flip open, and he's resurrected. A miracle? Of course. Once again, he has died so he can be reborn. How? It doesn't matter. Either we believe it or we don't; the willing suspension of disbelief is required. He has overcome the limitations of his own mind; he has chosen to wear the mantle of "the One."

I think *The Matrix* is one of those films that embodies a future direction in movies: technology integrated into a classical, mythical story line that becomes larger than life. Does it follow the "traditional form" of beginning, middle, end; Act I, Act II, Act III? Absolutely. But that's not what makes it work so well; it's the filmmaker's vision, the ideas behind the film that are integrated into the story and which heighten the filmic reality.

I don't arbitrarily set down any "rules" when I go to the movies. There's only one "rule" I follow: *if it works, it works, and if it doesn't, it doesn't*. It doesn't matter whether it's a "conventional" film or an "unconventional" film. I'm exhilarated when I see a film like Mike Figgis's *Time Code*, Spike Jonze's *Being John Malkovich*, Ang Lee's *Crouching Tiger, Hidden Dragon* (Wang Hui Ling, Tsai Kyo Jung, and James Schamus) or Christopher Nolan's exceptional *Memento*, because they push the form in new directions. It doesn't matter if certain parts of the films don't work. If I'm emotionally taken by the vision of the filmmaker, I'll go out of my way to support it. It could be a movie like Steven Soderbergh's *Erin Brockovich* (Susannah Grant), or his slightly off-kilter and wonderful *Out of Sight* (Scott Frank), or his dynamic *Traffic* (Stephen Gaghan); in each case, Soderbergh pushes the form of the story in new ways. If a movie works, it works, and it doesn't matter whether it's a nonlinear or a multilayered story line. If what I see on the screen moves or touches me, I want to take it apart and see how and why it works.

Which is what happened when I first saw *Magnolia*. I didn't have the opportunity of seeing it when it was first released, and I hadn't seen *Boogie Nights* either, or *Hard Eight*, so I literally knew nothing about the work of Paul Thomas Anderson other than what I had heard or read about him. Though there had been a lot of talk and press about *Magnolia*'s being nominated for several Academy Awards, including Best Screenplay, I had heard from friends that it was overlong, melodramatic and "unrealistic"; several people whose opinion I respected told me they didn't like it, and a few even walked out, taking issue with the frogs falling from heaven.

When I finally got a chance to see it, it was late in the afternoon and a light drizzle was falling. I had just finished a very tough chapter in this book, and I was drained and did not feel like continuing to work. When I saw that *Magnolia* was playing nearby, I jumped into my car, drove to the theater, paid my $8 and walked inside. I got my popcorn, found a seat and waited for the film to begin, all the while thinking of what I wanted to cover in the next chapter of my book. The previews came and went and the movie began.

I was totally unprepared for what I saw on the screen. I had had no preconceptions about *Magnolia*, so when I saw the newsreel-type shots of the hanging of three men—Green, Berry and Hill—in the prologue, I wondered what was going on. Then, hearing the voice-over narrator explain how a scuba diver wound up in the top branches of a tree struck me as so ludicrous, so strange, I started to get interested. The final part of this little introductory three-part prologue, where the boy Sydney gets killed attempting suicide, was so odd, so bizarre, so riveting, I was hooked. And when the narrator says, "This was not just a matter of chance," I still didn't know what was going on—nor did I care, because the filmmaker had me; I was ready to go anywhere Paul Thomas Anderson wanted to take me.

As the movie progressed I saw there were ideas here—ideas of death, of reconciliation and forgiveness, of chance, destiny and fate and the interconnectedness of all things—as well as serious issues—the relationships between fathers and sons, and fathers and daughters. I was totally engrossed by the superb acting as well as by Anderson's filmmaking prowess. As I sat in the dark it seemed to me that Anderson's style of filmmaking was more poetry than a series of staged dramatic actions. If there's any one word that describes *Magnolia* for me, it's "fluid." The movie flows from one sequence to another, one story to another. The camera itself is a fluid force, a bird in flight, not drawing attention to itself, but integrated as an essential part of the story. When young Stanley (Jeremy Blackman) and his father arrive for the taping of *What Do Kids Know*, the camera follows them inside. We wait while they talk to a production assistant, then the camera leaves Stanley and follows the assistant, who takes us to the next character, who leads us to Jimmy Gator (Philip Baker Hall) preparing for the quiz show. Powerful and inventive, it was reminiscent of the masterful opening sequence Orson Welles created for *Touch of Evil*.

After the prologue, each character is set up and the images flow from one into another. There are two different emotional levels working here, both dealing with the relationship between sex and love. First, we first see Frank T. J. Mackey (Tom Cruise) pitching his "Seduce and Destroy" infomercial on television. Over this, we hear Aimee Mann's rendition of Harry Nilsson's "One," setting up the theme about the quest for love. Frank maintains that sex is a way to destroy the opposite sex, yet the song says we all seek love. These themes are illustrated in the next scene, when we see Claudia (Melora Walters) being "hit on" in a bar; in the first scene, the middle-aged stranger says "Hi," then we cut to them walking into her apartment, see them do a few lines of coke, then he says "So?" and we cut to them having sex. So simple that we in the audience have to fill in all the unspoken and unseen actions. Great screenwriting.

From there, we go to Jimmy Gator, Claudia's father, being told by a doctor that he does not have long to live; then we meet young Stanley as he gets ready for school; then we cut to the former Quiz Kid, Donnie Smith (William H. Macy), at the dentist being measured for braces; then to Phil (Philip Seymour Hoffman), the hospice caretaker, arriving to care for the dying Earl Partridge (Jason Robards); leading to Linda (Julianne Moore), Earl's wife, leaving the house; and then to Officer Jim Kurring (John C. Reilly) as he prepares for his day. We listen to his voice-over recording on the answering machine telling us who he is, what he's looking for in a relationship and what he wants out of life.

The characters are all introduced and set up visually, and we're with them as they prepare for the day ahead so the real story can begin. Then we see an insert of the weather forecast: "82% chance of rain."

At this point, I still didn't know what the relationships were between the characters, or what part they played in the story, but I knew Paul Anderson did, so I willingly surrendered and let the story unfold. For me, that joy of discovery is what going to the movies is all about.

When I talk about *Magnolia* in my seminars and workshops, some people object and tell me it's too long. I agree. But so what? They say it's too melodramatic. I agree. But so what? They tell me it pushes the boundaries of reality. Yes, thank God. For me, it's the brilliance of Anderson's vision, the intelligence of the emotional tapestry he weaves into his fluid style of filmmaking, which makes the film such an overridingly powerful experience.

Many people insist that *Magnolia* is an excellent example of an "unconventional" film because it doesn't follow the "conventional" guidelines of the narrative film. When people insist on telling me how unconventional it is, and ask if I think it follows a "traditional" structure, I reply "Definitely," pointing out that "form always follows structure"; structure is only the start point, not the end point.

It may seem that *Magnolia* is a disjointed, nonlinear story experience, but that's not the case at all. The nine stories told in *Magnolia* are all connected and related to each other. The actions of each character are superimposed, one upon the other, and the film's structure begins at the beginning of the day and ends with Earl's death, at the end of the day.

As I studied the film, I saw that the film really revolves around the death of Earl Partridge. On this, the very last day of his life, Earl wants Phil, his nurse, to find his son, Frank T. J. Mackey. Earl, as seen on the background credits on the always-playing TV, is the owner-producer of the *What Do Kids Know* TV show, where

Stanley is a key contestant. Linda is Earl's wife. Jimmy Gator works for Earl, and, as we'll learn later, Jimmy molested his daughter, Claudia.

As I began to see the connections of the individual stories, I had the image of an old wagon wheel, where the hub at the center connects all nine spokes to the outer rim. That image stayed with me as I analyzed the film; Earl is the hub of the story and his past actions are the glue that holds the story together in terms of the present. Earl's guilt over leaving his wife so many years before, and letting his fourteen-year-old son Frank take care of his dying mother, has taken a heavy toll on Earl's conscience. The dying man has hidden that fact, and only now, as the cancer eats away at him and he is riddled with pain and memory, does he seek forgiveness.

Magnolia deals with the themes of reconciliation and forgiveness, revealing what the parents' past actions have wrought upon their children. Ibsen's great play *Ghosts* deals with the same theme of the sins of the father passing on to the son. Certainly, this is the subject of Earl's incredible deathbed monologue as he confesses his "sins" to Phil, telling him he walked out on his wife and son, leaving Frank to tend to his dying mother. "It's the biggest regret of my life," he says. "I let my love go."

When Phil drops the liquid morphine into his mouth, it's the end, but as it turns out, Earl's death is really a new beginning, the catalyst that brings everyone together. As the rain thunders down we see the nine characters singing about their pain and guilt and lack of self-worth, knowing it's just not going to stop "till you wise up." Claudia asks Jim Kurring, "Now that you've met me, would you object to never seeing me again?" Until they can accept themselves for who they are, until they can forgive themselves and accept their sense of self-worth, until they can let somebody love them for who they are and let the past go, it's not going to stop. They have to "wise up" first.

When I first saw this scene, I was taken aback. All the characters in this emotionally charged movie were singing about the truth of their lives. I guess that's why some people refer to *Magnolia* as being "operatic." To have the characters break into song, expressing their pain and discomfort in a musical lyric, is an extraordinary accomplishment. James Brooks tried to do this in his 1994 film *I'll Do Anything*, and it didn't work. After cutting the movie with several different approaches, Brooks finally had to drop the songs and tried to structure the film in a different way. But it never really worked. Paul Anderson makes it work in a masterly fashion.

Then there are the frogs. I didn't quite know what to make of this when I first saw it. But personally, I love this collision of reality and unreality. I learned this while working with one of my students, the brilliant Mexican screenwriter Laura Esquivel; Laura taught me about the heritage of the Mexican literary tradition referred to as "magic realism." Working with her on the screenplay of *Like Water for Chocolate*, I was introduced to this concept of "exaggerated reality," where the clash of reality and unreality blends into the framework of the story line. Intrigued, I began researching it, and discovered that the falling of the frogs is taken from the Bible—Exodus, Book 8, where a plague of frogs descending from the sky is the Pharaoh's punishment for betraying Moses and the Hebrews in the land of Egypt. As I began exploring the backgrounds of the scenes in the film, I kept seeing references to "8:2," in the audience at the TV show or on an outdoor sign on Magnolia Boulevard in the San Fernando Valley.

In the end, as Jim Kurring tells us in his voice-over narration, "Sometimes people need a little help. Sometimes people need to be forgiven. . . ." In the very last scene, this narration takes us to Claudia, who stares vacantly into the camera. Then she smiles. So simple, so bright, so elegant; I had not seen her smile once during the entire film. I was so moved to see that smile after all the pain she's lived in and been through, it brought tears to my eyes.

The voice-over narrator sums it all up: "There are stories of coincidence and chance and intersections and strange things told and which is which who only knows . . . and we generally say, 'Well, if that was in a movie I wouldn't believe it.' And it is in the humble opinion of this narrator that these strange things happen all the time . . . and so it goes and so it goes and the book says, 'We may be through with the past, but the past is not through with us.'"

And so it goes and so it goes.

I think *Magnolia* and *The Matrix*, or *Crouching Tiger, Hidden Dragon*, are examples of films that are guiding us into the new millennium. From what I'm seeing on movie screens around the world, we're perched on the edge of a revolution in storytelling; we have new tools, a new technology and a plethora of new filmmaking techniques. Even now, as I sit writing this, there is a film by Irish screenwriter Roddy Doyle, *When Brendan Met Trudy*, which has the main character's movie fantasies merging with reality. Scenes from Godard's *Breathless*, John Ford's *The Searchers* and other great films are incorporated into the emotional reality of the characters and express what the characters are saying and feeling. It seems we're standing on the threshold of a new frontier in the movies, and there are no rules as to what we can or cannot do. The question Jean Renoir posed so many years before, *"Qu'est-ce que c'est le Cinema?"* is as relevant today as it was when I first heard it.

When I first began my career as a writer and teacher, I asked myself what I would like to accomplish in my teachings and books, and the answer that came up was this: I wanted filmmakers to make great movies that would inspire audiences to find their common humanity. I knew that future technologies would emerge and there would be new, more advanced ways of telling stories with pictures. I felt that if people understood what makes good movies, what makes a good story, it would be of value to filmmakers and audience alike. When I uncovered the *Paradigm*, I didn't really discover anything new; this concept of storytelling has been around since Aristotle's time. I simply uncovered what was already there, gave it a name and illustrated how it worked in contemporary movies.

What's happened over the years is that the understanding of dramatic structure in the movies has become the focus of debate. The discussion rages over the differences between conventional and unconventional methods of storytelling. I find that good, because it may lead to conversations of discovery, new points of departure in film. Structure will not change, only the form, the way the story is put together, will. And if that leads to new ways of telling stories with pictures, then I've accomplished what I set out to do. So while "we may be through with the past, the past is not through with us."

As I sit in a darkened theater I'm sustained by an unbridled hope and optimism. I don't know whether I'm looking for answers to my own questions about life, or whether I'm sitting in the dark silently giving thanks that I'm not somehow up there on that monster screen actually confronting the struggles and challenges I'm seeing. Yet I know that in those reflected images I may glean an insight, or awareness, that may embrace the personal meaning of my life.

I think about this as I look back upon the footprints of my life. I see where I began my journey, gaze over the ground I've covered, the trails I've traversed, and understand that it's not the destination that is so important; it is the journey itself that is both the goal and the purpose.

Like the Oracle in *The Matrix*, I believe that the silver screen is a mirror, reflecting our thoughts, our hopes, our dreams, our successes, our failures. Going to the movies is an ongoing journey, for those dancing shadows of light are simply a reflection of our lives, where the end might be the beginning, and the beginning the end.

Just like in the movies.

Index